From Woe to Go!

A Training Text for Christian Counsellors

Graham Barker and Clifford Powell

Copyright © 2014 Graham Barker and Clifford Powell.

All rights reserved. No part of this book may be used or reproduced by any means, graphic, electronic, or mechanical, including photocopying, recording, taping or by any information storage retrieval system without the written permission of the publisher except in the case of brief quotations embodied in critical articles and reviews.

Scripture quotations are from the Holy Bible, New International Version @1973, 1978, 1984, by International Bible Society unless otherwise stated. NRSV New Revised Standard Version Bible, copyright @1989 The Division of Christian Education and the National Council of Churches of Christ in the United States of America. Used by permission. All rights reserved.

Balboa Press books may be ordered through booksellers or by contacting:

Balboa Press
A Division of Hay House
1663 Liberty Drive
Bloomington, IN 47403
www.balboapress.com.au
1 (877) 407-4847

Because of the dynamic nature of the Internet, any web addresses or links contained in this book may have changed since publication and may no longer be valid. The views expressed in this work are solely those of the author and do not necessarily reflect the views of the publisher, and the publisher hereby disclaims any responsibility for them.

The author of this book does not dispense medical advice or prescribe the use of any technique as a form of treatment for physical, emotional, or medical problems without the advice of a physician, either directly or indirectly. The intent of the author is only to offer information of a general nature to help you in your quest for emotional and spiritual well-being. In the event you use any of the information in this book for yourself, which is your constitutional right, the author and the publisher assume no responsibility for your actions.

Any people depicted in stock imagery provided by Thinkstock are models, and such images are being used for illustrative purposes only. Certain stock imagery © Thinkstock.

Printed in the United States of America.

ISBN: 978-1-4525-1268-6 (sc)
ISBN: 978-1-4525-1269-3 (e)

Balboa Press rev. date: 01/28/2014

To Alexis,
bright star in the constellation of my life

And
to Marion,
precious gift of God,
lifetime companion on the Way

Contents

Foreword John Townsend, Ph.D. xiii
Thanks and Acknowledgments xv
Introduction xvii

Part 1—Establishing a Framework 1

Chapter 1—The History of Christian Counselling 3
- The Conception Phase—the Ministry of Jesus.................3
- The Embryonic Phase—Twenty Centuries of Slow Progress...4
- The Infancy Phase—Narramore, Tournier, and Others.........7
- Childhood Phase—The Struggle for Legitimacy....................8
- The Adolescent Phase—"Who Am I?"—Models of Integration...10
- The Young-Adult Phase—Growing in Confidence and Acceptance..12

Chapter 2—Major Counselling Theories 15
- Psychodynamic Psychotherapy...15
- Cognitive Behavioural Therapy...19
- Humanistic Therapy...24
- Systems Theory..28
- Contemporary Therapies...35
  - Narrative Therapy..35
  - Solution-Focused Therapy..36
- Critiquing theories..38

Chapter 3—Essential Counsellor Qualities.............................41
- Relationship with Jesus..41
- Empathy 43
- Respect 45
- Integrity 46
- Humility 49
- Commitment to Life-long Learning and Growth................50

Chapter 4—Effective Listening— NEW GRACE 53
- Channel #1—N: Nonverbal communication 54
- Channel #2—E: Emotion 57
- Channel #3—W: Words..58
- Channel #4—G: God 61
- Channel #5—R: Responses within the Counsellor's Self 67
- Channel #6—A: Absent or Avoided information 69
- Channel #7—C: Context..71
- Channel #8—E: Experience...72

Chapter 5—The Incarnational Counselling Model 74
- Foundation Propositions... 74
- Task 1: Connecting 83
- Task 2—Correcting 86
- Task 3—Concluding 89

Part 2—Incarnational Counselling: The Expanded Model......... 95

Chapter 6—Task 1—Connecting 97
- Subtask 1—Connecting with the Person................................. 98
  - Containing.. 101
  - Direct Advice and Psycho-Education............................... 102
- Subtask 2—Collecting Relevant Data 104
  - Structured Interviews... 105
  - Life-History Questionnaires 105
  - Indirect Gleaning 106
- Subtask 3—Reflecting on Issues and Data........................... 106

Chapter 7—Correcting.. 111
- Subtask 1—Correcting Distorted Thinking........................... 111
- Subtask 2—Correcting Disruptive Emotions........................ 116
- Subtask 3—Correcting Destructive Behaviours................... 121

Chapter 8—Concluding... 125
- Subtask 1—Consolidating 125
- Subtask 2—Coaching 126
- Subtask 3—Celebrating 129

Part 3—Practical Skills Training 131

Chapter 9—The Skills of Connecting 133
- Establishing Rapport 133
- Attending 134
- Listening 137
  o Listening to Nonverbal Information 137
  o Listening to Emotions 139
  o Listening on More Than One "Channel" 141
- Paraphrasing 141
- Questioning 145
- Reflective Responses 148
- Summarising 161

Chapter 10—The Skills of Connecting II 164
- Grounding and Containment Skills 164
  o Sensory Grounding and Containment 165
- Self-Calming Skills 167
  o Diaphragmatic breathing 167
- Assessment Skills—(Collecting Relevant Data) 168
  o General Indicators of Progress 168
  o Scaling 171
  o Formal Assessment Instruments 175
- Diagnosis and Counselling Themes—(Reflecting on the Person's Issues and Data) 176
- Selecting Intervention Approaches 178
- Case Formulation 182

Chapter 11—The Skills of Correcting I:
Correcting Distorted Thinking 186
- Psycho-Education 187
- Normalising 189
- Self-Disclosure 191
- Discovering Client Strengths 192
- Challenging Irrational Beliefs 195

- Replacing Negative Thinking Patterns with Alternative Balanced Thoughts 199
- Disconnecting from Unhelpful Thinking 202

Chapter 12—The Skills of Correcting II:
Correcting Disruptive Emotions 205
- Helping People Manage Disruptive Emotions 207
- Physical Exercise 207
- Journaling 207
- Self-Calming Skills 209
  o Progressive Muscle Relaxation 209
  o Breath-Focused Relaxation 212
  o Mindfulness 216
- Sentence Stems 217
- Trial Sentences 221

Chapter 13—The Skills of Correcting III:
Correcting Destructive Behaviours 224
- Self-Monitoring 225
- Behaviour Rehearsal and Role Playing 227
- Behavioural Experiments 230
- Between-Session Tasks 234
- Conversation Skills 235

Chapter 14—The Skills of Concluding 239
Subtask 1—Consolidating 241
- Summarising 241

Subtask 2—Coaching 242
- Predicting and preparing for lapses 242
- Networks of support 243

Subtask 3—Celebrating 244
- The who and how of celebration 244

Part 4—Integrating Spiritual Resources 247

Chapter 15—Using Prayer in Counselling 251
- Prayers of Praise and Thanksgiving 253
- Supplication and Intercession 254
- Deliverance 255
- Inner Healing 258
- Physical Healing 259
- Seeking Guidance 259
- How Should We Pray? 259
- What General Guidelines Are There for the Conduct of a Prayer Time? 260

Chapter 16—Using Scripture in Counselling 262
- Incarnational Scripture 262
- Paraphrased Scripture 263
- Direct Use of the Bible 264
- How Should We Use Scripture? 265
- "Psalm Therapy" 269

Chapter 17—Confession and Forgiveness in Counselling 272
- Forgiving Those Who Have Wronged Us 274
  - We teach what forgiveness is not! 274
  - Why should we forgive those who have wronged us? 277
  - How do we incorporate a time of extending forgiveness into our counselling? 277
- Seeking Forgiveness for Ourselves 278
- Additional Important Notes 280

Chapter 18—Hearing God 281
- How Does God Speak? 282
- Why Might God Need to Speak to Us, as Counsellors? ... 283
- Revelation, Interpretation, and Application 286
- How Will I Recognise God's Voice? 290

Part 5—Leaving the Woe, Embracing the Go! 295
    A. Life-History Questionnaire 299
    B. Supervision Competency Checklist 307
    C. Concluding Therapy—A Sample Counsellor Letter 317
    D. Psychopharmacology for Counsellors 319

References 325

Foreword
John Townsend, Ph.D.

For many years, the phrase "Christian counselor" was an oxymoron. People would hear it and ask themselves questions such as:

- *Why do we need Christian counselors?*
- *Hasn't God been healing people for thousands of years before psychotherapy?*
- *Isn't the Bible enough for us?*
- *Is this a way to allow secular thinking into our churches?*

These are legitimate questions, and there are certainly harmful and unbiblical practices in some counseling corners. But over the years, academics, counselors and theologians have been landing on the idea that Christian counseling can be very helpful and very biblical, and that those who are hurting, depressed, anxious, addicted or in a relational struggle, can experience deep and transformational help in the process.

The body of Christ is a fundamental part of the equation. The Bible teaches us to do more than just read the Bible and pray. We are also to engage with each other in different ways, depending on the context: "And we urge you, brothers, warn those who are idle, encourage the timid, help the weak, be patient with everyone (I Thessalonians 5:14)." When God's people understand God's Word and connect with those who are hurting, good things happen.

With all this good news, there has also been a significant need for a coherent history and encyclopedic overview of the "big picture" of Christian counseling. Drs. Graham Barker and Cliff Powell's new book is a treasure chest of information about both the "how" and the "what" of the field. They have done massive research on how

Christian counseling has been part of humanity for thousands of years, and organized it in stages that make sense, and create clarity. They have also found the essential principles of what makes a good Christian counselor, no matter what the theoretical orientation, so that the reader can see what is truly important.

You will find that no matter what level of training you are at, whether just beginning the journey, or as an experienced clinician, there will be benefit for you. And Graham and Cliff are not only great in their information, but they write in a warm and accessible style.

The answers to the 4 questions above are all answered, along with much, much more. You will enjoy and gain from your reading experience.

God bless you.

John Townsend, Ph.D.
Psychologist, organizational consultant and leadership coach
Co-author of the 2 million bestseller *Boundaries*
Newport Beach, California USA
June 2013

Thanks and Acknowledgments

For Cover and illustrations: Rebecca Hallett of Boographics.

To Gordontraining.com for permission to use the extract on pp. 149-154. The original extract is from Gordon, T. (1970). *PET: Parent Effectiveness Training*, New York: Plume.

To Guilford Publications, Inc. for permission to use the extract on pp. 158-160. The original extract is from Miller, W., & Rollnick, S. (2002). *Motivational Interviewing* (2nd Ed.), New York: Guilford Press.

To Paul Meier M. D., psychiatrist, conference speaker and author for appendix D, Psychopharmacology for Counsellors.

To Teri Kempe for editing, structuring, and typesetting *From Woe to Go*. A God-provision for us in preparing this book for publication.

To Balboa Press and Jonah Marquez for invaluable assistance in finalising the publishing of *From Woe to Go*.

For the administration, staff, and hundreds of students from Wesley Institute in Sydney, Australia, whose contribution to our thinking and the development of the model of Incarnational Counselling over more than twenty-five years of teaching and training is beyond measure.

Thanks.

Dr. Graham Barker can be reached at docbarker01@gmail.com.

Dr. Cliff Powell can be reached at cliff@themindspace.com.au.

Introduction

What do we mean by Christian counselling? Does it differ from Christian psychology or Christian psychiatry or even pastoral care? In this book we are focusing upon the vocation of counselling conducted within an Evangelical Christian worldview with Christian principles as its driving force. This means that at times, some, all, or only one-of-the-above ministries may be represented. From our framework, the entire above have at different times contributed to what is generally recognised today as the movement labelled "Christian Counselling."

In our book, From Woe to Go!, we seek to integrate a comprehensive counselling model for Christian counsellors and a detailed skills-training program together with an extensive incorporation of spiritual resources.

> *From Woe to Go! seeks to integrate a comprehensive counselling model for Christian counsellors and a detailed skills-training program, together with an extensive incorporation of spiritual resources.*

Both of us have now spent more than twenty years in training and equipping people, mostly Christians, for the profession of counselling. Most of this has been done through the graduate programs in counselling at Wesley Institute in Sydney, Australia, where Graham has served as the head of the Graduate School of Counselling. Over the years we have provided the primary training for literally hundreds of Christian counsellors in Australia and overseas. Because of its respected international reputation, Wesley Institute continually draws large numbers of overseas students, so large numbers of international students have also been trained using our approach.

The model we outline in this book we have labelled *Incarnational Counselling*. While the concept of incarnational ministry is certainly not original, focusing on the importance of this foundation—that Christian counsellors should seek to both *incarnate*, or bring the *indwelling presence* of Christ with them into counselling, and also to exemplify the healthy process and advocated changes that go with that reality—seems to us to merit emphasis. Readers of this book, and especially those who work through the training process we have developed at Wesley Institute, will gradually appreciate the *experiential* reality, not just a theoretical understanding of the concept of incarnation.

Incarnational Counselling, as we develop it here, is a *growth-oriented* theoretical model. There are literally hundreds of models and approaches to counselling, and many of them appear to be focused on *problem-management*. This approach places the emphasis on understanding the problem and working to develop skills and life adjustments that enable it to be better managed. It is not our aim to disparage such approaches. We appreciate and make use of much of what is contributed via this kind of focus, but we do not endorse problem-management as the central task of counselling, nor as a descriptive label for our model.

Another theoretical approach, increasingly popular because of its claim to be brief, comes with the descriptive label, *solution-oriented* or *solution-focused*. Once again we recognise the value in putting greater emphasis on seeking solutions rather than excessively analysing the problem. Though both of us work with quite different counselling "styles," and though both of us recognise the importance of an accurate understanding of the problem, neither of us espouses "archaeology for archaeology's sake." We do not seek to "dig up the past" more than we believe is useful, and we *do* recognise the importance of giving emphasis to seeking solutions for people in distress. But we eschew the label solution-focused because it suggests that life and its attendant difficulties are problems to be solved, rather than processes through which we are to grow.

Accordingly, we believe the descriptive emphasis for our model is best captured by the label growth-oriented. We see the overall call of Scripture, and life itself, as being a call to growth for every person. The book of Proverbs in the Bible tends to call this goal of growth "wisdom," and it instructs us to seek this growth above all else.

> "Happy are those who find wisdom, and those who get understanding, for her income is better than silver, and her revenue better than gold. She is more precious than jewels, and nothing you desire can compare with her" (Proverbs 3:13–15 New Revised Standard Version).

In our Google-driven, Internet-cafe world, where there are a hundred thousand articles on every topic we could research, it is important to distinguish "wisdom" from "knowledge." When the Bible talks of wisdom, it is really talking of the capacity to see things from God's perspective and to incarnate and live out of that understanding—something quite different to the concept of having a lot of factual knowledge, or a bunch of university degrees.

Elsewhere in Scripture, the word that most closely captures this continuing call to growth is "maturity."

> "The gifts he gave were that some would be apostles, some prophets, some evangelists, some pastors and teachers, to equip the saints for the work of ministry, for building up the body of Christ, until all of us come to the unity of the faith and of the knowledge of the Son of God, to maturity, to the measure of the full stature of Christ." (Ephesians 4:11–13 NRSV)

We all have different skills and capacities, different vocations under God, but the goal and purpose remains the same for everyone—to progress towards maturity, to develop towards *the measure of the full stature of Christ.*

James, the brother of Jesus and early church elder, picks up this theme of God's call to growth for followers of Jesus, with particular emphasis on the process. In some of the most extraordinary verses in the Bible, he encourages us: "My brothers and sisters, whenever you face trials of any kind, consider it nothing but joy, because you know that the testing of your faith produces endurance; and let endurance have its full effect, so that you may be mature and complete, lacking in nothing" (James 1:2–4 NRSV, emphasis added).

For James, life is a pilgrimage that will bring "trials," or distressing circumstances, to all of us. He is writing his letter to Jews of the Dispersion, scattered because of persecution, so he cannot guide them with Pollyanna-ish instruction! As he writes his letter, they are actually living through trials, so that is where he starts his teaching. The task is not to *manage* or *solve* these trials but to *grow through* them.

Approached with the right understanding, "trials" can be growth-producing experiences that we can use to further develop our capacity to endure, and endurance will be a crucial building block in our growth as followers of Jesus. James wants us to know that if we can adequately glimpse the possibilities that a trial brings for our growth, it is possible to grow through it, even to "consider it nothing but joy"! This maturity, or "growing-upness," is the end point towards which we journey, the fulfilment of God's call to us. While we know that its completion and finality will only be reached in glory, the call is there daily for each of us.

> *The task is not to manage or solve these trials, but to grow through them.*

The call to growth for us, as Christian counsellors, is not a call to *self-fulfilment* in the sense that humanistic counselling theories have advocated in the past. It is not a call to get as much as we can, nor to be as happy as we can. It is certainly not a call to possessions, fame, or fortune. It is not even a call to developing all the inherent capacities and capabilities that we have, pursuits that are better than bank robbing but, in the end, still merely have a *self* focus. Rather, it is a call to growth in God-focus, to Jesus-likeness, to living a life that matters, to submission to God, to seeking to bring glory to God no matter what the external circumstances! While the outworking of this will be unique in each person's life, the purpose, the end-point, the *why* remains the same—to honour the One who gave us life.

So, clearly we see the biblical call to growth as God's call to *everyone*. It specifically and directly applies to us as counsellors and also to those we counsel. This call to growth involves ongoing transformation in the way we function at every level and in every dimension of our lives. We see it as a call to growth in the emotional, cognitive, behavioural, spiritual, personal, familial, relational, professional, and all other dimensions of our lives.

The ramifications of this are immense for trainee counsellors. Before we can, with integrity, seek to be helpers of others, we must be wholeheartedly committed to our own journey of personal growth in God. And this, we believe, is a lifelong task. If we are not constantly being transformed, constantly growing incarnationally, moving closer towards "the measure of the full stature of Christ" ourselves, then we really are dependent on purely secular skills and understandings in our seeking to help others.

We recognise that this growth will often be slow and difficult, but we encourage trainee counsellors to be focused in their personal commitment to growth, so they can call others to this same journey. We certainly do not want them to use counselling as a vehicle to *preach at* people, but we do seek to stir them to embody, to *incarnate*, this value of life-long "growing-upness," and to sensitively and appropriately model this perspective in their work of counselling.

So, we invite you to reflect on these emphases as we develop them in *From Woe to Go!* Above all else, our desire is that this book and its contents would make a worthwhile contribution to the training literature for Christians and, thus, enhance the growth of both trainee counsellors and those who seek counselling at their hands.

Graham Barker PsyD
Cliff Powell PhD
December 2013
Sydney, Australia

PART 1

Establishing a Framework

CHAPTER 1

The History of Christian Counselling

This chapter briefly surveys the history of Christian counselling using the metaphor provided by the stages of human development. This perspective recognises that Christian counselling underwent a "conception" stage with the ministry of Jesus. Since that time, there have been identifiable developmental advances not unlike the stages of normal human development.

* * * * * * * * *

The Conception Phase

It can be argued that the beginnings of Christian counselling should be grounded in the interactions of Jesus with his disciples and followers. Others might argue that the roots go even further back, in the early patriarchal dealings of ancient Israel and the wisdom literature, such as Psalms and Proverbs with their wealth of psychological insights. While we acknowledge these ancient underpinnings we begin this brief survey with accounts of the ministry of Jesus.

When we read the accounts of Jesus's interactions with people, it does not take long before we realise that his interactions included times of comforting, confronting, affirming, celebrating, and instructing. Some

> *Jesus used a variety of communication styles and techniques yet always matched the need with his approach.*

were with a single enquirer, such as Nicodemus or the woman charged with adultery. Other encounters involved small groups, such as Jesus's instruction times with Peter, James, and John. Still others involved even larger audiences, such as the crowds who heard him speak on the mountain, in the temple grounds, or on the Galilean shore.

It is interesting to note that Jesus used a variety of communication styles and techniques yet always matched the need with his approach. It is hard to place Jesus into one counselling orientation or another. He was truly flexible, able to be situation-specific yet was not locked into any one fixed style or methodology.

The conception stage can be expanded to include the era of the New Testament writings when the apostles and others dispensed pastoral counsel to the new Christians and their leaders. They used no single, prescribed model, and it can be seen that the approach was adjusted to meet the particular need. But it also demonstrated the personality of the author. We can observe that James, the half-brother of Jesus and early leader of the church in Jerusalem, was very pastoral, while Peter, the dynamic and impulsive apostle, was usually quite directive and forthright.

The Embryonic Phase

As the church expanded, so did its commitment to meeting the pastoral and physical needs of its adherents and their communities. In the early centuries of the first millennium, when Greek and Roman thought still dominated, it was the common belief among clergy, philosophers, and laypeople that psychological problems were actually "spiritual problems." Emotional problems were considered the results of spells and magic cast by witches and warlocks, or they constituted a punishment for performing acts displeasing to the gods.

Many of the early church apologists were among the most vocal in resisting the intrusion of natural philosophies and "scientific pursuits" into the realm of Christian belief. Possibly the most influential voice came from Tertullian (150–225), who railed against such influences. Bettenson records Tertullian's stance:

> "What is there in common between Athens and Jerusalem? What between the academy and the Church? What between heretics and Christians? Away with all projects for a Stoic, a platonic, or a dialectic Christianity!" (1963, p.6).

In the centuries that followed, the Church's condemnation of the application of human sciences to life's problems moderated. Augustine (AD 400) and Jerome (AD 420) tended to view science with a cautionary eye while freely quoting from such works. However, their cautionary eyes did not prevail, and by the end of the first millennium, a more pronounced hostility was once again evident. The influential cardinal and bishop of Ostia, Peter Damien (1007–72), denounced any elevation of human reason or scientific investigation as un-Christian. A recent writer, Inglis (1979), noted that, two centuries later, Pope Alexander pronounced that clergy involvement in "non-spiritual" enterprises, such as healing and "medicines," were the Devil's deception.

This conflicted relationship dominated the church until the Protestant Reformation in the sixteenth century. The Protestant reformers vehemently defended the principle of *Sola Scriptura*, claiming the Holy Scriptures, rather than tradition or other sources of validation, were the highest authority for Christian faith and practice. At no stage, however, did they endorse *Nuda Scriptura*, the claim that the Scriptures alone held authority in every sphere.

In his *Institutes of the Christian Religion* (2.2.15–16), John Calvin (1509–64) proposed a position not unlike that of contemporary integrationists.

> Therefore in reading profane authors, the admirable light of truth displayed in them should remind us that

the human mind, however much fallen and perverted from its original integrity, is still adorned and invested with admirable gifts from its Creator. If we reflect that the Spirit of God is the only fountain of truth, we will be careful, as we would avoid offering insult to him, not to reject or condemn truth wherever it appears... If the Lord has been pleased to assist us by the work and ministry of the ungodly in physics, dialects, mathematics and other similar sciences, let us avail ourselves of it.

This embryonic stage proved to be an extraordinary gestation period of twenty centuries. The works of Johann Christian August Heinroth, the inaugural chair of psychiatry at Leipzig University, are a notable milestone where science and theology met in an academic setting. Heinroth suggested a theory of personality based on Romans 7 in the Bible. He believed that the personality was comprised of the basic drives, the ego, and the conscience. He held that these three areas were in conflict, producing a tension that could only be relieved by yielding to the Holy Spirit. It can be argued that Sigmund Freud, the "father of psychoanalysis," adapted Heinroth's theory and developed his notions of id, ego, and superego.

Heinroth's publications *Disorders of the Soul* (1818) and *A System of Physical-Forensic Medicine* (1825) are considered his most important works. In them, he proposes that "sin," in its broader sense of a lifetime of indulgence in unhealthy and immoral behaviours, is the cause of mental illness. He believed the healing of these involved addressing these "spiritual" issues as genuine realities in the person's life. Heinroth, however, was a singular voice.

The advent of experimental psychology in the nineteenth century and the rise of Freudian thought in the early twentieth century prompted the development of two streams of thought regarding spirituality and scientific enquiry. One stream heaped derision upon spirituality as an anti-intellectual and emotionally unhealthy pursuit. Any public acknowledgement of a distinctive, spiritually based understanding of human behaviour was generally scorned by scholars. The other stream was supported by the notable William James and his pupil, E. D. Starbuck. Each attempted to study the phenomenon of religious experience from a scientific perspective.

The 1901–02 Gifford Lectures by William James were published under the title *The Varieties of Religious Experience*. In these lectures, he presented his beliefs regarding the interaction of the spirit and the mind. James acknowledged that the pursuit of the spiritual in life was most natural and not to be ignored in clinical investigation. His work led to a significant re-legitimising of the integration of scientific and "Christian-based" study.

Anton Boisen (1876–1965), whose own mental crisis led to a crusade to educate theological students in psychological intervention, warrants acknowledgement. His efforts eventually morphed into the Clinical Pastoral Education Movement in the 1930s. The CPE movement gained significant support from more liberal traditions within Christianity but was viewed with scepticism, and even some alarm, by the more conservative branches of the church.

The Infancy Phase

The Christian counselling movement gained impetus among the evangelical branches of Christendom in the aftermath of World War II in the United States. It was there that Christian psychologists, including Clyde Narramore, advocated the integration of Christian and psychological truths. Narramore's radio program *Psychology for Living* was influential in raising the profile of the integration movement among the broad Christian public. A major step in the movement's growth occurred in 1952, when the Christian Association for Psychological Studies (CAPS) was formed so that, finally, Christian counselling had both a voice and a home.

During this period, there were also stirrings on the European continent led by the writings of Swiss physician Paul Tournier. In 1940, his first book, *Médecine de la Personne* (translated in 1957 as *The Healing of Persons*), advocated that man is more than just body and mind. Man is also a spiritual being and, thus, needed to be addressed and treated as an integrated whole. This theme was further developed in all of Tournier's subsequent popular publications.

Concurrently in the United Kingdom, G. J. McKenzie's book *Psychology, Psychotherapy, and Evangelicalism* (1940) addressed the interface of the evangelical church of the day and the increasing influence of psychology. McKenzie called for adequate interdisciplinary training for both religious workers and psychologists to avoid the unnecessary trauma created when either was omitted.

This infancy phase was considerably shorter than its predecessor. The dynamics had changed. The majority of the church had accepted the validity and benefits of genuine scientific research and embraced the application of this research to human need.

Childhood Phase

During the ensuing decades, there was considerable growth as a new generation of Christian psychologists and counsellors began to develop and structure the integrative process. As with a young child learning to walk, the initial steps in the integration of Christian faith and psychological understandings were tentative. The United States was again the major venue for these developments as practitioners and scholars sought to define what Christian counselling looked like. Some key events transpired at this time.

- Fuller Seminary began its graduate school of psychology in 1965. This heralded the formal marriage of evangelical theology with psychology.
- Christian psychologists and counsellors began to publish their thoughts and challenge the church about its negative response to the efficacy of psychological research and its guilt-by-association-to-Freud attitude to the practice of modern psychiatry and psychotherapy.

Authors such as Gary Collins, Larry Crabb, Everett Worthington, and the Minirth-Meier team began to publish for an expanding US evangelical market. At the same time in the United Kingdom there were significant publications proposing the same integrative process; Frank Lake, a psychiatrist with a background as a missionary, published *Clinical Theology* (1966), and Roger Hurding, a physician, followed with his book *Roots and Shoots* (1986). Both publications acted as polemics to the sceptical evangelical populous.

The childhood phase proved difficult to negotiate. There were a number of antagonists who resisted any attempt to integrate Christian belief with psychological theory and practice. The most notable was Jay Adams, a professor at Westminster Seminary in the United States. In his book *Competent to Counsel* (1970), he claimed that any attempt to integrate Christianity and psychology would undermine the authority of the Christian Scriptures. Adams believed the Bible contained all the truth necessary to bring healing to a sinful world. Adams gained a large following and in turn published multiple volumes in support of his position.

Author Tim Stafford, in the May 11, 1993, edition of *Christianity Today*, stated that Adams's critique seems to have ironically spurred on the growth of Christian psychotherapy, making it more self-consciously evangelical. This was partially the result of Arthur F. Holmes and Gary Collins entering the debate with their watershed publications. Holmes's *All Truth Is God's Truth* (1977), and Collins's *The Rebuilding of Psychology* (1977), successfully challenged the Church and the psychological fraternity to consider the legitimate foundations of the integrative movement.

The childhood stage of Christian counselling was frequently characterised by a struggle for legitimacy and acceptance within the evangelical Christian community and the Western public in general. This struggle continues in some areas, and at the time of this publication, there still exists some divide between those who advocate integration and those who oppose the notion.

The Adolescent Phase

As in human adolescence, the Christian-counselling movement began asking itself, "Who am I? What should I look like? How do I make sense of the large number of fixed and variable factors in my makeup?" As these questions were addressed, there emerged several differing models as to the identity of this integration movement.

One of the earliest models, described as "Biblical Counselling," but distinct from the movement that followed Jay Adams' writings, was proposed by Larry Crabb. He re-shaped Albert Ellis' Rational Emotive Therapy (RET) into a cognitive therapy acceptable to the Evangelical Church. Crabb acknowledged that the psychological community had made many significant discoveries that warranted "plundering" in the cause of Kingdom ministry.

Perhaps the greatest influence came with the 1979 publication of *The Integration of Psychology and Theology*. In this book, Rosemead professors, Carter and Narramore posited four possible integration models based on Richard Niebuhr's 1951 classic *Christ and Culture*. Carter and Narramore use the four models, "Against," "Of," "Parallels" and "Integrates," to describe the more common approaches to integration. This publication was the forerunner of many publications by other authors, such as William Kirwan and Siang-Yang Tan, proposing their understanding of the Scriptural model of counselling and psychotherapy.

We have found that the various models reflected three philosophical positions that better describe their intentions:

- Those opposed to integration reflect a Reductionist position that rejects the possibility that truth can be accessed from outside the chosen discipline.
- Those who embrace complementary approaches take a Revisionist position, in which supportive "truths" from alternate disciplines are accommodated upon revision.
- Those supporting an integrative approach appear to hold a Restorationist position that believes all truth is God's truth and seeks to restore that unity.

The struggle for identity continued as differing schools of thought duelled over territorial rights. Colleges and associations were formed to promote the various "faces" of Christian counselling, and denominational conflicts emerged over which position was the more "Biblical "or "scriptural."

Bufford (1997) noted: "By 1992 there were ten distinctive themes that could be identified in the Christian counselling movement." To name a few, the list of themes included: Christian anti-psychology; Biblical counselling; Christian lay-counselling; pastoral counselling, and the Christian Recovery Movement. These themes represented the competing "identities" of the adolescent phase of the Christian counselling movement at the end of the twentieth century.

The Young-Adult Phase

If we are to continue following Erik Erikson's developmental model, then the Christian counselling movement is entering a more mature phase where there is a real attempt to suppress the egocentric narcissism of youth and to embrace the value of moving forwards together and avoiding the splinter effect of isolation.

James Fowler (2004) conveniently interprets Erikson for us at this juncture:

> Intimacy means developing the capacity to engage in closeness with others... without needing to use or manipulate the other, and without allowing or fearing the loss or abuse of oneself. Intimacy inherently involves boundaries and mutual commitment. (p. 2)

This definition correctly identifies two aspects of the current phase of the integration debate:

- The ability to engage in closeness with others; and
- doing so without the fear of losing one's own identity or boundaries.

These two aspects must be present if there is to be ongoing dialogue over the identity and future of Christian psychology. In the past, the absence of these aspects has created division and inhibited unity.

When the movement was in its adolescent phase the *distinctives* were key factors in the identity search. It resembled a re-enactment of the Corinthian Church splits ("I belong to Paul"; "I belong to Cephas") only, this time, it was not church members identifying with their mentors. Rather, it was counsellors and psychologists who labelled themselves and others by their perceived harmony with Scripture. Somehow it evolved to the point where it was considered acceptable to be a cognitive behavioural therapist and in harmony with Scripture, but to practice Gestalt therapy was clearly suspect, and so on. At its worst, many groups of Christian practitioners and laypeople "circled their wagons" around their particular position.

In retrospect, this divisive era had more to do with integration-minded psychologists focusing on the theoretical assumptions of the "models" rather than about granting each other the respect to be able to be selective in their adherence to those assumptions. If someone practiced client-centred counselling, this did not necessarily mean he or she embraced all of Carl Rogers's humanist beliefs but that they appreciated his respect for the client and saw this as entirely compatible with Jesus's approach to people. Similarly, if someone practised psychoanalysis, this did not mean the practitioner believed all of Freud's assumptions, but he or she was respectful of his observations and the analytic process.

Thankfully, the movement has "grown up" to the point where, for the most part, there is respect for the practitioner whether she or he follows some perceived "ideal approach." or not. The commonalities rather than the differences are now much more in focus. In this phase of early adulthood we need to pay our respects to the pioneers in this field, heed their warnings, and embrace their invitations, all the while continuing to explore the practicalities and healing applications of our approach to Christian counselling. Roger Bufford (1997) expresses an important truth regarding what constitutes Christian counselling: Christian counselling is not about the style of counselling or the techniques used. It is primarily about the character of the counsellor.

> *Christian counselling is not about the style of counselling or the techniques used. It is primarily about the character of the counsellor.*

We agree with Bufford, a person can be a Christian counsellor and adhere to evidence-based therapies

13

or therapy-based evidence. From our understanding, the choice of theoretical orientation may well have more to do with personality traits than philosophical commitment. However, we hold strongly to the position that it is not possible to be a Christian counsellor, unless we ground our practise in Scriptural wisdom, and seek to relate with hurting people out of a living and vital relationship with Jesus. These are foundation tenets for Incarnational Counselling.

Further Reading

Carter, J, Narramore. B. (1979). *The integration of psychology and theology.* Grand Rapids: Zondervan.

James, W. (1982). *The varieties of religious experience.* New York: Penguin.

McKenzie, G. J. (1940). *Psychology, psychotherapy, and evangelicalism.* London: Allen and Unwin.

Stevenson, D. H. (2007). Introduction in *psychology, Christianity and integration.* Batavia IL: CAPS.

Tournier P, (1957). *The healing of persons.* New York: Harper and Row.

CHAPTER 2

Major Counselling Theories

There are some three hundred models of counselling from which a trainee counsellor can choose his or her preferred practice modality. This can be an overwhelming number from which to choose.

In this chapter we present a distillation of these models into five classic and basic theoretical positions: psychodynamic psychotherapy; cognitive behavioural therapy; humanistic/existential therapies; systemic therapies; and contemporary therapies.

* * * * * * * * *

Psychodynamic Psychotherapy

Introduction

Psychodynamic psychotherapy is a longer-term therapy that provides people, through the medium of a relationship with a therapist, the opportunity to explore how their views and reactions to people, the nature of their relationships with others, and how they cope with these interactions show up as recapitulations of unconscious templates developed in their earliest years.

The origins of current psychodynamic therapy lie in the psychoanalytic works of Sigmund Freud and the Viennese Society of Psychoanalysis in the late-nineteenth and early twentieth centuries. This school was absorbed in the study of how man's unconscious drives influenced his daily life. Freud proposed that the twin drives of sex and aggression were foundational to most of an individual's emotional distresses. Other members of this society included Abrahams, Jung, Adler, and Rank.

Freud introduced the concept that the mind is divided into multiple parts, including the irrational and impulsive Id (a representation of primal animal desires), the judgmental Super-ego (a representation of society inside the mind); and the rational Ego, which attempts to mediate the divide between the other two parts. His basic therapeutic idea was that mental illness was caused by mental tensions created by repressed desires and that mental health could be restored by making conscious this repressed knowledge, using the "talking cure."

Since the middle of the twentieth century, newer models of psychodynamic therapy have been developed by therapists Anna Freud, Klein, Winnicott, Guntrip, and Bion as a result of continuing research into the unconscious and early childhood development. These "neo-Freudian" models are much less concerned about struggles between the theoretical parts of the mind and much more concerned with how people understand and represent their relationships with other people.

> *Neo-Freudian models are much less concerned about struggles between the theoretical parts of the mind, and much more concerned about how people understand and represent their relationships with other people.*

Major Tenets

- **A person's unconscious mind is the major contributor to his or her thought processes, emotional responses, and behaviours.**

    This proposition holds that individuals respond to any situation from an information and emotional memory bank established in infancy and modified as they grow. These "unconscious banks" create "response templates" upon which the individual draws whenever interpersonal issues arise.

- **Most emotional problems are interpersonal in nature, revolving around issues of attachment, separation and individuation.**
  Throughout their lives, people face issues that recapitulate the developmental templates from childhood and, <u>unless they have developed newer coping methods, they will tend to regress to their childhood responses</u> with self-defeating and relationally devastating results.
- **Familial experience is the first and most significant source of emotional templates**
  The family of origin provides the source for the majority of templates carried in a person's unconscious. The recapitulation of dysfunctional family dynamics in an individual's marriage, workplace and social settings can create emotional distress for all parties.

- **The therapeutic relationship becomes a microcosm of the person's life and holds the key to resolving emotional problems**
  The recapitulation of a person's problem within therapy is a regular and predictable phenomenon since the therapeutic process is a metaphor of the conflicted interaction that clients have with other past and present relationships.
- **The therapeutic relationship is the basis for a** *corrective emotional experience.*
  A corrective emotional experience occurs when the therapist responds to the individual in a manner that challenges the template-based expected response. This process is the fundamental premise of psychotherapeutic change.

Therapeutic Goals

- to complete any incomplete developmental tasks from the person's past

- to replace dysfunctional templates with more functional ones
- to resolve any attachment, separation and individuation conflicts
- to develop a more cohesive emotional structure within the person

Steps in Psychodynamic Therapy

1. **Connect to the client.**
   Connect to the client's personal history.
   Connect to the client's core issues.
   Connect to the client's psycho-dynamic patterns.

2. **Correct their interpersonal deficits.**
   Correct the client's developmental deficits.
   Correct the client's transferential responses.
   Correct the client's emotional structure.

3. **Conclude the therapy.**
   Conclude the therapeutic process.
   Conclude the relationship.

Therapeutic Methods

Identifying and working through transference

Transference is usually thought of as the unwarranted displacement of attitudes, feelings and impulses experienced towards people in the past, onto people in the present. There are three major forms of transference; paternal, maternal and erotic.

Identifying and utilising counter-transference

Counter-transference is viewed as the dynamic by which the therapist engages with the client's transference issues and thereby gains insight into the therapist- client relationship.

Strategic Confrontation

Contrary to common perception, in this approach to therapy, psychodynamic confrontation is a constructive process. It is used to describe the technique by which the therapist highlights the detrimental repetitive behaviours in which the client is engaged. These behaviours may be conscious or unconscious.

Interpretation

This is the intervention used by the therapist to "connect the dots" between the person's current attitudes and responses, and the dynamics of their earlier templates, thereby creating a rational context for the client's behaviour.

Interpretation of Resistance

This is the interpretive technique in which the therapist connects the client's reluctance to fully participate in the therapeutic process of self discovery, to early psychodynamic defensive templates.

Cognitive Behavioural Therapy

Introduction

Cognitive Behavioural Therapy (CBT) is a set of psychotherapeutic techniques used to correct a range of psychological difficulties and disorders by challenging faulty belief systems and unrealistic expectations. CBT is built on the pragmatic notions that people have innate potential for rational thinking and behaviour, and that a person's psychological problems arise as a result of their irrational and self defeating beliefs. CBT is an evidence-based therapy that promotes change through the use of scientifically validated methods to alter an individual's beliefs, thoughts and behavioural patterns.

> *CBT is built on the pragmatic notions that people have innate potential for rational thinking and behaviour, and that a person's psychological problems arise as a result of their irrational and self defeating beliefs.*

CBT had its origins in the foundational work of behaviourists Watson (1920) and Skinner (1948), and cognitive therapists Piaget (1920), Kelly (1955), Beck (1960) and Meichenbaum (1971). Since the introduction of Managed Care into the delivery of therapeutic services, CBT has become the treatment of choice for many psychological disorders and dysfunctions. It has a very good record as the first line of treatment for depression, anxiety disorders, including panic attacks, and is successful in combination with drug therapies in most clinical disorders.

Major Tenets

- **People develop belief systems** (schemas) about themselves and their world based on their perception as to whether events or persons create positive (reward) or negative (punitive) thoughts and /or feelings.
- **People are vulnerable to forming irrational belief systems** and faulty thought processes based on faulty perceptions of other people or events.

- **Emotional problems are the result** of irrational beliefs and faulty thinking about life events.
- **The reorganisation of a person's thoughts and beliefs** will, in turn, reorganise his or her emotional responses and behaviours.

Therapeutic Goals

- to identify and replace self-defeating, negative thinking with positive, rational thoughts
- to reduce automatic negative behaviour patterns and symptoms with positive, thoughtful responses
- to substitute unrealistic demands on self and others with more realistic preferences

Steps in Cognitive Behavioural Therapy (CBT)

Although there are different ways to conduct CBT, the Mayo Clinic has identified five generic steps:

1. **Identify troubling situations or conditions in your life.**

These may include a range of issues such as a medical condition, divorce, grief, anger, and specific mental illnesses, such as panic disorder or bipolar disorder.

2. **Identify thoughts, emotions and beliefs about these situations or conditions.**

The content here may include self-talk about a person's experience, his or her interpretation of the meaning of a situation, and his or her beliefs about self, others and events.

3. Identify negative or inaccurate thinking.

People's thoughts about a situation or condition can affect the way they react to it. Inaccurate or negative thoughts and beliefs about something or someone can lead to undesirable reactions.

4. Challenge negative or inaccurate thinking.

Examine and test the validity of any influential thoughts and beliefs. This may include asking whether the person's view of an event fits the facts and logic, and whether there might be other explanations for a situation.

5. Change thoughts and beliefs.

The final step in the cognitive behavioural therapy process is to replace negative or irrational thinking with positive and more rational thoughts and beliefs.

Therapeutic Techniques

Cognitive Rehearsal

In this technique, the person is first asked to recall a problematic situation from the past. They then work together with their therapist to find a solution to the problem and rehearse the process.

Validity Testing

In this process the therapist tests the validity of the individual's beliefs or thoughts. Initially, the person is allowed to defend his or her viewpoint by means of objective evidence. The faulty nature or invalidity of the belief system is exposed if he or she is unable to produce any kind of objective evidence.

Thought Record/Writing in a Journal

This involves the practice of maintaining a diary to keep an account of the situations that arise in day-to-day life. The thoughts which are associated with these situations, and the behaviour exhibited in response to them, are recorded in the diary.

Systematic Desensitisation

In using this technique the individual is systematically exposed to an offending stimulus in a graduated manner, while simultaneously maintaining a calm and stable emotional state. As the stimulus is exposed concurrently with a calm state, the stimulus is associated with a positive emotional state rather than a negative.

Modelling

In this technique the therapist and the individual perform role-playing exercises aimed at responding in an appropriate way, in order to handle better future difficult situations. The individual makes use of the therapist's behaviour as a model to solve future problems.

Homework

The homework is usually a set of assignments or tasks from a manual or workbook, or may be designed cooperatively, then given to the person for completion between sessions.

Systematic Positive Reinforcement

Systematic positive reinforcement occurs when a person's desired behaviours are rewarded with positive reinforcement. A reward system is established for the reinforcement of certain positive behaviours. Similarly, withholding the reinforcement may be deliberately used in extinguishing a maladaptive behaviour.

Humanistic Therapy

Introduction

During the 1950s, humanistic psychology began as a reaction to the domination of psychoanalysis and behaviourism. Psychoanalysis was focused on understanding the unconscious motivations that drove behaviour, while behaviourism studied the conditioning processes that produced behaviour. Humanist thinkers felt that both psychoanalysis and behaviourism were too pessimistic, either focusing on the most negative of emotions, or failing to take the role of personal choice into account.

Humanistic psychology seeks to minimise the effects of the unconscious mind, focusing instead on the uniquely human capacity to understand one's place in the world and relationships with others. It focuses on a person's potential, and stresses the importance of growth and self-actualisation. The fundamental belief of humanistic psychology is that people are innately good and only need encouragement to use those healthy parts of the personality such as creativity and choice, to move towards increasing psychological health. Two major theorists associated with this approach are Carl Rogers and Abraham Maslow.

> *The fundamental belief of humanistic psychology is that people are innately good and only need encouragement to use those healthy parts of the personality such as creativity and choice, to move towards increasing psychological health.*

In 1962, Abraham Maslow published *Toward a psychology of being* in which he described humanistic psychology as the "third force" in psychology. The first and second forces were psychoanalysis and behaviourism respectively.

In humanistic therapy a person's psychological journey towards maturity should be internally driven, rather than externally controlled by social forces. According to Dombeck and Wells-Moran (2012), humanist theory holds that every human being has the right to become all they were born to be; to fully explore their inborn interests and to make a unique contribution to society. This theoretical pinnacle of self-expression is referred to as a "self-actualised" state.

The main therapies considered to be humanistic are Person-centred, Gestalt, Existential and Transpersonal therapies.

Major Tenets

- **An individual's present is the most significant aspect of his or her "reality."**
  Humanistic therapists emphasise the "here and now" instead of examining the past or attempting to predict the future. Their freedom within the moment, and the choices they make in the here and now, determine whether or not they are healthy.
- **Each person is inherently worthy.**
  Each person is born with a natural desire and drive for health and goodness. This inherent state is, however, vulnerable to the less-healthy influences from social forces such as authoritarian parents, social systems, and religious beliefs.
- **People must take personal responsibility for both their positive and negative actions.**
  While any given action may be negative, such actions do not cancel out someone's value as a person. However, healthy psychological development requires that people take responsibility for their choices and actions.

- **People are influenced by environmental experiences as well as internal thoughts and desires.**
  According to humanistic theory, culture, family, and other external influences play a prominent part in moulding a person's view of self and others. In order to change someone's view of self and others, aspects of their environment need to be changed.
- **A person's healthy choices are driven by a hierarchy of needs.**
  According to Maslow's "needs hierarchy" (1943), people must first secure their basic needs of food, clothing, and shelter. They next seek to achieve a feeling of adequate safety, a sense of belonging, and a sense of self and social respect. The top level of the hierarchy, self-actualisation, incorporates the drive to do all a person desires to do with his or her life. Maslow theorised that this could only emerge after all the earlier needs in the hierarchy were adequately satisfied.

Therapeutic Goals

- **to promote the individual's growth and self-actualisation** through the creation of a therapeutic relationship that is warm and accepting
- **to develop the freedom and wholeness inherent within clients** by engaging with them, enlarging their sense of possibility, and increasing their self awareness and capacity for choice
- **to help clients find philosophical meaning** in the face of their central problems of anxiety, loneliness, and, ultimately, death by choosing to think and act authentically and responsibly

Steps in Humanistic Therapy

Carl Rogers outlined the conditions for therapeutic change as follows:

- therapist-client connection through empathy and respect
- the presence of a minimum state of motivational anxiety
- the presence of a genuine and psychologically healthy counsellor
- the presence of unconditional positive regard in the counselling relationship

Rogers also believed there were five stages in successful client-centred therapy:

- release of any pent-up emotions and irrational thinking
- the "breakthrough" period of catharsis
- the acceptance that the problem constituted a failure to believe in one's self
- the acquiring of insight into the realities of the person's life and world
- the development of a framework for positive self-action

Therapeutic Techniques

The closest a humanistic therapist comes to the use of "techniques" is what are considered core skills. The American Psychological Association, Division 32, lists these as the abilities to

- empathically understand and grasp the world of the client;
- accept, affirm, value, or prize the client; and
- facilitate and participate in co-constructive dialogue with the client.

Most humanistic therapists also try to optimise the relational process by

- presenting their own real self-in-relation to the client; and
- genuinely engaging in a "meeting of persons" with the client.

The APA (1997) notes the following:

> Humanistic therapists aim to provide an optimal relational process within which a client can reflect upon the patterns of his or her life, experience him or herself more deeply, access or mobilize his or her own capacity for agency, and experience and explore the formation and function of relational bonds.

Humanistic therapists keep their attention primarily focused on the client's existential moment and on the ongoing emerging process between himself or herself and the client. They sensitively track the experience of the client as the client struggles with issues and experiences; and they track emerging themes and bring in suggestions, ideas, and techniques when they are relevant to what is happening in the moment. <u>The therapist keeps his or her attention focused more on what is unique about this particular client than on what is common about him or her with respect to others.</u>

Systems Theory

Introduction

Family Systems Theory emerged from Ludwig Von Bertalanffy's (1901-1972) work on *general systems theory* which offered the world of the mid-twentieth century an alternative view of science to the mechanistic models of the time. Von Bertalanffy's general systems theory argued that organisms are complex, organized, and interactive. In simple terms it means that organisms, including families, have their own distinct way of organising themselves and dealing with disturbances from within or without the system. What interested students of human behaviour was the notion that if one part (person) in the system changed (e.g., became asynchronous), the remainder of the system is forced to alter its normal behaviour pattern and adjust. The Systems approach shifted the focus of family interactions away from a linear causal model to a model that required a broader, *holistic* orientation in order to understand family dynamics. By the close of the Twentieth Century Family Systems Theory had become one of the major theoretical foundations guiding empirical investigations into the study of families, out of which clinical interventions with families were developed.

> *In simple terms it means that organisms, including families, have their own distinct way of organising themselves and dealing with disturbances from within or without the system.*

Murray Bowen (1913–90) developed the most articulate model of family systems, viewing the family as an emotionally interdependent unit. His core assumption was that an emotional system that evolved over several billion years governs all human relationship systems. According to Bowen, family members are often so intensely emotionally connected that they affect each other's thoughts, feelings, and action. Family members solicit each other's attention and approval and support and react to each other's needs, expectations, and distress. Consequently, a change in one person's functioning is predictably followed by reciprocal change in others.

Heightened tension within the family tends to intensify the dynamics and processes that interconnect them in unity and teamwork. When such occurrences create disturbances in the system's harmonious functioning, problems tend to arise and the system has to adjust. An example would be that when a family member becomes anxious, his or her anxiety can escalate by spreading infectiously among other family members. As the anxiety increases, the emotional connectedness of family members becomes more stressful than supportive, and eventually, one or more members feel overwhelmed, isolated, or out of control and try to accommodate the demands of others to reduce the tension.

Major Tenets

Triangles

Bowen conceptualised the idea of *triangulation* to describe the action in which a family member, who feels distressed with another member, seeks out an alliance with a third member in order to regain some equilibrium. This action, however, turns the excluded member into an "odd man out." The anxiety of anticipating exclusion, or the reality of exclusion, is what Bowen termed triangulation.

Multigenerational Transmission Process

This term refers to the way family emotional processes are transferred and maintained over generations. As the family continues its patterns from one generation to the next, they often refer back to previous generations ("He's just as irresponsible as his uncle Jim"). The transmission of the process occurs on several interconnected levels ranging from the conscious teaching and learning of information, to the automatic and unconscious programming of emotional reactions and behaviours.

Differentiation of Self

The basic building blocks of a "self" are present at birth, but a person's family relationships during childhood and adolescence can determine how much actual "self" the person develops. The less developed a person's true self, the more vulnerable he or she is to the influence of others on his or her functioning, and the more he or she will try to control, actively or passively, the functioning of others. A person with a clear sense of his or her real self is able to identify times of dependence on others but can stay calm and clear headed enough in the face of conflict, criticism, and rejection, to distinguish between rational, factual thinking and thinking clouded by emotionality.

The Nuclear Family Emotional System

The nuclear family emotional system describes the four basic relationship patterns that govern the development of family problems during periods of heightened and prolonged tension.

- **Marital conflict**
  As family tension increases, each spouse externalises his or her anxiety into the marital relationship. Each tries to control the other, and each resists the other's efforts at control.
- **Dysfunction in one spouse**
  In this pattern, one spouse pressures the other to think and act in certain ways, and the other yields to the pressure. Both spouses accommodate to preserve harmony within the system, but one dominates.

- **The identified "impaired children"**
  The parents often transfer their anxieties onto one or more of their children, thereby relieving the pressure from their own relationship. The more the parents focus their anxieties on the child, the less the child is able to individuate and act from his or her own sense of self. Thus, the child becomes more prone to act out or internalise the family's tensions.
- **Emotional distance**
  This term refers to the practice of emotionally removing oneself from a person or situation in order to reduce the

increasing emotional intensity. The benefit for the person is that he or she regains some sense of self and, thereby, lowers the tension but at the same time runs the risk of emotional isolation.

Family Projection Process

The family projection process describes the primary way parents transmit their emotional problems to their child. The most commonly projected problems, which affect their lives, are relationship sensitivities, such as

- heightened needs for attention and approval;
- difficulty dealing with expectations;
- the tendency to blame oneself or others;
- feeling responsible for the happiness of others, or that others are responsible for one's own happiness; and
- acting impulsively to relieve the anxiety of the moment rather than tolerating anxiety and acting thoughtfully.

The projection process follows three steps during which the parent

- focuses on a child out of fear that something is wrong;
- interprets the child's behaviour as confirming the fear; and
- treats the child as if something is really wrong with him or her.

Emotional Cut-Off

This concept describes how people manage their unresolved emotional issues with parents, siblings, and other family members by reducing or totally cutting off emotional contact. Emotional contact can be reduced by moving away and rarely returning home, or it can be reduced by staying in physical contact with the family but avoiding sensitive issues. People who attempt to reduce the tensions of family interactions this way risk elevating the significance of new relationships and may unthinkingly attempt to recreate their family of origin within them.

[Handwritten note: I MOVED AWAY BECAUSE IT WAS TOO HARD.]

Sibling Position

The basic idea of sibling positioning is that people who share the same sibling position predictably share important common characteristics. For example, oldest children tend to gravitate to leadership positions while the youngest often prefer to be followers. Systems theorists stress that the characteristics of one position are not "better" than those of another position but that they are complementary. Individuals that share the same sibling position, however, can exhibit marked differences in functioning. For example, rather than being comfortable with responsibility and leadership, an oldest child, on whom parents focus anxiously, may grow up to be markedly indecisive and highly reactive to expectations. Consequently, a younger child may become a "functional oldest," filling a void in the family system. *[Handwritten: interesting]*

Therapeutic Goals

- **Reframe the presenting problem** as a systemic, multigenerational issue that has external causal factors unrelated to the individual.
- **Lower the level of anxiety and emotional turmoil** so the family can reflect and respond more calmly.
- **Increase the differentiation of the parental dyad** in order to improve personal anxiety management and the ability to transition into parenthood and thus promote the family's emotional well-being.

- **Form a relationship with the identified "problem member"** and assist him or her to individuate and thereby resist triangulation and emotional fusion.

Techniques

Apart from nondirective questioning and the use of genograms (a pictorial display of a person's family relationships and medical history), the Family Systems therapist tends to avoid overt techniques. They do, however, engage in process-enhancing activities, including

- **the prohibition of open conflict** because this raises anxiety levels;
- **therapist neutrality** and the refusal to enter into triangulated relationships;
- **the promotion of members' differentiation** through the use of "I" statements;
- **the encouragement of excluded members to return to the family**; and
- **the use of descriptive labels** such as "pursuer" and "distancer" to help members understand the dynamics that work between them: that following distancers only causes them to run further away, while pursuers need to create a safe place that invites the distancer back.

Family Systems Theory has been adopted by most family therapists and has been adapted by those therapists working with "surrogate" family structures, such as schools, industry, hospitals, and the military. The principles seem to make easy transitions and demonstrate the wide application of Systems Theory.

Contemporary Therapies

Narrative Therapy

Narrative Therapy is a therapy approach that builds on the idea that people live their lives according to the "stories," or narratives, they construct about who they are and can be; dominant stories and alternative stories; dominant plots and alternative plots; events linked together over time that powerfully shape their lives. These stories can act like a lens, filtering out those "alternative stories" which fail to harmonise with the dominant narrative. Narrative therapists are interested in joining with people to explore their stories, their relationships, the effect of those stories, their meanings, and the context in which they have been formed.

> *Narrative therapists are interested in joining with people to explore their stories, their relationships, the effect of those stories, their meanings, and the context in which they have been formed.*

Major Tenets

- **Problems are separate from** the person.

- **People possess the skills**, attitudes, and motivation to change the relationship with the problems in their lives.

- **There are many valid pathways** that a therapeutic conversation can take to arrive at a resolution.
- **The individual consulting the therapist** plays a significant part in determining the pathways to be taken.

Goals of Therapy

- to separate the problem from the way the person sees himself or herself

- to assist the person to deconstruct and revise the problem-based narrative of his or her life
- to strengthen the right of the person to define his or her own reality
- to reconstruct, or reorganise, what the person sees, hears, feels, and remembers into a more meaningful story or narrative of his or her life

Techniques

- Honour the person's experience.
- Externalise the problem(s).
- Look for unique outcomes—times when the problem is absent.
- Develop the new/old story.
- Apply new knowledge to the present and future.

Solution-Focused Therapy

Solution-Focused Therapy is one of several therapies that have their roots in Family Systems Theory. Its roots are largely attributed to Steve de Shazer and Insoo Kim Berg of the Brief Family Therapy Centre in Milwaukee USA. Their work in the early 1980s built on that of a number of other innovators, among them Milton Erickson and also the group at the Mental Research Institute at Palo Alto California. The approach focuses on the present and future, rather than the past. Solution-focused therapists help individuals:

- Identify the things that they wish to change
- Attend to the positive things that are currently happening
- Identify times in their current life that are closer to their desired future.

The therapist helps the person repeat the successful things he or she does when the problem is not there or is less severe, and thereby moves him or her towards the preferred future he or she has identified.

> *The Solution-Focused therapist helps the person repeat the successful things he or she does when the problem is not there or is less severe.*

Major Tenets

- **Traditional therapy is in error** by focusing on the causes of clients' problems, thereby reinforcing their passive and helpless role.
- **People need to be encouraged to shift the focus** to what they are doing right and take responsibility to utilise their resources to reach their goals.
- **As people change the language that shapes how they think** about the problem, they change the language that shapes how they think about the solution.
- **A problem need not be understood in order to be fixed.**
- **The solution may not even look like it will fit or resolve the problem.**

Goals of Therapy

- Support people to articulate and take responsibility for their preferred futures.
- Explore when, where, with whom, and how pieces of that preferred future are <u>already happening</u>.
- Utilise the existing positives to move people towards their preferred future.

Techniques

- The therapist becomes a part of the system for a short time, learning the language and accommodating the therapist's views to the client world.
- The *miracle question* helps the client envisage how the future will be different when the problem is no longer present.
- The use of *Scaling*, involves rating the complaint on a scale of 1 to 10, with 1 being "extremely bad" and 10 being "problem completely gone." This can help an individual shift from problem-talk to solution-talk.

Critiquing theories

There are several ways to critique theories:

- for their evidential basis
- for their broad- or narrow-population band
- for their ease or difficulty in understanding, and application
- in the case of this book, on the basis of their harmony with the Christian faith

We are both of the view that there is value in most theories, and in the hands of a competent therapist, any of these theories can be beneficial to a counselee.

Of course all theories have a variety of hybrids that must be assessed in their own right. For example, CBT has morphed over the years into several versions, including Rational Emotive Brief Therapy (REBT) and Acceptance and Commitment Therapy (ACT). Each of these is distinct in its approach and needs to be critiqued as such.

Overall, there are some basic measures that can be used to help evaluate any theory of counselling, insofar as it harmonises with the Christian faith.

First, *consider whether any aspect of the theory or application directly contradicts clear teaching in Scripture.* Scripture demands that we not partner with error, since light does not coexist with darkness (Ephesians 5:8–13), so there is no room for collusion with falsity or deceit in the life of a Christian counsellor.

Second, *consider whether all aspects of the theory or application are compatible with the clear teaching of Scripture.* On this foundation we would rule out any counselling approaches that are manipulative or disrespectful of people, since Scriptures such as Genesis 1:26 remind us that all people are created in God's image. It is true that people commit heinous crimes and create untenable webs of deceit, yet they deserve to be seen as redeemable creations of a holy and merciful God.

Third, *consider whether the theory or application complements the clear teaching of Scripture.* A relevant example here might be the question of whether meditation should be used. The Bible authors recommend meditation on verses of Scripture for renewal of the mind and the seeking of God's wisdom (Joshua 1:8; Psalm 1:2, 4:4). It appears that it is the content upon which one meditates that is the crucial component.

Further Reading

Antony, M.M. & Roemer, L. (2011). *Behaviour therapy.* Washington: American Psychological Association.

Corsini, R.J. & Wedding, D. (2011). *Current psychotherapies.* Belmont, CA: Brooks-Cole.

Jones, S. & Butman, R. (1991). *Modern psychotherapies.* Downers Grove Il: IVP.

Rogers, C. (1961). *On becoming a person.* New York: Houghton and Mifflin.

Sommers-Flanagan, J. & Sommers-Flanagan, R. (2012). *Counselling and psychotherapy theories in context and practice.* New Jersey: John Wiley and Sons.

Westbrook, D., Kennerley, H., & Kirk, J. (2007). *An introduction to cognitive behaviour therapy skills and applications.* London: Sage.

CHAPTER 3

Essential Counsellor Qualities

Many writers and theorists have set out to list the *essential* qualities that are needed for counsellors to be effective. Carl Rogers (1961), out of his lifetime of theorising and practice in the field of counselling, concluded that these "core conditions" could be encapsulated by just three qualities:

- empathy;
- genuineness; and
- unconditional positive regard. *(unconditional love)*

His list is rich soil for consideration, and we borrow freely from it here, but we start with another quality that we see as foundational for the Christian counsellor seeking to follow an incarnational approach. In truth, we see all of these qualities as representative of the *incarnational* presence of Jesus in the Christian counsellor.

Relationship with Jesus

The first requirement for anyone wanting to contribute *as a Christian counsellor* in healing and restorative work with distressed and troubled people, is a vital relationship with Jesus. This will always be the "foundation distinctive" for Christian counsellors. There will be plenty of room for differences in our theories of counselling and in our application of

> *There will be plenty of room for differences in our theories of counselling, and in our application of techniques, but without a relationship with God, through Jesus Christ, we will not really be Christian counsellors.*

techniques, but *without a relationship with God, through Jesus Christ, we will not really be Christian counsellors*. The very term "Christian counsellor" implies that we are "Christ-one counsellors"; in other words, we seek to counsel as Christ would.

Some would see the understanding and application of biblical principles as the foundation distinctive for Christian counsellors. While we as counsellor trainers in no way want to dismiss the importance of our study and understanding of Scripture, it is our contention that knowing the Bible is not the *foundation* distinctive. Rather, we see the foundation distinctive as the requirement for us as Christians who counsel, *to be involved in a vital, relationship with the risen Christ, through his Spirit!*

In Acts 4:13 we read of the response of the Sanhedrin to the testimony of Peter and John, who had been arrested for creating a commotion when they healed the man at the Gate Beautiful. "When they saw the courage of Peter and John and realised that they were unschooled, ordinary men, they were astonished and they took note that these men had been with Jesus." The presence and functioning of these two disciples was so irradiated with wisdom and courage, that the "politicians" of their day were pushed for an explanation. It wasn't the knowledge of Peter and John. It was something different. Essentially it was a relationship. They had been with Jesus!

Whatever other qualities we need as counsellors, we must start with the priority that we guard our personal relationship with Christ and are committed to keeping it alive and growing through the use of devotional practices such as Scripture reading, times of solitude and times of prayer. We present the relationship as the *sine qua non* ("without which, nothing") of Christian counsellor qualities.

Empathy

As we noted above, Carl Rogers (1961) identified empathy as one of the "core conditions" for effective counsellors, and so it is. Empathy, as it has been defined in counselling texts, implies both the capacity to enter into the feeling states and understandings of another person but also the capacity to communicate this to the person. It would, of course, be a useless counsellor quality if I were able to "feel along with" the other person, but he or she never knew that I was "with him or her" because of my inability to communicate this.

The word empathy means much the same as the biblical word "compassion." We read that Jesus often "had compassion" on those he ministered to. An example would be Matthew 9:36: "When he saw the crowds, he had compassion for them, because they were harassed and helpless, like sheep without a shepherd." (See also Matthew 14:14, 15:32, 20:34; Luke 7:13.)

Jesus was a man of compassion who felt deeply for those who were suffering. That he conveyed his "in-tuneness" with the situations and feeling states of people is evident by his acts of compassion—feeding the hungry (Matthew 14:14–21, 15:29–38), touching and healing lepers (Matthew 8:1–4), taking little children in his arms (Matthew 19:13–15), weeping over God-rejecting Jerusalem (Matthew 23:37), and expressing care for his mother even while in the throes of crucifixion (John 19:26–27).

However, it is not merely that we follow and serve a person of compassion and, therefore, this seems like the sort of quality we should aspire to. Beyond the obvious model of Jesus, we are also *instructed* to be people who are compassionate, people who enter into the feeling states of those we serve, so that they know they are not alone.

In Romans 12:15 Paul instructs us, as part of our "yielding our bodies as a living sacrifice" to God: "Rejoice with those who rejoice, weep with those who weep." We are to enter into the rejoicing of those for whom life is full of sunshine, and we are also to participate in the emotional state of those caught up in the darkness of life! We are to share and serve not as some kind of "act" that we put on, but as a genuine overflowing expression of our love and care for their situation. This is not to be false in any way, but rather to be a natural outworking of our membership of the Body of Christ, and an expression of the gifting that God has given us (see verses 4–6). Similarly, Hebrews 13:3 (NRSV) instructs Christians: "Remember those who are in prison, as though you were in prison with them; those who are being tortured, as though you yourselves were being tortured." This instruction is set in the context of verse 1: "Let mutual love continue," and provides some detail on how we are to live out our love for others in practical ways. As Christian counsellors, we are called to enter into the emotional state of someone in prison, or someone undergoing torture (or someone who has suffered abuse; has lost a loved one; is overwhelmed with depression; has been torn with guilt over an action he or she has taken; is experiencing the control of addictive behaviours; is tormented with fears; or has been shattered by an infidelity).

This kind of empathic or compassionate engagement with a person in a distressing situation is not an end point in itself. It is not that we are called into depression along with the depressed person. That would simply disempower our helping. That would indeed be purposeless, unhelpful, and unloving. No, we are called into feeling *with* their mental and spiritual anguish in order to be powerfully motivated to care for them. Such "tasting" of their feeling state enables us to connect with God's caring heart for them. This kind of empathic connection accomplishes at least three purposes:

- It validates the experience of the person in the situation.
- It strengthens them by conveying that they are not alone.

It crystallises and focuses our love-motivated interventions on their behalf.

[handwritten margin note: ?what exactly does this mean]

It is the kind of love-grounded state that we observe in Jesus when he weeps over Jerusalem, because they have been blocked from recognising, in his coming, the time of God's visitation (Luke 19:41–44).

Respect

"Respect" is the most frequent term used in modern texts to attempt to convey all that Rogers meant by his cumbersome phrase "unconditional positive regard." While it may be inadequate in some ways, when properly understood, this term carries the connotation of valuing the other person, with no strings attached. The root meaning of respect comes from the Latin, meaning to "see again" or to "regard again." If we are to *respect* the other person we are required to see him or her again, *from God's perspective*, to relate to him or her as though he or she is a person of worth, regardless of what life has done or what the person has done in his or her life. Of course this is a biblical call for Christians.

> If we are to respect the other person we are required to see him or her again, from God's perspective.

Jesus accepted all who came to him. He made no *a priori* judgments about the worth of a person: he had time for children, for outcasts, for the wealthy, for leaders, for prostitutes, for adulterers, and even for someone we would see as a "raving lunatic." No matter what the other person had done or become, no matter what had happened in his or her life, for Jesus this was still a person made in the image of God.

We are called to be like Jesus, to "incarnate" his presence. Christian counsellors are called to see beyond the irritating, or off-putting, aspects of a person's behaviour and, empowered by God, to "call forth" the implanted elements of their God-image once more. We are called to see beyond the aggressive, timid, angry, meek, proud, defensive, violence-producing, self-excusing aspects of others and, in God's strength, to invite them to healing and change. Often the most challenging person is the most hurt person. When we get past the initial horror reactions to the abuser or the murderer and hear his or her story, it is frequently not hard to feel deeply for that person. And somewhere behind *that* compassionate response is the foundation for treating the person with respect.

[handwritten: REALISING THAT BOTH MOM AND DAD DID BEST THEY COULD W/ WAYS THEY WERE HURT]

Of course we would want to acknowledge that each of us has limitations in our capacity to connect effectively with others—particularly if their behaviour offends or frightens us too much. If we are seeking to counsel some such people but find ourselves too caught up with their offensive behaviours, it is appropriate to seek to refer them to another counsellor. But even in doing this, our best actions will be governed by respect for the possibilities of the person.

[handwritten margin note: ALSO KNOWING THAT I COULDN'T BLAME THEM FOR WHAT DID]

Integrity *(Being Real)*

Integrity is the counsellor quality of "being real." Carl Rogers used the words "genuineness," or "congruence," to try to capture the flavour of this counsellor quality. The implication of integrity is that the way we present ourselves to the other person "lines up with" our truest feelings towards them and our best understandings of them. Everything about the counsellor should "ring true." This requires the counsellor be a person who is not deceptive or manipulative in his or her relationship with the person seeking help. On this basis a relationship of deep trust can be built and this relationship will be a vital part of the person's journey of healing.

Integrity is demonstrated in our seeking to relate as openly and honestly as possible with the other person. We are not "bunging on an act"; we are seeking to be WYSIWYG- (What You See Is What You Get) type people.

Obviously, we are not to lie to people or manipulate them, so as to build a relationship with them. The Scriptural standard is to "speak the truth in love" (Ephesians 4:15). These two parts—truth and love—together are important in our understanding of how we are to live out integrity. The counsellor who operates only from the standard of "truth speaking," could easily harm the fragile person or discourage the tentative person. "Speaking the truth" can even be used as a weapon to hurt, and then, justify, sinful behaviour under the claim that we are "just speaking the truth"!

How many times has a husband or wife launched a scathing and damaging attack on a partner and then tried to justify his or her action by the words, "Well, I was just being truthful." We are not to be "just truthful"; we are to "speak the truth *in love.*" Once we bring in the qualifier *in love*, we cannot deliberately speak the truth in order to cause hurt.

The point of this is to clarify that, for us as counsellors, being people of integrity does *not* mean we are always compelled to share our thoughts, particularly if our thinking could be damaging. We are not to *attack* people with our opinion, believing our opinion is *truth*. We are *not* to be insensitive to the feelings of those seeking help. There will clearly be times when we avoid a direct answer because we seek to function from a base of love.

This requires strong wisdom

We are called to incarnate the presence of Jesus. Isaiah, using words echoed by Jesus in Matthew 12:20, describes the Messiah's approach to those in need, with the words "a bruised reed he will not break, and a dimly burning wick he will not quench" Isaiah 42:3 NRSV).

It is enlightening to look again at how constrained Jesus was in his conversations with people. Many times he appears to say little when much could be said. He does not "lecture," "preach sermons," "attack with truth," or "wage ministry" at damaged people unless someone needs to be confronted, and then usually by a succinct and arresting piece of truth. For example, our accounts record very little said to Zacchaeus, or the woman caught in adultery. What is said is sufficient. His most extensive confrontation with painful truth seems to have been reserved for the scribes and Pharisees in Matthew 23. And all the evidence indicates that the intensity of his anger expressed here is a reflection of the intensity of his love for the people of Jerusalem who are being blinded to the truth of his Father's love for them, by the hypocrisy of these religious and political leaders. The intensity of his barrage is also a measure of the "rusted-in-place" state of these leaders.

A final word about integrity. Being people of integrity does not allow us to be "tricky" in our counselling approach. There are some techniques and approaches that we consider to be quite manipulative, in the sense that counsellors use these to bring about an undeclared purpose while, on the surface, pretending and proclaiming another purpose. The issue here is the transparency of the approach. Of course all counsellors ask questions and make responses with the *intended* purpose of helping to clarify and bring to the surface understandings that will be helpful to the client. This is simply to acknowledge that all people communicate purposefully—we communicate with a "rhetoric of intent."

The issue at stake here is: Is our *intent* transparently directed towards effective counselling, or is it "manipulative" or "tricky"? We would hold that, if the counsellor cannot be open and honest about the techniques he or she is employing, the techniques should be eschewed. The approach is transgressing the call to be people of integrity.

Humility

Humility is another quality that we see as central to the task of being an effective Christian counsellor. The word humility derives from the Latin word *humus,* which means "earth or soil." To be humble is to be "close to the soil" or "lowly." Built into the "fruit of the Spirit" (Galatians 5:22–23), humility is a quality that Jesus demonstrated, and spoke of quite a lot.

In Incarnational Counselling we see humility as a core quality. Counsellors need a clear sense of their personal inability to bring healing to anyone. We are in the position of the person knocking on the door of a neighbour in Jesus' parable of The Friend at Midnight (Luke 11:5–8). As counsellors, we are left with a simple statement of fact to remind ourselves of our total dependence upon God: "A friend of mine on a journey has come to me, and I have nothing to set before him" (Verse 6).

Jesus reminds us in John 15:4–5 (NRSV): "Abide in me as I abide in you. Just as the branch cannot bear fruit by itself unless it abides in the vine, neither can you unless you abide in me. I am the vine, you are the branches. Those who abide in me and I in them bear much fruit, because apart from me you can do nothing." This truth prevents us from thinking that we, as counsellors, have all the answers or even any answers. It reminds us that we are completely dependent on God for wisdom and healing.

The best counselling will come from our taking the position of humble dependence upon God for his enlightenment and wisdom, in the work of counselling. (This of course is not to be an avoidance of our responsibility.) We are to use the best of our understanding, we are to read and consult others whom we respect, but ultimately, we are to recognise our limitations as imperfect vessels, and we are to seek God's wisdom.

Of course, this will take us to prayer on behalf of the people we counsel. We believe that we can never get past this responsibility. In Chapter 15 we talk about the various ways we can make use of prayer.

In secular counselling approaches, an approximation of this counsellor quality that we are identifying as humility is described by a variety of phrases. Some speak of the importance of a "not knowing" approach, or "anthropologist's mind," while narrative counsellors advocate valuing "local knowledge," or listening to and learning from the experience of the person seeking counselling. We appreciate all of these terms and support their intent—the desirability of removing the counsellor from "expert status" and placing him or her instead in the role of a fellow learner, a colleague, or a coach. We endorse the intent behind these emphases.

Even so, we see our dependence and the foundation of our humility in somewhat different terms. We recognise that we are also sinners, completely dependent upon God for wisdom and grace. So, as well as seeking the wisdom of the person being counselled, we actively seek God's greater wisdom and seek to be open to his Spirit.

Commitment to Life-long Learning and Growth

As disciples of Jesus we recognise that we will never reach complete Christ-likeness until we finally reach heaven. But God calls us to be committed to growing in godliness all the days of our lives. The Bible becomes our sourcebook of instruction in righteousness as we study and open ourselves to its teaching through the Holy Spirit.

However, for each of us as Christian counsellors, another important part of this ongoing personal growth is the quest to understand our own self. Often we find that we are a mystery to ourselves. We do not fully know who we are. If we do not understand ourselves, how will we understand the other person? And if we do not understand *our* needs, unresolved issues, unconscious desires, fears, and values, how will we keep these from getting tangled up in our counselling with the other person?

These elements of *my*self, my reactions and patterns of functioning that can intrude into my counselling are what psychodynamic theorists mean by counter-transference. They are aspects of *me* that, if I am unaware of them, can "muddy" my understanding of other persons and interfere with my ability to be an effective helper. *As a Christian counsellor, I am obligated to continue the quest for self-understanding so that I am better able to keep "me" from getting tangled up in my understanding of the "other."*

For this reason, with "beginner's mind," we need a lifelong commitment to understanding self and our deeper motivations. It is usually important for counsellors to seek personal counselling so they may better understand their own wounds and hurts, motivations, desires, and reasons behind their functioning in certain ways—all the elements of functioning that make them who they are. At the very least they need to ensure they have a supervisor for their counselling, someone who can be objective and can help separate counsellor issues from the issues of the client.

Growth in understanding also requires a commitment to undertaking ongoing professional growth in the field of counselling. All accredited counsellors have to undertake regular professional development as part of their commitment to growth. For the Christian counsellor, this means attending workshops and seminars to stay abreast of advances in the fields of counselling and psychology, and of Christian approaches in these fields. It means taking seriously the responsibility to be up to date in the reading of professional journals and books. Without this kind of commitment there is always the danger of becoming stale and lifeless and burnt out or, even worse, a danger to the people we want to help.

Even more, beyond the understanding of ourselves and deepening our knowledge and skills in counselling, we need to be committed to ongoing growth in godliness. As Christians this means an unrelenting commitment to becoming more like Jesus Christ, the process that we have come to know as sanctification. The supreme catalyst for this level of personal growth is our contemplation of the glory of our Lord, and our savouring the wonder of his grace towards us. (See 2 Corinthians 3:18 NRSV.) "And all of us, with unveiled faces, seeing the glory of the Lord as though reflected in a mirror, are being transformed into the same image from one degree of glory to another; for this comes from the Lord, the Spirit."

Summary

These then are the counsellor qualities that we seek to emphasise and develop in students as they undertake their training: a vital relationship with Jesus, empathy, respect for others, integrity, humility and a life-long commitment to ongoing learning and personal growth. There are many other qualities that could be emphasised because they also are important for the Christian counsellor. But we believe these six are foundational.

Further Reading

Cozolino, L. (2004). *The making of a therapist.* New York: W. W. Norton and Co.

Kottler, J. (2010). *On being a therapist,* 4th Ed. San Francisco: John Wiley and Sons.

Skovholt, T. M. (2012). *Becoming a therapist: On the path to mastery.* Hoboken, NJ: John Wiley and Sons.

CHAPTER 4

Effective Listening— NEW GRACE

Listening is absolutely foundational to the task of counselling. Although there are many skills involved in helpful counselling, we see listening as distinctive. Many of the other skills are, in fact, an aspect of listening. We position it here among our foundation chapters, because it is always relevant in counselling and, in the absence of the development of this as a skill, counselling will always be profoundly limited. In this chapter we unpack some of its complexity, clarifying key elements of the skill and emphasising the importance of committing to lifelong practice for all counsellors.

* * * * * * * *

It seems so obvious that listening is a key skill in effective counselling. What is not nearly so obvious is the fact that listening is not a simple skill—in fact, it is probably true to say that, rather than listening being a skill, it is a complex group of skills. It certainly involves our ears, our hearing. But it is clear that it also involves our eyes, our observing. And it involves our mind, our reflecting and thinking. It is an externally directed skill, in the sense that we listen to the clients' communications and observe what is going on with them. But it is also an inwardly directed skill, in that it involves us in noting what goes on in ourselves, and it involves us in listening to deductions, responses, hunches, intuitions, and inspirations that arise within ourselves.

Normally we are trained to listen to the words that the other person speaks, and this is important. Unfortunately, either indirectly or directly, our usual Western socialisation process also teaches us that it is impolite to notice other communications that are coming from the client. Hence, in clarifying communication, we often put much emphasis on understanding the words, but we neglect the other channels of communication that are open in the interaction between ourselves and other people.

Listening, however we define it or think of it, is important. Many times in counselling, people report at the end of a session, "I feel much better." When the counsellor probes to find out why, since the counsellor is often not aware he or she has intervened in any exceptional way, more often than not the answer is, "Well, it just helps to have someone listen. I think that's what helped." When a person feels he or she has been listened to, somehow the person feels validated, and some of the internal pressure associated with the problem starts to dissipate. Not surprisingly, the psalmist expresses his love for God in Psalm 116:2 because "he turned his ear to me"—God is a listening God!

> *When a person feels he or she has been listened to, somehow the person feels validated, and some of the internal pressure associated with the problem starts to dissipate.*

In our counsellor training approach we think of listening as a complex skill that requires the counsellor to attend to at least *eight* "channels of communication," outlined below. We list these under the acronym NEW GRACE. When people feel they have *really* been listened to, it has the capacity to feel like they have been "graced." The more common experience of feeling unheard, uncared for, gives potency to this *new* grace, this feeling that you really care, that you have really connected at a deep level with them.

Channel #1—N: Nonverbal communication

Perhaps it might seem unusual that we should make this the first "channel of communication." However, there are some good reasons why it deserves this place. Mehrebian (1971), in one of his studies, looked at three aspects of communication to determine their relative contribution to *whether the receiver felt positive or negative about the communicator*. He looked at the contribution made by the speaker's words, the speaker's tone of voice, and the speaker's nonverbal communication that went along with the words. What he found was that 55 percent of the impact for liking or not liking the speaker was contributed by the nonverbal information. Another 38 percent was contributed by the voice tone of the speaker. Finally, only 7 percent of the impact for liking or disliking the speaker was contributed by the actual words spoken. While there are other points that can be made, this study emphasises the central significance of non-verbal information that we take in when we are listening. It is vastly more important than we generally recognise.

So what does this mean in the process of listening in a counselling situation? It means that the effective listener will be tuned in to a range of very subtle information which the other person is transmitting, including such things as facial expressions; finger and hand movements; tremors; facial twitches; eye movements; tiny changes in facial or neck colouration; body posture; general body movement; the glistening of a tear; and so on. All these aspects of the nonverbal channel provide important information for the listener. They may be communicating information about the person's general emotional state, emotional changes occurring in the here-and-now, their degree of comfort or discomfort with us as the counsellor, the accuracy of what they are sharing with us at any given moment, and a variety of other bits of important information.

It is important to be aware that nonverbal information is ambiguous. We will make important mistakes if we think that we can "read" a person's nonverbal communication without checking our accuracy. Nonverbal information is useful for generating hypotheses, but we must remember to check the accuracy of our hypotheses rather than simply assume we know what is going on!

One client that came into our clinic gave all the manifestations of incredible anxiety—facial movements of the tongue and lips, including licking her lips. Everything seemed to say, "This woman is incredibly anxious." However, there was nothing particularly anxiety-producing in her current situation, and when questioned she claimed to not be anxious. The explanation emerged as the history-taking went on. She had been treated with antipsychotic medication in the past, and the facial movements were an unfortunate side effect, called tardive dyskinesia, that occurs with some people. Nothing to do with anxiety, although that's what it looked like! Remember, nonverbal information is ambiguous. It needs to be checked with information coming from other channels before we jump to conclusions about its meaning.

When we see people moving uneasily in their seat, it may be telling us that they are feeling uneasy because of the content in focus at the moment in the counselling session. However, it may also be telling us that they need to go to the bathroom! We need to be careful not to get carried away by our brilliant ability to "read" nonverbals, without checking the meaning of what we are seeing.

When nonverbal information does not match with what the person is telling us, and there appears to be a discrepancy, it is likely that the nonverbals contain the truth. A person is most likely not telling the truth when he or she colours with embarrassment when we enquire about his or her sexual functioning, only to have the person hasten to also reassure us he or she is comfortable talking about this. Of course we need to know what the embarrassment is really about before we conclude the person is covering the truth, because it *is* possible it has another source. However, we would certainly be justified in *forming a hypothesis* that it is uncomfortable for him or her to talk about this particular topic.

We need to set ourselves, then, to listen to the nonverbal information that people transmit. It should be a lifelong task. It is one channel we are not normally trained to listen to, yet it often communicates vital information to the counsellor. The counsellor who is skilled at listening to this channel will find herself or himself with a much fuller understanding of the clients' issues.

Channel #2—E: Emotion

When people share on some problem or issue that is causing them some distress, they don't simply communicate *ideas*. They also communicate feelings. The effective counsellor will have worked at developing the capacity to "listen" to the emotional quality of the person's sharing.

How do we hear the feelings behind another person's words? How do we hear the other person's emotional state? There is no single way but, rather, a number of ways for us to "hear" emotions.

Sometimes we hear it in the quality of their voice. The voice tone becomes strong and aggressive, indicating anger. Or it's very controlled, perhaps indicating suppressed anger. Or it becomes very soft and tentative, almost like a little child's voice, although the client is an adult of thirty-five. We need to ask ourselves: *What emotion am I hearing now? Is it fear, uncertainty, vulnerability?* Perhaps there is a tremor in the person's voice, suggesting nervousness or anxiety. There may be sadness or hopelessness conveyed in the tone.

Often there will also be nonverbal clues that help us hear the person's emotional state. Slumped shoulders, tears, a smile, animation, a sudden squaring of the jaw, tensing of fists as they talk of a parent's involvement in their life—these and a myriad of other minute nonverbal cues give rise to hypotheses about what the person is feeling. We need to be aware, in our wondering about nonverbal signals, that tears can indicate almost every emotion—sadness, anger, guilt, shame, joy, and so on.

Finally, the words people use give us information about their feelings. They may label their feelings directly—"I feel so angry at her"; "I'm frightened to talk about this"; "I feel sad when I think of my life." The effective counsellor listens to feeling words and will often reflect them, allowing the client to process his or her feelings more in the counselling.

It should be obvious that our interpreting of emotions needs to be tentative, just like our interpreting of the meaning of nonverbal information. Effective counsellors check out people's feeling states rather than simply assume they always know how the other person is feeling.

It is important to remember that listening to the emotion in another person is not something we do in many normal interactions. Clients frequently report they feel really "listened to" by their counsellor, when what they mean is that the other person heard, and acknowledged, not just the *content* they talked about but also their *feeling* state. It feels like a deeper level of being listened to, a new grace!

Channel #3—W: Words

Obviously the words spoken are a primary source of information for anyone counselling another person. We often begin the first counselling session, after some initial data collecting, by asking, "What is it you wanted to talk about?" The point is that if someone has come seeking help in counselling, the person usually recognises that he or she will need to convey to the counsellor what is bothering him or her. Their primary way of doing this is by "telling their story" in words.

Sometime during the fourteenth century, an unknown British priest wrote a spiritual classic, which has become known as *The Cloud of Unknowing* (Wolters 1978). His basic thesis was that God calls us to spiritual watchfulness, or contemplation, and to the task of reaching out towards him, *even though we do so from a position of never being able to fully understand or comprehend.* This is a useful metaphor for the task of the counsellor.

In counselling we are called to the task of effective listening, recognising that we operate from the position of never really being capable of fully understanding the other person, in all the richness of their experience of life. We operate out of our own "cloud of unknowing." Recognising this is a humbling but useful position for us to take. It forces us to operate out of the awareness that, even when we hear the words of the other person, we can easily misunderstand the *phenomenological* import of those words. That is, we may easily misunderstand what those words carry in the way of meaning, impact, and significance in the other person's experience. We remind ourselves, and our trainees, that it is valuable to operate under "the Rule of Unknowing."

> "The Rule of Unknowing requires that we listen carefully to the words that are used, and avoid falling into the trap of assuming that we know exactly what the other person means by the words he or she uses.

The Rule of Unknowing requires that we listen carefully to the words that are used, and avoid falling into the trap of assuming that we know exactly what the other person means by the words he or she uses. Everybody carries different connotations with the words they use. Sometimes they carry different denotations, as well. This may be because they are not clinicians and only have a rough idea of the meaning of clinical words. For example, one client at our clinic sat down and described his problem as "depression." He had been struggling with depression for some months. Now the definition of depression is well understood, so really there was no need to ask any more about what he meant. However, *the Rule of Unknowing* requires asking further questions, to say nothing of the fact that accurate diagnosis requires more than the client supplying a diagnostic word. Questions such as, "And what do you experience when this depression is troubling you?" needed to be asked. In seeking more information about what he had been experiencing, it fairly quickly emerged that this person was not suffering from depression at all but from acute anxiety symptoms! We need to listen to the words people give us, and we need to remind ourselves that, just because we have heard the words, does not necessarily mean we understand what they mean. We will often need to hear *more* words, descriptive words, explanatory words, to bridge the gap of understanding between them and us. We need to try to enter the phenomenological world of the other person as best we can in order to understand what he or she means by his or her words and what is distressing the other person.

When we focus our attention on the words people say to us, it is important to be aware that sometimes a particular word stands out. When talking about his first romantic relationship at age eighteen, a client stated: "I never realised until years later how angry I felt about the relationship. It was horrendous! I was completely overridden by the force of her personality, so I just went along. But I felt trapped, and somewhere deep inside I hated it. I hated her!" There are a number of particularly strong words used by this person—"horrendous," "trapped," and "hated." Effective listening requires that the counsellor hears these key words, these emotive words, and notes the strength of them. Effective listening probably requires that the counsellor ask more about them, to move to deeper understanding. For example: "Trapped? That's a pretty strong word. Could you tell me more about what it felt like when you were feeling trapped?" This is the process of actively listening to the words the client shares, without assuming a facile understanding.

The purpose of listening to the words—indeed, of listening to any of the "channels of communication"—is to *understand* the client. The word "understand" is made up of the two words "stand" and "under." It implies a position of inferiority, a readiness to take a stance under or lower than the other person in order to be instructed by him or her. It requires us to assume the position of "unknowingness."

If we listen to a person's words, or any other communication he or she may give us but fail to take a position of "standing under," then our listening misses something vital and is unlikely to be helpful to the other person. The counsellor who functions from the position of the expert who knows everything can be quite damaging. Our most effective position is that of the learner, the one who does not yet know, and, as such, we need to ask for help in understanding.

Channel #4—G: God

Incarnational Counselling holds that God is active in our world, and at a personal level, in our lives. We believe that "the Kingdom of God is among us" and that God, through the agency of the Holy Spirit, actively speaks into our lives, sometimes in quite extraordinary ways. As such, we emphasise that counselling is a process that requires us to listen to God, at the same time that we are listening to the client. If we neglect doing this, we neglect potentially the most important "channel of communication" relevant in our counselling. In this section, we simply want to introduce you to the concept; later, in Chapter 18, Hearing God in Counselling, we will develop this further.

The Christian who is training to be a counsellor recognises that he or she is ultimately dependent upon God in this difficult task of helping others. How do we hear his word in relation to the person in distress before us?

It is important to recognise that God communicates with his children in many ways. Primarily, he instructs us through his Word, through the Scriptures. We hold that <u>there is no substitute for spending time reading his Word and opening ourselves to the guidance of God given there.</u> If our hearts are open in prayer for a person we are seeking to help, there may be moments in our personal devotional time when a verse or passage comes alive for us, because of its connection to the person's situation. Of course what we need to do with a passage that seems to "take life" in this way is a matter for prayer. We need to ask God for wisdom in what to do with such a passage. Has he enlivened this word so that we should share it with the client? Or is it a word that is intended to guide us in understanding how to approach the task of helping this person? Or is it a word given just to encourage us about the outcome of working with this person? There are many possibilities.

Or perhaps a verse of Scripture comes into our mind not during our personal devotions but in a counselling session. In some respects the issue is the same: "God, what do you want me to do with this? Am I to share it with this person now, or is there some other reason for bringing it to my mind? Or is it just my mind wandering?" with the implication that we are not attending sufficiently to the person. We would simply emphasise two points. The first one is that God speaks through his Word, and the second one is that we always need to inquire from God what he wants us to do with the passage or verse. <u>Sometimes the message will be for the client; sometimes it may be just for us.</u>

In devotional reading at one point, God stirred into life the verse from Job 22:21 (NRSV): "Agree with God, and be at peace; in this way good will come to you." It was a word of instruction for a client who, right at that point in her life, was playing with the idea of going her own way, in rebellion towards God. Although this verse could be used as a general application verse to many such people, on this particular morning God activated it and connected it to this client in such a specific way that it was obvious that it was for her. Not surprisingly, when it was shared in a caring, but nonconfrontational manner, she broke into tears, and a significant turning point in her life occurred as she made a choice.

But God communicates in other ways as well as through Scripture. He may give an impression, or at times a "picture," or a revelatory word, which is somehow relevant to the person. It may be in the session or at some other time. Some people call this experience a "word of knowledge." The terminology is probably not important. What is important is to recognise that God *does* sometimes speak by direct revelation to us, and in the counselling task, we want to listen for his voice, in addition to the other channels of communication. The point is for us to be prayerfully open to direct communication from the Holy Spirit in the counselling process. If we have a heart that is listening for his guidance, there will be times when significant breakthroughs are made in people's healing journeys.

Two issues need to be made clear. First, we are imperfect hearers of God. Honesty, and godly humility, require that we be aware that, at best, we hear God with a lot of "static" in our hearing. We may be accurate, or we may be way off target. Therefore, we need to be careful about how we handle what we take to be revelation from God. People who assume they always hear accurately are, frankly, likely to be dangerous as counsellors.

Secondly, as Christian counsellors we need to be guided by ethical behaviour and sensitivity to our clients. We have worked with clients who have been given "words of knowledge" that have been damaging. One female client was told that she had been sexually abused, even though she had absolutely no knowledge, nor any symptoms to suggest that this might have occurred. Not surprisingly, she was distressed at this "information" and afterwards went through a turbulent emotional time trying to make any sense of the "word from God" that had been "dumped" on her.

If we are going to share a word of knowledge with a client, it is crucial to be aware of the importance of *how* to do this. The "counsellor" in the example above, who told the woman that God had revealed to him that she was sexually abused, was breaking crucial ethical guidelines. He was introducing *his* explanation (accurate or not) *as though this was indisputably accurate,* and this practice certainly leaves him open to charges of introducing "false memories" and of harming his client. He also failed to exercise due care in terms of how she received this bombshell. The truth is she was shocked and distressed, and he simply sent her off home! Such practice is quite culpable. She could easily have been in a dissociated state after being told something like this, yet she had to drive her car home. She could even have responded by becoming suicidal. For these sorts of reasons, it is *never* ethical to "tell" someone he or she has been abused. Any such discovery needs to arise from the client's own experience, or wonderings, without the counsellor "leading" him or her! If, as counsellors, we have some sense that abuse may be an issue, whether we believe this is a word from God or not, it is not appropriate to express this openly but simply to hold it as a hypothesis in our thinking.

When a counsellor believes he or she has received a revelation from God, it needs to be handled ethically and sensitively. Usually this requires two things: first prayer and secondly God's wisdom about whether to share. Maybe the "word" is just for the counsellor. If the counsellor decides to share the revelation, it is safest to say something like, "I'm not sure if this means anything to you, but I thought I was getting ["a picture of a baby crying," or the words "billycarts (a children's wagon) and bicycles," etc.]". A gentle approach like this allows the client to respond with an affirming response or to shake his or her head and look puzzled. In either case the counsellor has not violated the client's autonomy by "laying" something on him or her from the elevated position of "expert."

One more thing needs to be said about "listening to God." Usually, if a revelation is accurate, it is quite an emotional moment. As counsellors we can and should be positive and hopeful in such a situation. If God has clearly given some helpful revelation, then we are justified in having a faith-filled and expectant position that he is at work for healing, in quite a significant way. However, experience and the model of Jesus himself alerts us to the fact that we should also not get too carried away by the miracle that we have just experienced. Often it represents a significant step forward in understanding, but it does not "fix" everything. Usually the journey goes on, and there is much change that a person still needs to work through in terms of his or her patterns of thinking, feeling, and behaving. The client and the counsellor would naturally like everything to be fixed in one hit. It is rarely, if ever, the case.

Are words of knowledge simply another term for what Egan calls "advanced empathy" in his book *The Skilled Helper* (2010)? From our position, we would say no. The essence of advanced empathy is usually that, out of the counsellor's skills and experience *as a counsellor*, he or she "senses" things that are only hinted at, issues that underlie the client's sharing but that often lie beyond the client's conscious awareness. Thus, advanced empathy may lead us to sense unrecognised anger underneath the client's words. This is quite a different experience to having the words "billycarts and bicycles" suddenly emerge in the counsellor's mind, as he is listening to a client talking about her conviction that she is jealous about something but is completely blocked as to what that is about. There was absolutely no context for this phrase to arise, so the counsellor,

[margin note: Like with Marissa and describing the cycle of depression]

on this occasion, tried to put it aside, eventually feeling quite foolish when the "word" was shared. ("Look I'm not sure if 'billycarts and bicycles' means anything to you, but it just seemed to come into my mind there…") The client shook her head and simply looked puzzled.

However, not content to leave the issue because of some inner prompting, it was pursued a little further. Did she have any significant recollections to do with "billycarts and bicycles"? She recalled that, when she was growing up with her brothers and sisters they had a billycart, but there was nothing significant attached to the memory. She also recalled that she alone, amongst her brothers and sister, was never given a bicycle by her parents since she had been scapegoated as a child. However, there was no emotional connection to the feeling of jealousy.

A little more encouragement from the counsellor: Even if there was no awareness of jealousy about the fact that her brothers and sister had been given bikes but she had been left out, would she be willing to just lay it before God and ask him to forgive her if there was any jealousy attached? A gracious client, willing to humour a crazy counsellor, she nodded. As soon as she began to pray, the word "babies" came to mind, so after the end of the prayer it seemed appropriate to suggest, "I think it's 'babies.'" This time she began to weep and eventually shared that her unmarried sister was pregnant, and so was a next-door neighbour who already had three children. The pain for her was attached to the fact that doctors had diagnosed her with endometriosis and told her (some time earlier) that she would not have any more children. It was simple for her now to bring this issue before God and seek his forgiveness for the jealousy.

There is much that is mysterious in this illustration, but the simple truth is that God provided a revelation that was beyond any counsellor's capacity to create and used it for healing in her emotions. Sometime later, in a prayer time over the phone, this client had a vision of lying in a hospital bed holding a baby girl, a vision that came to pass within the following year. This is hardly the experience-based intuition of advanced empathy referred to in Egan's writings. This is God bringing revelation.

Channel #5—R: Responses within the Counsellor's Self

When we are involved in the process of actively listening to someone as he or she shares about his or her struggles in life, we will sometimes find our body manifesting idiosyncratic responses. We may become aware that we are starting to feel sleepy, or that our neck and shoulder muscles are tightening, or that we are sitting farther away from the client. We may become aware that we are talking more, and increasing the energy in our voice. Or perhaps we notice that we are holding back, almost as though we are afraid to say anything. We may become aware that our voice is shaking a little and our lips are a little dry. All of these represent another "channel" of information that the trained counsellor will want to monitor.

Of course there may be many times when we recognise that there is information coming in from this channel but not feel any need to do anything directly with it. For example, the shaking voice was not anything that needed to be commented on or to draw to anyone's attention. The counsellor noticed it and was well aware that it was just his human response to the fact that this was a crucial moment in the counselling. If he could not "reach" this person in the next few moments, there was every chance that a marriage, which had no compelling reason to finish, was probably going to end. The point is that this channel was responding to inner experiencing within the counsellor by broadcasting information through his body's functioning. There was no need to puzzle over what the source was on this occasion.

However, there will be times when the information coming from the channel of our own responses may be quite crucial. If we fail to pick it up, we may miss something of significance that might otherwise have been very helpful. For example, is our sleepiness just our own tiredness, or is it a regular and "normal response" to this person's lack of life in his or her tone or "boring" self-presentation? And if it is the kind of response that others also experience, dare I take the risk of sharing this response that I am having? Of course we know that Carl Rogers came to this point with one of his clients and finally shared the information in a caring confrontation. He found it a significant moment in the counselling. The person was able to receive it, and so began a process of change.

The key questions here are ones like: Are the responses that I am experiencing at this moment being triggered by aspects of the client's functioning that he or she is unaware of? Do others feel controlled by this person's demeanour, or voice tone, and also find themselves disengaging? Do others feel intimidated in the presence of this person and find themselves feeling angry? Do others feel drawn into having to "try harder" to help or "fix" this person's problems?

Of course physical and emotional responses in the counsellor's own functioning may not be "regular and normal" responses to the client's functioning at all. Sometimes there will be *counter-transference* responses in the counsellor. This simply means that some aspect of the client's functioning is triggering responses in the counsellor, which were laid down with *another* person in the counsellor's earlier life. Thus the counsellor may be feeling some rising anger, not because of the client but because the client is reminding them, in some way, of someone from their earlier life, to whom they attach anger. The client has a beard like the counsellor's father, or reminds them in some way of that school teacher who humiliated them in Year 9. In this instance, the response in the counsellor is not truly a response to the client, but rather a response *to someone else* that is being triggered by some aspect of the client's functioning. It is the nature of transference and counter-transference that these responses are unconscious. They are not in conscious awareness. Hence it is vital that, as counsellors, we listen in on this channel so that when we start to pick up information from unexpected responses that we are having with a client, we can begin the process of sorting out whether this is *their* material or *ours*! If it really is counter-transference material, and we are not aware of this, we will find ourselves caught in a very muddy, and probably quite unhelpful, counselling relationship. For this reason we encourage trainees to monitor this channel, and to take time to process unexpected personal responses to their clients, in supervision.

> *Sometimes there will be counter-transference responses in the counsellor. This simply means that some aspect of the client's functioning is triggering responses in the counsellor, which were laid down with another person in the counsellor's earlier life.*

Another vital piece of self-awareness. As counsellors we need to be aware that if we fail to understand our counter-transference, we can slip into responding to the transference offered by the client in a way that creates collusion. This is particularly dangerous when the offered transference is of a romantic or erotic nature.

Either way, whether the counsellor's responses are directly linked to client functioning, or whether they are the counsellor's own personal material, we need to listen to this channel. Its information will be vital at times.

Channel #6—A: Absent or Avoided information

Sir Arthur Conan Doyle's short story *Silver Blaze* tells the story of a champion racehorse that disappears from its stable on the moors. As usual the case is brilliantly solved by Sherlock Holmes, while the unimaginative detective, Inspector Gregory, struggles to figure things out. At one point the inspector asks Holmes to help him establish what happened.

Sherlock suggests that Inspector Gregory attend to "the curious incident of the dog in the night-time."

The Inspector replies, "The dog did nothing in the night-time."

"That was the curious incident," replies Holmes. The point was that the dog did *not* bark, which led Holmes to the deduction that whoever stole the horse was familiar to the dog. The *absence* of expected behaviour, or information that would normally be anticipated, can sometimes be quite significant as a channel of communication.

At times in counselling we are struck by what the client omits, or avoids, in his or her sharing. We are not aware of the significance of this omission or avoidance, but it is important that we recognise that it *is* communication. It is telling us something, although at the time that we notice it we may not be able to decipher precisely what this absence of material means. Understanding will almost always require further exploration. Nevertheless, it is important for us to be aware of this channel, lest we overlook an important source of information in helping us understand the client's world.

We may have asked the person about his or her family and heard the person speak of Dad and two sisters but suddenly notice that all mention of Mum seems to have been omitted. And because we are listening on the channel of absent information, we think: *I wonder what that means.* Or, when we enquire about their sexual relationship, one partner of the married couple gives the answer, "Oh that's fine!," and we feel that it's a little bit too glib, suggesting perhaps a desire to avoid talking about *that* area. Obviously in these examples there is more to ask, although we may decide not to push into the area straight away. *When* to probe more deeply must always be a matter of judgment. We would make a mistake if we thought that the omission of expected information always means we must probe there *right now!* However, we need to hear, and wonder about it, and obviously make a decision to follow it up at some point. The absence or avoidance may be telling us that this is a significant, albeit difficult area for the person to deal with.

Channel #7—C: Context

We also need to be aware of the particular context the client is operating in or, otherwise, we can easily mishear the import of his or her sharing. We may assume things that simply are not accurate, because we are judging from our own particular context.

Both of us have frequent involvement in the training of counsellors from other cultures. Although we are not "experts" in understanding these other cultures, we have made it a priority to listen more carefully to the issues and concerns that arise because of the different context. Context is particularly important when we are working with a client who grew up in another culture. The norms and expected values for our culture may be quite different and if we are viewing from *our* societal norms then we may well not understand.

For example, one of us worked with a woman who had migrated with her family from Iran. As she described the situation at home, *from the standpoint of our Western culture,* it sounded as though she had no freedom and was quite badly treated by her husband. However, it was important to recognise that her context was completely different because of her radically different cultural background, and these things were *not* viewed as a problem for her. The problem that brought her to counselling was quite a different issue. If the counsellor had failed to "listen" to her context, he could easily have directed attention to issues that she clearly did not see as a problem at all.

But context includes more than different culture. It can include such things as "listening" to the unique context of the abuse survivor, the solo parent, the overstressed executive, the couple repairing their relationship after "an affair," or the person dealing with multiple griefs. With each client, we need to carefully listen to context. While much of the time it may not tell us anything of unusual significance, on occasions it will. If we miss these bits of information, we may well turn out to be far less helpful than we would hope.

Channel #8—E: Experience

As we gain experience as counsellors, we start to "hear" information that comes to us as part of our wider experience. We believe that, provided this is handled with caution, it also represents another channel of communication. In this case we are listening to the client and passing it through the grid of our experience, and listening to the information thus generated.

The danger with this channel, of course, is that we could easily end up stereotyping the client, because we have seen many clients with grief, or a number of clients with this particular problem. While we want to be aware of this danger, and guard against it by actively listening to all the channels of communication listed above, we also do not want to disregard the accumulated experience gained through work with other clients. There will be times when it is helpful in guiding us on how to best help. Provided we do not become glib or carried away with ourselves, provided we can genuinely work from a position of humble "unknowing," then accumulated experience will add valuable information to the mix that we receive in listening.

Wrapping up on Listening

These eight channels all represent potential sources of vital information for the task of helping someone who is in distress. When we sit down to begin the task of Connecting, it is essential that we have some sense of the multiple, and rich, channels of communication that exist, and that we seek to develop our capacity to "hear" on each of them. While this is truly a lifetime work, the progress we make in this complex of skills will bear fruit the whole of our lives in the work of effective counselling.

Further Reading

Brady, M. (2003). *The wisdom of listening.* Somerville, MA: Wisdom Publications.

Donoghue, P. J., & Siegel, M. F. (2005). *Are you really listening? Keys to successful communication.* Notre Dame, Indiana: Sorin Books.

CHAPTER 5

The Incarnational Counselling Model

Incarnational Counselling is a model of counselling that is Bible-derived. It builds from a commitment to the unity of truth ("All truth is God's truth") and the unity of persons ("Each individual is a body-mind-spirit, not merely a body, plus a mind, plus a spirit"). This chapter looks to build up the specific tasks of the Incarnational Counselling model.

* * * * * * * * *

Our starting place is to take the following propositions as foundations for a sound understanding of people and their behaviour. We see these propositions as grounded in Scripture.

Foundation Proposition #1—Every individual is created in God's image.

Genesis 1:26–27 records

> 26 Then God said, "Let us make man in our image, in our likeness, and let them rule over the fish of the sea and the birds of the air, over the livestock, over all the earth, and over all the creatures that move along the ground." 27 So God created man in his own image, in the image of God he created him; male and female he created them. (New International Version)

This passage informs us that every individual has intrinsic worth and dignity since each person has God's imprint within. It also provides every individual with the template for a relationship with his or her

Creator, the true source of health and wholeness. However, the news is not all good in that the original relationship between God and his human creation has been broken through people's lack of trust and betrayal. This leads us to

Foundation Proposition #2—Every individual is a flawed and alienated being.

> Genesis 3 records the precipitate event in this fashion:
>
> 1. Now the serpent was craftier than any of the wild animals the LORD God had made. He said to the woman, "Did God really say, 'You must not eat from any tree in the garden'?" 2 The woman said to the serpent, "We may eat fruit from the trees in the garden, 3 but God did say, "You must not eat fruit from the tree that is in the middle of the garden, and you must not touch it, or you will die.'" 4 "You will not surely die," the serpent said to the woman. 5 "For God knows that when you eat of it your eyes will be opened, and you will be like God, knowing good and evil." 6 When the woman saw that the fruit of the tree was good for food and pleasing to the eye, and also desirable for gaining wisdom, she took some and ate it. She also gave some to her husband, who was with her, and he ate it. 7 Then the eyes of both of them were opened, and they realised they were naked; so they sewed fig leaves together and made coverings for themselves. (NIV)

This record reveals to us that we have an enemy. In the events recorded here three core relationships were broken as a result of the encounter. We believe the restoration of these three relationships is the key to an individual's growth and wholeness.

Those three core relationships are as follows:

- intimacy with God
- intimacy with one's God-purposed self
- intimacy with others

> *In the security and safety of the counselling relationship the person can explore their dynamics and the defences that alienate their relationships.*

It should be obvious at this point why the relationship between the counsellor and the person becomes so important in the counselling process. In the security and safety of the counselling relationship the person can explore their dynamics and the defences that alienate their relationships and allow themselves, instead, to be known at an intimate level.

As the person experiences grace in the unconditional acceptance and empathy of their counsellor's journeying presence, he or she can begin to more confidently face the painful realities of his or her brokenness and ineffective strategies for dealing with life. The therapeutic interaction of grace and faith moves the person towards restoring his or her core relationships, and this in turn facilitates growth and wholeness.

This next foundation proposition may be more controversial in some Christian circles, but we believe it has a biblical foundation, though we acknowledge this is tenuous.

Foundation Proposition #3—Every individual has an unconscious dimension to his or her functioning, and this intrudes into, and affects, his or her behaviour.

We are confronted with the intimations of the unconscious mind when we consider the biblical references to the "heart" of man as deceitful (Jeremiah 17) and James's comments in the New Testament on the capacity of man to deceive himself (see James 1:22–24). In Psalm 139 we read that that King David implores God to search his "heart" and bring any deceit to his awareness.

> 23 "Search me, O God, and know my heart; test me and know my anxious thoughts. 24 See if there is any offensive way in me, and lead me in the way everlasting" (NIV).

David is acknowledging that there are parts of his being that he is not consciously aware of, and he is inviting God to "know" them and to free him from any "offensive" parts or patterns. In Psalm 19:12–13, King David asks: "Who can discern his errors?" and distinguishes "hidden faults" and "wilful sins," suggesting there are dimensions to our functioning beneath conscious awareness.

A clinical example, demonstrating the existence of unconscious mind, would be the woman client who came for a consultation because she had developed a relatively uncontrollable urge to spend time rearranging a group of ornaments on the mantelpiece at her home. Often as the last thing at night, she would find herself going to get a drink of water but then stopping to arrange the ornaments, stepping back to view them from the doorway, readjusting them, and checking to see how they looked, over and over. Sometimes she spent up to an hour arranging and rearranging these small ceramic ornaments. She genuinely had no understanding of the internal compulsion that kept her doing this. In all other areas of her life, things appeared to be relatively "normal."

Questioned about when the behaviour started, she was able to identify a time, some months earlier. The compulsion had grown since then. At first, when asked what else had occurred around that time, she was unable to think of anything. However, after some time, she was able to recall that a month or so prior to the first manifestation of the "problem," she had become a naturalised citizen. In her sixties now, she had come to Australia as a migrant in her teens and had never taken up citizenship, even though often pressed by her husband and children who were all Australian citizens. As a "surprise" gift to her family she had decided to take up citizenship, and she had invited them all to the ceremony. Was there any connection between the ornaments and this significant event?

With quite a start, as the connection hit her, she noted that the ornaments included a little ceramic cow and other pieces that came from Ireland, her birth country. The counsellor wondered aloud whether part of her did not want to lose touch with her "roots" as Irish. Tears suddenly appeared as the full experiential awareness of this "aha!" moment connected. She was invited to go and consider what she could do in response to the "message" generated by this *unconscious* part of her mind. The next session was all that was needed, as she reported that she had gone home and taken a small sun room, which she had now set up as her "Irish room." She had the ornaments on display, together with some paintings by an uncle from Ireland, and a few other features from her home country. She shared that she sometimes just sat there for a while, or read while in the room. Having given appropriate recognition to her Irish "roots," the compulsion to adjust the position of the ornaments completely disappeared.

The importance that an unconscious dimension of our minds exists lies in its clinical implication. Any given individual has a history of events and processes, along with their attending dynamics and learned behaviours. Many of these factors are lost to conscious awareness but the templates from those factors continue to influence the decisions the person makes every day. The common occurrence in which a person initially perceives the counsellor as an authoritative figure is a form of *unconscious* transference that exposes childhood response patterns. This transference issue becomes a focus of intervention in the psychodynamic theories of counselling.

Foundation Proposition #4—Living in truth leads the individual to freedom, while deception enslaves.

Another foundation belief upon which we base our model of counselling is the understanding that we, as fallen humans, usually avoid personal responsibility and seek the cause of our faults and failings in other people or external circumstances rather than within ourselves. We look "out the window" too much, seeing blame and fault "out there" rather than "in the mirror."

> *As fallen humans, we usually avoid personal responsibility and seek the cause of our faults and failings in other people or external circumstances rather than within ourselves.*

The Genesis 3 narrative illustrates this at work in an obvious way.

> 8 Then the man and his wife heard the sound of the LORD God as he was walking in the garden in the cool of the day, and they hid from the LORD God among the trees of the garden. 9 But the LORD God called to the man, "Where are you?" 10 He answered, "I heard you in the garden, and I was afraid because I was naked; so I hid." 11 And he said, "Who told you that you were naked? Have you eaten from the tree that I commanded you not to eat from?" 12 The man said, "The woman you put here with me—she gave me some fruit from the tree, and I ate it." 13 Then the LORD God said to the woman, "What is this you have done?" The woman said, "The serpent deceived me, and I ate." (NIV)

In this passage we observe Adam blaming God for his need to hide. It is God's fault because God put "the woman" in the garden! Rather than acknowledging his fault, Adam also blames Eve for his sin of disobedience, excusing himself with *"she* gave me…" Eve, in turn defends herself by blaming the serpent, shifting the fault elsewhere with her explanation, *"the serpent* deceived me…" Neither takes responsibility or ownership of their sinfulness, but each chooses avoidance and self-preservation over truth. We have this same dynamic recorded in the biblical image of our tendency to see the speck of sawdust in another's eye while failing to see the plank in our own eye. "Why do you look at the speck of sawdust in your brother's eye and pay no attention to the plank in your own eye?" (Luke 6:41 NIV)

In counselling, people take major steps towards growth when they shift the focus from avoiding truth to accepting any such painful pieces of reality, particularly the reality of their own sinful internal processes.

We place an emphasis on these foundation propositions because we believe that everything we do in counselling needs to be biblically sound. We align ourselves with St. Augustine, who stated, "All truth is God's truth," though we also recognise that there are many opposing voices espousing "God's truth."

The safest way to ensure we are on God's pathway to truth is to take that which he has declared propositionally to be true and use it as a measure for other claimants. Accordingly, we

- consider a theory or strategy a candidate for inclusion into our Incarnational model if it is consistent with, or complementary to, biblical teaching; and
- exclude any theory or strategy from our model if it is inconsistent with, or contradictory to, biblical teaching.

At this point we want to introduce our basic three-stage model. We label this *Incarnational Counselling*, for the reasons outlined in the Introduction.

A counselling model is, of course, a kind of map. Its primary purpose is to provide a guide for the counsellor involved in navigating the process of counselling with another person. Like any map, a counselling model is simply a conceptual representation—not to be confused with the reality of the counselling experience. Just as a road map is not actually the bitumen, hills, valleys, stoplights, and traffic of the journey but merely a conceptual guide for the person undertaking the journey, so the model of counselling is simply an attempt to provide the counselling novitiate with a useful theoretical representation of the process of counselling. It is aimed at being a rough guide, enabling the counsellor to check where he or she is up to, in the process of counselling. There is always the danger that we could take it too seriously and give it too much *actuality*, as though it is somehow the reality, rather than an imperfect guide to the process of counselling.

However, we believe a useful model should also provide an outline of the *structural processes* involved in counselling. A useful model serves as a template, outlining the differing tasks that counsellor and client need to move through in the counselling experience. We wanted our stage labels to provide some direct scaffold—to virtually say to the counsellor, "Emphasise this now!," "Focus on this task at this point!," "Make sure you've covered this process at this time!" Such a model can provide guidance for the beginning counsellor who might wonder where he or she ought to be focusing energy at any one time. While our model does have a developmental aspect, it is more appropriately seen as a task model rather than a stage model.

We believe that any useful model has to be easily remembered. It needs to be the kind of "map" we can carry around in our head, rather than one we need to go and look up. A map that is too complex to recall will not help the counsellor sitting in session and inwardly asking: *What should I be focusing on now?*

Counselling models attempt to provide a conceptual representation of a *generic* process. We recognise that, in truth, every counselling experience will be, to some extent, idiosyncratic—because counselling is a dynamic process it will not fit perfectly with any generic model! While the model on paper appears to describe a process that is neat, sequential, and linear, the actual counselling experience may be more like the tangles in a plate of spaghetti! At the broadest level our model is sequential and developmental, in that the emphasis shifts from one task to the next as the counselling journey moves ahead.

However, again we acknowledge the reality that the task emphasis is likely to shift back and forth as new issues are brought up, or deeper insights gained, and that more than one task may be being furthered, all at the same time! So with the above points kept clearly in mind, here is our "bare-bones" task model of Incarnational Counselling.

Incarnational Counselling Model

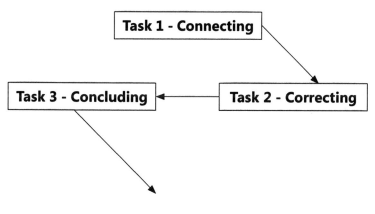

Figure 1

Task 1—Connecting

We identify three subtasks as part of this primary task in counselling:

- *Connecting* with the person
- *Collecting* relevant data
- *Reflecting* on the person's issue(s) and data

The first stage of counselling involves the task of sitting down together and establishing a relationship. We call this stage Connecting. The word connect derives from the Latin root *connecto*, meaning "I fasten together, I unite." Centrally, we see this first stage as a time of fastening together or uniting the counsellor and counselee in a relationship aimed at assisting the counselee grow in handling the issues they have come seeking help for. Connecting brings associations to do with the development of trust and mutual respect. In some models or theoretical approaches, this is titled the working alliance, the rapport stage, exploring the problem, or simply the beginning phase. We choose to call it Connecting because we believe this better reflects the vital, *relational* aspect of two people coming together with mutual trust and goals, engaging one another, and establishing a focused, therapeutic relationship.

With some people, the relational essence of this Connecting task will be covered in the first session, or even a part of the first session. Trust is underway, and the person is feeling safe or comfortable in the relationship with the counsellor. However, for others, this stage will be a longer, more drawn-out process, involving periods of unconsciously "testing" the relationship, possibly by behaviours that appear to block progress or resist change.

It is important to note that while we see Connecting as the first stage of the counselling process, and we place considerable emphasis on training novice counsellors to be able to work well in this stage, we are aware that, in truth, the process of relational connecting continues and develops right through counselling. It continues even when other aspects of the work are more in focus. However, we identify *Connecting to the person* as the first sub-stage in Stage 1 because we see it as crucial for the development of any successful counselling. This is the foundation for the ongoing therapeutic relationship. If we fail to *connect* therapeutically, we will not be helpful to the other person.

> *If we fail to connect therapeutically, we will not be helpful to the other person.*

However, we take the concept of connecting further. While the dominant force of this label for us will always apply to the development of a therapeutic relationship, we recognise that the counsellor's tasks also include *connecting* to aspects of the client's "story." This involves *connecting* to the data, the dynamics, and the dysfunction—all vital aspects of the person and his or her "story." We label this aspect of the work as the *Collecting* subtask of Connecting. We will focus more on this subtask of Connecting in the next chapter.

So, as we have seen, the counsellor is engaged in *connecting* not only with the person but also to a body of important information and understandings. Finally, the counsellor also *connects* to his or her wider body of understandings, as another aspect of helping the person. Clearly there are many points during counselling when it is important for the counsellor to give considered thought to the information already gathered. It is important that, from the earliest stage, we take time for unhurried reflection, looking for ways to make sense of the client's world and his or her experience in that world. We see this aspect of Connecting as the third subtask—*Reflecting*—reflecting on the person's issue(s) and their "story." This subtask is also "fleshed out" in more detail in the next chapter. Incorporating these subtasks, the Incarnational Counselling model now looks like this:

Incarnational Counselling Model

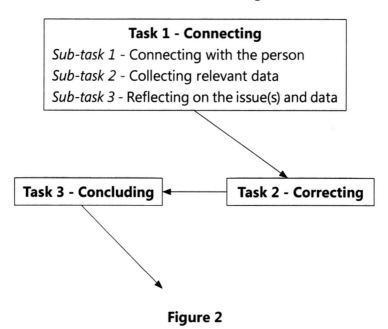

Figure 2

Of course in the early period of counsellor training, a key opportunity for thinking through issues to do with the material we have been collecting will arise through supervision sessions with a more experienced counsellor. We emphasise supervision sessions as a nonnegotiable requirement for ethical and effective training in counselling.

Task 2—Correcting

Three subtasks are caught up in the central task of Correcting:

- Correcting distorted thinking
- Correcting disruptive emotions
- Correcting destructive behaviours

The second major task in our model of Incarnational Counselling, we label Correcting. One of the Latin roots here is the adjective, *rectus*, meaning "straight" or "upright." The implication is that aspects of the counsellee's life that have somehow become "bent" or "fractured" in some way, parts of their life *that no longer work as they were meant to work* are being re-shaped to bring a restoration of "rightness" or healthy functioning. Our label, Correcting, in the sense we want to use it, also has links to the Latin root, *recte,* meaning "favourably" or "safely." We want this part of the counselling process to be conducted with the emotional safety of the person retained as a priority. As with the other labels for stages of the counselling process, the *"co"* part of *correcting* conveys the sense that this is a *joint* process. Client changes are worked out collaboratively as much as possible. Although we hold some reservations regarding the client's ability to understand what changes are needed for their life to run the way they would want it to, we also agree with the perspective that sees the client as, in some measure, the person with the most intimate knowledge of their issues, including causes and possible solutions. We want to make use of this potential by making sure that the client is invited into the process of restorative change.

By taking this position in Correcting, we are trying to avoid two equally undesirable errors. The first error *is the attitude of counsellor arrogance* – —the tendency for counsellors to assume they know best, that their wisdom is always superior, and that they don't make mistakes in their interventions aimed at bringing positive change for clients. We emphasise with trainees that this is not a stage where they are able to play the role of the "all-knowing" counsellor who imposes his or her brilliant suggestions for change on the "nice but clueless" client! We have already written about this in Chapter 3, where we gave attention to the importance of *humility* as an essential counsellor quality. The counsellor who lacks this is, to put it simply, dangerous, and could inflict severe damage on his or her clients, sometimes without even realising it.

The second error we want to avoid is that of assuming that the client, because of his or her struggles with some aspect of life, has no reservoir of wisdom or insight to bring to the counselling venture. This second error is *the assumption of client ignorance*. In our training of counsellors we emphasise what counsellors working from narrative theory have called "local knowledge"—the personal, intimate self-awareness that the client carries regarding his or her life and struggles. Obviously this reservoir of understanding is vital in all stages of the counselling process.

> *Correcting functions as a participative, interactive part of the counselling process, in which the counsellor and client talk together about the "how" of client change.*

So Correcting functions as a participative, interactive part of the counselling process, in which the counsellor and client talk together about the "how" of client change. Engaging in this task, counsellor and client discuss possible interventions, adjustments and changes in ways of thinking and behaving, and they "run experiments" in which the client tries to do some things differently in his or her functioning, to see if life is better, to see if he or she feels a positive difference in his or her experience of day-to-day functioning. The focus now is clearly on outcome. "How is your life working now that you are making this change? Are you experiencing an improved sense of well-being?"

This stage is usually grounded in the particular theoretical approach from which the counsellor works. Interventions aimed at helping the person grow will tend to be developed out of the counsellor's understanding of human behaviour, the counsellor's beliefs about the process of change, and his or her understanding of what aspects of the person's functioning to focus on in order to initiate and maintain positive changes.

What is the focus of our correcting? Amongst other things we want to give special attention to Correcting Distorted Thinking, Correcting Disruptive Emotions, and Correcting Destructive Behaviours. These three areas will be given more detailed attention in Chapter 6.

Incorporating these subtasks, the Incarnational Counselling model now looks like this:

Incarnational Counselling Model

Task 1 - Connecting
Sub-task 1 - Connecting with the person
Sub-task 2 - Collecting relevant data
Sub-task 3 - Reflecting on the issue(s) and data

Task 2 - Correcting
Sub-task 1 - Correcting Distorted Thinking
Sub-task 2 - Correcting Disruptive Emotions
Sub-task 3 - Correcting Destructive Behaviours

Task 3 - Concluding

Figure 3

Task 3—Concluding

The Latin root for our English word Concluding is the verb *concludo*—"I bring to a finish," or "I fulfil." If counselling has been effective, there is a point in which the client reports a level of improved functioning. Perhaps the depression has lifted, the grief has become manageable, the fear has diminished, the anger is more under control, the relationship has mended (or ended), and so on. Recognising the appropriate time for counselling to be brought to an end is not always easy. We see the word *concluding* as having a situation-specific application. We encourage trainee counsellors not to aim at fixing every issue or imperfection. The goal is not to try to reconstruct personality. They are simply aiming to bring to a point of *conclusion* the distressing issue(s) for which the person has sought help.

It appears to us that there are three ways counselling can conclude: traumatically, developmentally, and organically. Each warrants a brief explanation.

Traumatic Conclusions

A traumatic conclusion occurs when therapy is stopped because of a severe deterioration or disruption of the therapeutic alliance. Irrespective of whether the alliance can be repaired or not, it is advisable to have a closing session where there can be clarification as to what happened to make it possible for the client to resume with another therapist or with the same one. The key is for the therapist to not be defensive or punitive.

Developmental Conclusions

This is a conclusion that occurs prior to the completion of counselling where the client feels they need to "go it alone" for a while or they feel they are ready to graduate even though the issues remain. This usually occurs when the client feels more confident and independent from the counsellor. The counsellor needs to support the client in their move yet leave the door open for a return if needed. Beware of interpreting this attempt at independence as resistance or acting out.

Organic Conclusions

ANGIE? (handwritten)

There are some clients who "last the distance" and finish well. This usually is accomplished through several phases. It is a general rule that the longer the counselling and the deeper the therapeutic issues involved, the longer these phases take. An organic conclusion is worth celebrating!

The questions raised for the counsellor at this juncture of counselling include the following:

- How will I know when the presenting problem is at a sufficient point of conclusion?
- How will I know that it is time for counselling to be completed?
- How should I go about this process of concluding?
- What is involved in concluding well?
- What can I do to ensure that gains made by the client are not lost?

These issues largely form the content of chapter 8.

However, at this point we can say that Concluding, like all of the tasks in our model, is best conducted with due attention to the client's wisdom as well as the counsellor's. In truth, the most frequent guide for the right time to begin the process of finishing counselling is likely to be the reports of the client that he or she is doing much better, that significant, or sufficient, changes have occurred and that the distress that brought him or her into counselling is no longer as difficult for the person to cope with. Under most circumstances, the client becomes the best indicator of the appropriate time to begin the process of finishing counselling.

> *Under most circumstances, the client becomes the best indicator of the appropriate time to begin the process of finishing counselling.*

Of course this will not always be the case. There will be times when the counsellor's judgment differs from that of the client. The client believes he or she is ready to terminate counselling, but the counsellor believes it is too soon. Or the client, fearful of abandonment, believes he or she needs to continue while the counsellor sees the time as right for him or her to experience more of his or her strength by venturing forth on his or her own for a period. Although these differences of viewpoint tend to be rare rather than common, they are always difficult situations to negotiate. The most important thing to share at this point is that they need to be negotiated slowly, rather than precipitately. Room needs to be made for underlying concerns to be expressed, and the client needs to feel heard in the process.

In terms of specific focus, this Concluding stage involves, as subtasks, Consolidating, Coaching, and Celebrating. We will have more to say about these subtasks in Chapter 8.

The full Incarnational Counselling model incorporates these tasks and subtasks:

Incarnational Counselling Model

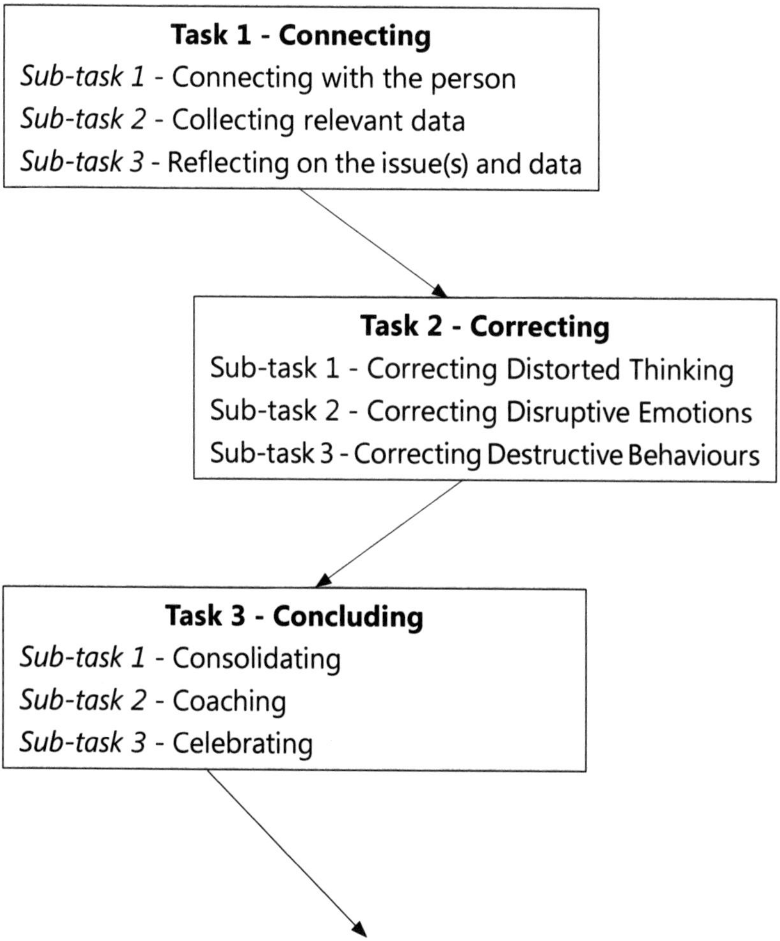

Task 1 - Connecting
Sub-task 1 - Connecting with the person
Sub-task 2 - Collecting relevant data
Sub-task 3 - Reflecting on the issue(s) and data

Task 2 - Correcting
Sub-task 1 - Correcting Distorted Thinking
Sub-task 2 - Correcting Disruptive Emotions
Sub-task 3 - Correcting Destructive Behaviours

Task 3 - Concluding
Sub-task 1 - Consolidating
Sub-task 2 - Coaching
Sub-task 3 - Celebrating

Figure 4

PART 2

Incarnational Counselling: The Expanded Model

CHAPTER 6

Task 1—Connecting

This chapter takes up the first task of Incarnational Counselling—the task of Connecting—and fleshes out the subtasks involved for the counsellor. These include Connecting with the person, Collecting relevant data, and Reflecting on the issues(s) and data in order to develop a strategy for change. All of these are vital aspects of the counsellor's work in effectively handling this task.

* * * * * * * * *

We have emphasised that in Incarnational Counselling we put the highest priority on developing a therapeutic connection with the person seeking help. The process of counselling begins with Connecting. There is no magic way to ensure that this connection takes place, or that it takes place quickly and efficiently, since it depends both on the readiness of the person to trust and to share concerns openly, and also on aspects of the counsellor's functioning. On the counsellor's side, the counsellor qualities detailed in Chapter 3 and other factors such as the perceived trustworthiness and expertise that the counsellor brings to the process are clearly important. More and more there is evidence to suggest that the person's resistance in counselling or, alternatively, their level of openness, is an outcome of *the quality of the interaction* rather than simply an aspect of the counselee's functioning or personality. Obviously, resistance manifests in the counselee, but it is a product of the quality of the interaction. Thus, it might be more accurate to say that it manifests between the client and the counsellor.

From a considerable pool of observations and research, Miller and Rollnick (2002, p.46) conclude that *client resistance behaviour is a signal of dissonance in the counselling relationship.* The reciprocal is also true. High levels of openness and trust exhibited by the counselee is a sign of a positive connection between the two people. These findings place the trainee counsellor on notice that, from the outset, connecting empathically, respectfully and authentically (to draw on Carl Rogers's three "core conditions"), and to establish an effective rapport, is an *interactive* process. Obviously, the counsellor has a vital contribution to make in enabling the Connecting to occur.

Subtask 1—Connecting with the Person

The person entering counselling for the first time will usually have questions, often unvoiced, about the process. They wonder:

- Will the counsellor be "safe"?
- Will the counsellor believe what I say?
- Will the counsellor think I'm "crazy" or "bad"?
- Will the counsellor *care* about me and my struggles, or is he or she just interested in making money, or seeing me as a "project"?

The beginning counsellor needs to be aware that these questions are a normal part of the initial stage of counselling, though they may be unvoiced. The demonstrated quality of the counselling relationship will, over time, give the person the answer.

Of course it is true that people come into counselling with varying degrees of readiness to connect, to take the risk of sharing deeply with a counsellor. If people are highly motivated to seek help and have no significant history of having had trust abused, they are likely to be open to the process and allow themselves to connect quickly. On the other hand, if trust has previously been abused, or the person has a history of experiencing rejection, the task may be much more difficult, and there is likely to be a period of "checking out" the counsellor, taking time to assess what sort of a person he or she is, and determining what skills he or she brings. Even though we do not usually have reliable, objective measures of the degree of "connectedness" that exists between ourselves and another person, we have a strong awareness of this quality when it is *present*, and, conversely, a strong awareness of its *absence*, when we are *not* emotionally connected. Effective counselling depends upon it being developed from the first session.

It is safe to assume that most people coming into counselling for a first session will have given thought to what they want to share. They are likely to have "mentally rehearsed" what they want to say. For this reason the most useful starting place in connecting, beyond the greeting and any other agency requirements, is to ask,: "What do you want to talk about?" This avoids the risks of "agenda setting" by the counsellor or inadvertently "leading the person" and, instead, gives counselees the freedom to share what they want.

Once the person has begun to "tell his or her story," the most vital skill for the counsellor in promoting the task of Connecting is the overall quality of his or her listening. Because the capacity to listen well is so important, we devote a full chapter to the elements involved in effective listening in Chapter 4. At this point it is sufficient to emphasise that effective listening in counselling, as noted already, goes way beyond *hearing* the words and understanding their general meaning. It certainly includes this receptive attitude but requires a lot more. In addition to the eight "channels" of communication identified in chapter 4, effective listening is a composite of a number of micro-skills.

- It is an *active* process, which involves sitting and hearing both words and data from other channels.
- It is also an *internal process* in which we are engaged as we give focused attention to the other person's communication.

- Beyond even that, effective listening in the counsellor's repertoire of skills also involves what we *choose to do in response* to what we have received.

Other counsellor skills involved in aiding this task of Connecting, using the broad descriptor *listening*, include establishing rapport, attending, reflective responding, asking questions, and summarising. In some senses, all of these counsellor responses are aspects of active and effective listening. While they are particularly important in aiding the first task of Connecting, they remain "bread-and-butter," foundation skills for every aspect of the counselling enterprise.

> *Often the first task for a counsellor is to provide the counselee with a safe "holding environment" where he or she can confidently and confidentially tell his or her story without fear of criticism or condemnation.*

Often the first task for a counsellor is to provide the counselee with a safe "holding environment" where he or she can confidently and confidentially tell his or her story without fear of criticism or condemnation. As we have noted already, some counselees are likely to find a first encounter with a counsellor to be a fearful experience. To share with a counsellor may be contrary to all the "rules" of the client's upbringing or may fly in the face of the belief system he or she was exposed to growing up. It may also mean the client will have to let go of a false sense of self or make accusations that tear at his or her family's fabric. The beginning counsellor, who assumes every person who enters counselling will be relieved and will look forward positively to the experience, is likely to be "educated" differently quite quickly.

Containing

This raises the question of how the counsellor should respond when counselees share highly emotional content. We need to help counselees "contain" their intense emotional responses by modelling the capacity to do this. The counsellor quality of genuineness frees us to be emotionally moved by stories of horrific treatment or dreadful experiences, and the counsellor quality of empathy affirms that it is okay to share these responses. So it is legitimate for us as counsellors to show that we are emotionally affected by client sharing, if this is a genuine response. Even so, we need to *contain* or manage our emotions. There is a huge difference between tearing up a little on the one hand and allowing emotion to overwhelm us on the other. If we as counsellors show signs of being overwhelmed, we model for the clients that their experience *is* overwhelming, and we fail to provide the safe, containing environment they may need. We might, in effect, implicitly teach them not to share difficult content because they see we cannot handle it.

Little things can make a big difference to apprehensive first-time counselees.

- Make sure the voice that answers their call for an appointment is pleasant and informed on all procedures so they feel reassured.
- When they arrive, make sure they come into a secure, comfortable, and relaxed environment where they can feel safe to share.
- Do not overwhelm the person with clutter or colour.
- Modulate voice tone and pace of speech so you convey reassurance, safety, and genuine care.
- Be reasonably organised in your use of time.

Overall, Connecting advances in proportion to the counsellor's consistency in simply being there for the person.

Direct Advice and Psycho-Education

When someone starts counselling, he or she usually expects some degree of direct guidance and instruction (Pekarik 1980). It is important to "tune in" to the expressed needs of the person, to know whether he or she is looking for you to "fix" the problem, or whether he or she is really just needing to "download," hoping you will provide a more helpful perspective. It is always useful to ask, early on, "What are you hoping to get out of our counselling together?"

Of course our capacity to provide "answers" to the struggles in people's lives is always limited, so it is entirely legitimate to defer giving advice. Counselling has a long and respected history of not rushing to give advice. More and more we have come to understand that "rushed solutions" are mostly unhelpful. They play a part more in calming the counsellor's need to feel useful than in actually *helping* the other person. So don't rush with "answers," and do be truthful when confronted with direct questions that stump you, such as, "So what do you think I should do?" It is completely appropriate, if it is the truth, to respond with, "To be honest, I don't really have any ideas at the moment. It's pretty early in our work together, and I'd like to know more before I venture any thoughts. I really don't want to do that too lightly. However, I'm aware that this is a serious concern for you, and I'm hopeful that, if we're both working hard on it, some way ahead will emerge."

Our point here is that we need to know what outcome the person is seeking. If the person is looking for direct advice, we will need to be aware of it and shape our counselling with that awareness in mind. If we ignore it in the interests of "not intruding our own wisdom," we will be less helpful. If someone is looking for our wisdom about a situation and we fail to hear this or to make any response, the task of Connecting will be made much harder.

In the big picture, Christian counselling aims to raise the self-awareness of counselees and empower them in the use of their God-given resources, so they are better equipped to work their way, productively, through future times of difficulty. In the first session, doing some psycho-education, or taking some time to teach people about relevant aspects of human functioning, will often be helpful. The provision of some information about the causes of depression, or the normal symptoms of a trauma experience, or helping the person understand how panic works, or guiding them in journaling feelings, or some such intervention, can be very useful. Diagramming the information on a writing pad, or on a white board, can help them absorb the relevance even more effectively. Some psycho-education can contribute much to this period when we are laying down the foundations of Connecting.

> Christian counselling aims to raise the self-awareness of counselees and empower them in the use of their God-given resources, so they are better equipped to work their way, productively, through future times of difficulty.

As counsellors, it is important that we appreciate that people themselves are the most valuable resource, with regard to understanding and making the changes they want. They are usually aware of their own behavioural and relational history. Some beginning counsellors believe the process of expounding *their* (the counsellor's) knowledge and experience will promote Connecting. While this may be true at times, more experienced counsellors know that counselees rate genuineness and acceptance even more highly and they give attention to relating in ways that convey these qualities.

The experienced counsellor will work to have the clients increasingly more involved in their own reparative process. Initially, the counsellor may need to help link their past patterns with their current issues, or guide them. When the counsellor shares those linkages with the counselee they empower them for change and convey respect. This also aids the task of Connecting.

An opportunity to work at developing these important micro-skills is provided in the exercises in chapters 9 and 10.

Subtask 2—Collecting Relevant Data

This aspect of Connecting involves connecting to the data, the dynamics and the dysfunction—all vital aspects of the person and his or her "story." On the positive side, effective helping is likely to be optimised when we can place clients and their current distress in a larger context. This will usually involve learning something about their childhood and upbringing, including significant events that have influenced them. It may be important to hear about the "history" of the problem and how they have handled it in the past. Over the years, what part have family relationships played in the development, maintenance, or improving, of the problem? What dynamics flow in the river of their personality? Do they have a demonstrated history of being anxious, or dependent, or aggressive, or something else? How do these "currents" play into the distress they are experiencing at the moment? Have they had counselling, and if so, what was that like and how did they find it?

It will usually be important to know if they are on any medication, or if that has been suggested before, and if so, how have they responded. It may be important to get a clearer picture of their resources and capacities, including the strengths and achievements they have demonstrated in their life up to this time. Some counsellors like to build a genogram with the clients so they can both see significant themes and issues that appear in the family history. All of these are aspects of Connecting to the clients, but we have come to see them, more specifically, as the *Collecting* subtask of the Connecting stage.

Collecting can occur in three ways:

1. Structured Interviews

This method is most effective when a specific time is allocated for the counselee to respond to structured questions such as found in the Mental Status Exam (used primarily by psychiatrists and clinical psychologists), or some kind of reasonably standardised questionnaire. The advantage of this method is that it can provide comprehensive demographic and personal health information in a relatively short time. It does not, however, easily lend itself to detailed expansion or clarification during the actual interview, and it may end up collecting information that is simply not relevant to the person coming for counselling

2. Life-History Questionnaires

Life-history questionnaires allow clients to write out their answers to predetermined questions at their own pace in their own time at a location of their choice. This method has the advantage of providing a fuller, more considered outline of the main events and experiences in a person's life but removes the spontaneity and some of the cohesion achieved in the structured interview. They may ponder over their answers or complete the questions over a number of sittings, creating a more manufactured response. It also requires the counsellor to read and assimilate the information without the additional interpretive context provided by the person's active participation. Things can easily be missed or misconstrued, and although these can usually be corrected fairly easily, some misunderstandings can remain. We have included a sample of an extensive life history questionnaire in Appendix A.

To be effective, either of these two methods needs to be combined with a less-structured personal review time where the counsellor can seek more detail or clarification.

3. Indirect Gleaning

When a counsellor uses this less-structured method, he or she builds up the essential information from the general flow of conversation within the sessions. This approach often takes longer; however, an experienced counsellor can guide the conversation, directing it to the most relevant areas, thus collecting the central information. In fulfilling this task, it is important the counsellor seeks more detail and additional understanding as relevant information surfaces.

There is always a danger that the task of Collecting can become excessive, so that time is poorly used and unnecessary information is amassed. The general guideline for counsellors these days is that only such information as is judged to be important to the person's issue(s) is sought. Because most people, including counsellors, are usually time-poor, and because of the cost of counselling, data collection needs to be held to the minimum. A basic life-history questionnaire is often the most economic and easy way to begin this task, although it will need to be supplemented by questioning into areas that seem particularly important.

Subtask 3—Reflecting on Issues and Data

Data collection is intended to serve a purpose. As counsellors, we are not interested in digging up the past to merely fill time. We are not into "archaeology for archaeology's sake." The purpose is to aid our Connecting, to give perspective and insight into our involvement with the person and his or her struggles. But, of course, our Connecting will only be improved if we take the time to pause and reflect on the data we have collected. Thus, we include a third subtask as part of our Connecting—the process of *reflecting* on the data we have and the issue(s) the person presents with.

It is also important to be aware that the counselee has a perception of why the counsellor wanted the information and what he or she will do with it. Empower him or her with the truth.

Once the counselee has provided sufficient relevant information, and the counsellor believes he or she has an adequate understanding of the issues, the counsellor need to decide whether counselling is the treatment of choice, or whether another form of treatment is preferable. Thus, *reflecting* also includes the screening out of persons for whom counselling is an inappropriate intervention.

> *The process of reflecting... goes on throughout the whole counselling endeavour.*

There may be obvious factors that determine that a medical or psychiatric intervention is needed. These factors could include:

- Psychotic episodes
- Severe mood swings
- Disease or alcohol-based emotional dysfunction
- Accident- based emotional dysfunction

There are other factors that necessitate a more specialised skills-based intervention:

- life-threatening substance abuse
- domestic violence
- alcohol-induced dysfunction
- legal issues
- disorders for which the counsellor's training is inadequate

Whenever a counsellor encounters someone with these elements, or factors like them that will dramatically interfere with counselling, it is vital he or she consults his or her supervisor or refers the client to an appropriate professional.

The counselling task of "weighing things up" is taking place at some level right through the process. While it may not always be the specific focus, it goes on at some subterranean level during the whole of counselling. It certainly goes on during the early counselling sessions, as the interaction flows back and forth. But, additionally, we emphasise here the importance of having a significant period of evaluating and reflecting *outside the counselling session*. Counsellors tend to lead busy lives, and it is all too easy for them to slip into sessions that lack focus, or that merely "trouble shoot" on the events of the week. In terms of our model of growth-oriented counselling, we believe it is vital that a more deliberate process of consideration be undertaken, so that we connect accurately and helpfully to the dysfunction, disorder, or, perhaps, even the diagnosis that fits this person. We think of this as the Reflecting subtask of the Connecting stage. If we do this work well, a *plan for growth* emerges more readily and can be usefully implemented.

One important difference between the counsellor and the person seeking counselling is that the counsellor brings his or her wider understanding of human behaviour. The counsellor also brings one or more theoretical frameworks to guide the processes of evaluation, synthesis, and intervention—bringing together bits of gathered information to help in understanding the person's struggles. Finally, the counsellor also brings his or her life experience, including counselling experience, to the tasks of identifying key events and themes, so these can play into which areas need further exploration, or where the process of change needs to start.

Drawing on this world of personal knowledge, counsellors formulate understandings of the issues with which the person is dealing (Johnstone and Dallas 2006). The process of case formulation will largely be shaped by the theory of human behaviour that the counsellor is drawing from, whether this is cognitive-behavioural, psychodynamic, social constructivist, systems-based, or some combination. Early on in counsellor training, it is especially helpful for counsellors to consider, in some structured way, questions such as the following:

- What is/are the problem(s)?
- What brought the problem(s) into existence?
- What triggers them?
- What maintains them?
- What are the person's strengths?
- How does all this information fit together to guide me in thinking about where we should focus initially in counselling?
- What other issue(s) should we attend to?
- What interventions/homework might be useful?
- How will we go about measuring progress and change?
- What risk factors do we need to guard against, lest they block progress or cause a relapse?

This process of formulation is important because it gives shape to the counselling. There is always some danger that counselling can descend into the process of "putting out brush fires" each week and fail to have an overall direction that is specifically focused on the presenting problems. This is a danger for every counsellor, not just the trainee, and it is especially important for those starting out. While there is value in having some time for "checking in" on how the week went, unless there is a direction to the work, a strategy that is being followed, some sense that "we are moving forward," there is a real danger the person will lose heart and withdraw. Counselling needs to be more focused than simply listening to the counselee's experience of the past week.

This process of reflecting, as we have noted, goes on throughout the whole counselling endeavour. It is not unique to this primary task of Connecting. Even so, we include it in Connecting because it clearly contributes to the nature and quality of the counselling relationship and shapes the ongoing course of counselling. It is not the first thing a counsellor attends to, but it needs attention reasonably early, or there is a danger that the connection, and counselling itself, will flounder.

Further Reading

Windy Dryden, W. (2008). *The therapeutic alliance* as an *integrating framework*. Thousand Oaks: Sage.

Muran, J.C. & Barber, J.P. (2010). *The therapeutic alliance: An evidence based guide to practice.* New York: Guilford Press.

Horvath, A. O. & Luborsky. L. (1993). The role of the therapeutic alliance in psychotherapy. *Journal Of Consulting And Clinical Psychology.* 61, (4), 561–73.

CHAPTER 7

Correcting

Correcting is the second task in counselling. In many ways it is the central task, except that we recognise from research that successful Correcting depends largely on the quality of the counselling relationship. In other words, effective Correcting derives from and is dependent upon the success of the Connecting task.

In this chapter we give attention to the specific subtasks of Correcting—Correcting distorted thinking, Correcting disruptive emotions, and Correcting destructive behaviours.

The subtasks of Correcting take us directly into several of the theories of human behaviour, each with a distinctive emphasis on a dimension of human functioning.

Subtask 1—Correcting Distorted Thinking

It will come as no surprise that the beliefs we hold and the ideas we believe are key motivators for the way we behave. Clear, rational thinking usually leads to healthy positive actions while confused or distorted thinking seldom results in healthy positive actions. This idea is reflected in James Allen's literary essay "As a Man Thinketh," which contains the following:

> Mind is the master power that moulds and makes,
> And man is mind, and evermore he takes
> The tool of thought, and, shaping what he wills,
> Brings forth a thousand joys, a thousand ills—
> He thinks in secret, and it comes to pass:
> Environment is but his looking-glass.

The title was influenced by the book of Proverbs 23:7, "As a man thinketh in his heart, so is he" (KJV). Both Allen and the author of Proverbs acknowledge that the mind is the motivator of behaviour. St. Paul reflects this thought in his Romans 12 passage where he urges, "be transformed by the renewing of your mind." This phenomenon is the basis of cognitive therapy that seeks to change mood and actions through correcting "stinkin' thinkin'" or, in more psychological terms, "cognitive distortions."

A simple way of illustrating the way thought affects the way a person feels and behaves is to imagine our mind as a lens through which all data from our senses pass. The lens, however, is ground by many factors, some of which are positive, such as a sound educational experience or a healthy functional home, while others may be negative, such as a traumatic experiences or an impoverished childhood. These factors grind the lens that in turn influences the beliefs.

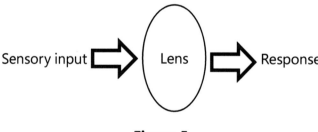

Figure 5

Aaron Beck, the founder of Cognitive Therapy has identified a number of common distortions encountered in the therapy room:

All or Nothing Thinking is sometimes referred to as "black-and-white" thinking. People with this distortion do not see middle ground, assuming there are only two polarised possibilities. For example, someone assumes that if he or she fails to achieve all credits in the assignments, he or she will be perceived as a failure and will be asked to leave the program.

Overgeneralisation: In this thought distortion, the person extrapolates to his or her entire future based on a single occurrence. For example, someone assumes that if he or she failed his or her first basic skills mini-test, he or she is just not cut out to be a counsellor.

Catastrophising: This thought distortion magnifies the outcomes or effects of thoughts or behaviours so as to create unmanageable anxiety. For example, someone imagines he or she will be asked to leave college because of two overdue library books.

Minimising and Maximising: This distortion discounts all accomplishments and magnifies errors. For example, someone berates himself or herself for scoring one below-average grade while ignoring the remaining credits.

Fortune Telling: This distortion leads people to predict that things will inevitably turn out for the worst, no matter what they do or say. For example, they are convinced that no matter how well their project is presented, no one will like it.

Emotional Reasoning: This distortion results in emotions ruling over thoughts and actions. For example, someone mispronounces the key concepts in his or her presentation and feels foolish and assumes other people see him or her that way too.

Shoulds and Oughts: What has been called "hardening of the 'oughteries'" (Ellis, 1997) occurs when someone focuses on what other people expect of him or her, rather than on his or her own needs. For example, someone feels he or she ought to help his or her project buddy with the buddy's part of the project, even though it will cost him or her time.

Magical Thinking: This distortion involves believing that your or another person's specific acts correlate with unrelated good fortune or threatened or actual calamities. For example, someone believes the failure to phone his or her husband resulted in his or her having a car accident on the way home.

Labelling: This distortion causes people to identify or label their mistakes and failures in personal holistic terms. For example, they say, "I *am* a complete loser" instead of saying, "I *made* a judgement error."

Albert Ellis, the founder of Rational Emotive Behaviour Therapy labelled distorted thinking as "irrational thoughts" that clutter our mind and prevent healthy functioning. The most common "irrational thought" seems to be, "I cannot be happy unless everyone likes me." Others include the following:

- When somebody disagrees with me, it is a personal attack against me.
- I have to be successful in everything I do, otherwise it's terrible.
- My true value as an individual depends on what others think of me.
- I am in absolute control of my life. If something bad happens, it is my fault.
- The past always repeats itself. If it was true then, it must be true now.

Everyone at some time engages in distorted thinking; it is one of our natural defences against a harsh reality or compensation for a perceived deficit. In most cases, these thoughts do not impair cognitive functioning. However, distorted thinking is often amongst a cluster of symptoms that exist with high anxiety and other neuronal misfiring. Below are some recognised strategies for dealing with distorted thinking. The skills that accompany these strategies will be presented in Chapter 11.

- **Identify the Distorted Thoughts and their Consequences**

Clients can compose a list of their most common troublesome or identified distortions and match them with their effects. Doing this exercise helps externalise the issues and aids in a more rapid reality check.

- **Challenge the Thoughts with Counter-Beliefs and Reality Checks**

When the neurons misfire and automatic distorted thoughts appear, they can be "neutralised" by counter-beliefs. For example, "I am stupid" can be countered with, "Sometimes I do make mistakes; however, other times I make sound decisions."

- **Self Care**

An alternative to devaluing "self-talk" is to talk to ourselves in the same respectful and caring way that we would talk with a friend in a similar situation.

- **Scaling the Problem**

Instead of thinking about our problem or predicament in an either/or polarity, evaluate things on a scale of zero to one hundred. When a plan or goal is not fully realised, re-evaluate the experience as a partial success, again, on a scale of zero to one hundred.

- **Reality Checks**

It can be helpful to seek the opinions of others regarding whether our thoughts and attitudes are realistic.

- **Reframe the Problem**

Rather than accepting total blame for the problems and predicaments experienced, identify external factors and other individuals who might have contributed to the problem. Provide a window through which to view your issue as an opportunity to learn or to eliminate a perception or behaviour.

We present a more detailed look at skills for changing thinking in chapter 11.

Subtask 2—Correcting Disruptive Emotions

Emotion can be understood as a spontaneous affective state of consciousness in which feelings and sensations are experienced, accompanied by certain physiological and cognitive changes.

It is worth noting that emotions were not always perceived in this way. The roots of emotion can be seen in the Latin word "motus" (movement), suggesting it has something to do with "motion." The premier Christian theologian Augustine (440 AD) thought so, as did Thomas Aquinas (1250 AD), both of whom wrote extensively on this issue. The problem, however, was that the concept of what we now call emotion was not known as such by the ancients. In the Greco-Roman period emotion was generally conceived to be a part of the "body" and therefore at odds with the mind. Not surprisingly, it was demeaned by the Gnostics and their sub-grouping of Stoics.

Augustine and Aquinas preferred the Aristotelian term "pathos" for the emotions. In this view, emotion was largely a passive state, located within a general metaphysical landscape contrasting active and passive, form and matter, and actuality and potentiality. The Roman Stoics frequently translated "pathos" as *perturbatio*, which came to have a particularly negative ring. Seneca (50 AD) used *affectus*, while others preferred *passio*, which explicitly connected the emotions with "undergoing," or "suffering."

All of these translations, however, emphasised passivity, particularly the psychological passivity of the emotions and the sense in which they are out of voluntary control and, indeed, not a proper part of humanity. These words were commonly used in the New Testament (NT) translations. The one word that was *not* in the NT was "emotion," although some well-meaning translators used the word freely.

In what became known as the central motif in the "classical Christian view," passions were considered involuntary, inappropriate, unruly forces in need of control by reason, will, and virtue, while those more godly and voluntary parts of man's soul were spoken of as "affections." The passions were lower appetites that *moved* towards the worldly or fleshly objects while affections were appropriate *movements* of the reasoned will towards goodness, truth, and, ultimately, towards God (Dixon 2003). The classical view was the dominant understanding by theologians, physicians, and philosophers of what we, nowadays, term emotion, until at least the eighteenth century. By the end of the nineteenth century, emotion had become a legitimate field of study for the scientific community, riding the wave of Darwinian evolutionary theory. The conservative theologians of the time such as Sewell (1840) and Gorman (1875) held to the mind's connection to and to its governance of the emotions and fought hard against the rising tide of naturalistic materialists that gained impetus from the works of the "Darwinian sect," including Huxley (1863) and Bain (1859). However, society in general had relegated to history the belief that emotions were a dimension of the Creator's image in man designed to assist in the successful living of an intelligent and moral life.

Peripheralist Theory of Emotion

A significant milestone in the current understanding of emotion was achieved when William James published his "peripheralist" theory of emotion in 1890. It immediately became the benchmark for all psychological theories of emotion.

The peripheralist theory of emotions proposes that emotion is experienced when the organism becomes aware of visceral and somatic changes induced by some event. Specific combinations of visceral changes produce different emotion states that we have experienced, and as a result, our autonomic nervous system creates physiological events such as muscular tension, heart rate increases, perspiration, dryness of the mouth, and so on. The bodily sensation prepares us for action, as in the fight-freeze-or-flight reaction. Emotions grab our attention and, at least, attenuate slower cognitive processing.

Centralist Theory of Emotion

The peripheralist position was largely supplanted by the Cannon-Bard theory or "centralist" position that proposed that emotions result from concurrent brainstem and cortical events (Colman, 2009). Normally the cortex inhibits the thalamus's intervention. An emotion-producing event removes this inhibition and the impulses that are released to the autonomic nervous system produce the emotional behaviour through physiological changes, such as muscular tension and sweating.

Two-factor Theory of Emotion

With the rise of Cognitive Behavioural Therapy [CBT] and neurological-based therapies, the emotions are more likely to be seen in the light of the Schacter-Singer two-factor-type theories that propose that emotions and emotional behaviour are produced as a result of information from two systems: the internal state regulated by the hypothalamus within the limbic system and the external environment or context in which the internal state occurs (Colman, 2009). Emotions are, therefore, perceived as cognitive interpretations of physical arousal. The response, therefore, would be moderated by an appraisal of the mind through its various schemas. This was actually a return of sorts to the Judeo-Christian model without a theistic worldview.

The Limbic System

The limbic system has long been referred to as the emotional brain. Anand (2006) notes the limbic system is an abstraction and not an anatomical referent. It is an attempt to integrate neurobiological and psychoanalytical thought on drives, affects, behaviour and learning. It is defined around the hippocampal formation which is the centre of sensory integration and, therefore, seen as the centre of emotional experience. The limbic system comprises the hippocampus, the parahippocampal gyrus, the amygdala, and the thalamus. It projects stimuli to the hypothalamus, which gives rise to emotional expression. The limbic system's functions of emotions encompass

- flexibility of behavioural response to reinforcing stimuli;
- motivation;
- communication;
- social bonding; and
- survival responses.

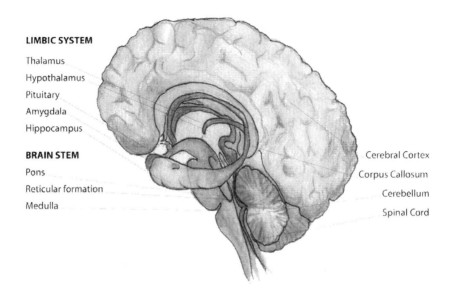

Figure 6—The Limbic System

As with cognitive distortions, disruptive emotions intrude upon all but the most psychotic of persons. We are all victims of our emotions at some time. However, when emotions dominate our lives or create chaos within them, we are dealing with a clinical issue. Following are several recognised strategies that are recommended for the correction of disturbing emotion, while a richer look at skills for change with emotions will be presented in Chapter 12.

Self-regulation

Self-regulation has been described as an "ongoing inner conversation" that allows us to find ways to control emotional impulses and even to channel emotions in useful ways. Through consciously choosing emotional responses to people and events, we are able to be less reactive

> *We are all victims of our emotions at some time. However, when emotions dominate our lives or create chaos within them we are dealing with a clinical issue.*

and more motivated and focused. Time is not wasted on negative emotions that inhibit the ability to achieve all that we want on a personal and professional level.

"Three-T" Solution: Time out, Think it out, and Talk it out

Step 1. Time Out: When we notice the start of physical steps of a reaction we need to declare a "time out" and put space between ourselves and the stimuli. This can be done physically by removing oneself from the situation, or mentally by switching the internal focus to another space.

Step 2. Think It Out: Here we ask ourselves, *To what am I reacting?* This is usually something prior to the immediate situation. Remember, a "$100 reaction to a $1 situation" tells us we are overreacting. Presumably we are withdrawing emotional currency from our stored-up emotional bank.

Step 3. Talk It Out: Children act out while adults talk it out, so we can ask ourselves, *What would be more helpful?* and act on that. Or having identified the source of an angry reaction, we could discuss the situation with the immediate party in a less-hostile manner. It also helps to accept responsibility for our responses. Remember, nobody makes us upset, we give ourselves permission to get upset.

Subtask 3—Correcting Destructive Behaviours

The Early Psychodynamic Approach

Changing behaviour can be a difficult task at the best of times, whether it is a golf swing or study patterns. If the behaviour pattern is of the entrenched destructive variety, then it is often even more difficult. The behavioural theorists have debated the causes and means of correction for more than a century. Sigmund Freud, in the early Twentieth century, postulated that we all have an unconscious self-destructive impulse that he called *thanatos*, which leads us to sabotage our good intentions and drives us towards self-destruction. This drive, according to the psychoanalytic community, is often observed in a person's resistance to any change that would enhance the *eros*, or drive for life. The presence of this impulse makes it difficult to correct destructive behaviours. The treatment prescribed, therefore, is the identification and resolution of the underlying psychic conflict that birthed the self-destructive drive. Secondly, we need to replace it with a more mature response pattern. For example, a bulimic patient would need to discover what his or her purging behaviour is seeking to accomplish on a conscious and an unconscious level, and then address the underlying core issue in a more conscious and developmentally mature manner.

Contemporary Approaches

Since the mid 1950s, behavioural researchers have put forward the theory that individuals engage in any given behaviour because it provides a rewarding experience. The behaviour may well be self-destructive in the long term; however, in the short term the reward outweighs the cost. This research has led to many treatment interventions where the operant conditioning principles espoused by Skinner (1938) and his adherents have been implemented. The more common term used for this approach is behaviour modification.

Behaviour modification is based on the belief that all behaviour is controlled by aspects of the environment. In this theory both internal and external aspects of our body constitute an environment. An excellent example can be seen in the swimmer who sees a shark and leaves the surf and retreats to the shore. According to behavioural theorists, the swimmer is not retreating because he is "scared." Instead, he is leaving the water because many of those who did not in the past were attacked. Therefore, the urge to retreat is primarily the result of this knowledge. In addition, the subjective feeling of being "scared" is considered a flight, fight, or freeze reflex, not an emotion. Physiologically, the heart races and production of the chemical adrenaline increases as the central nervous system reacts to the "environment" of the body. Therefore, according to this theory, all behaviours can be a target for behaviour modification.

To modify behaviour, the desired behaviour must be reinforced and any undesirable behaviour must be discouraged. The methodology often involves what Skinner termed "shaping." The desired behaviour is typically broken down into components so that the individual is reinforced for every action that increasingly approximates the desired behaviour. For example, a smoker attempting to quit is given a reward for each hour, then each day, and then each week that a cigarette is not smoked until the desired behavioural goal is achieved.

> *The key to correcting destructive behaviours emanating from "maladaptive schemas" with Schema Therapy is to identify and test the maladaptive schemas and identify and strengthen the more adaptive schemas.*

The more recent focus on Cognitive Behavioural Therapy has produced recognition of the role that thinking and cognitive schemas play in behaviour selection and, therefore, the role they can play in correcting destructive behaviours. A schema has been defined by Aaron Beck (1967) as "A structure for screening, coding, and evaluating the stimuli impinging on the organism... by which the individual is able to categorise and interpret his experiences in a meaningful way" and, in 1990, as "specific rules that govern information processing and behaviour." Some theorists refer to schemas as the "core beliefs" that determine behaviour.

The key to correcting destructive behaviours emanating from "maladaptive schemas" with Schema Therapy is to identify and test the maladaptive schemas and identify and strengthen the more adaptive schemas. In Chapter 13 we outline specific treatment skills and techniques that accompany each model of therapeutic behavioural correction.

Further Reading

Backus, W. & Chapian, M. (2000) *Telling yourself the truth*. Minneapolis: Bethany

Beck, J. & Beck, A. (2011). *Cognitive behaviour therapy, (2nd Ed.): Basics and beyond*. New York: Guildford Press.

Ellis, A. (1977). *Handbook of Rational-Emotive Therapy*. New York: Springer

Thurman, C. (1999) *The lies we believe*. New York: Nelson

CHAPTER 8

Concluding

When the task of Connecting has gone well and the change process involved in Correcting has also gone well, the person is able to resume healthy involvement in life, free from the restrictions and distress of the presenting problem(s).

In the counselling enterprise, the third task, also essential, now lies ahead. This is the task of Concluding—a task that involves

- Consolidating;
- Coaching; and
- Celebrating.

Subtask 1—Consolidating

Once clients have met their therapeutic goals, they tend to move in one of two directions. Some will view the process as a completed whole and want to move on as quickly as possible. Others will want to prolong the final subtask as long as possible and, perhaps unconsciously, avoid any painful separation issues. This is particularly true of those clients who have been involved in longer-term therapy. Both sets of clients will benefit from a period of review where they identify the key events that facilitated the desired changes and those times when they felt stagnant or disengaged from the process.

> *The counsellor needs to inform the client of the benefits derived from revisiting the entire process through which their gains were achieved and recognising the steps or phases they negotiated.*

The task of identifying the key points of change, stagnation, and disengagement aids in consolidating the gains achieved during their therapy. The "primacy" and "recency" effects will probably focus their thoughts on the beginning and ending periods of therapy rather than the work that occurred during the middle, usually the most difficult, period. The counsellor needs to inform the client of the benefits derived from revisiting the entire process through which their gains were achieved and recognising the steps or phases they negotiated. In so doing, the client will further own the changes they achieved and be better grounded in these.

The same process is important for those clients for whom therapy has been a less-than-successful experience. In these cases their understanding of the point or points where they believe the therapist or the therapeutic process aided, or possibly, failed them, will enable them to make more informed decisions concerning their future participation or non-participation with another therapist. They will also leave knowing they are still on an incomplete journey to health.

Subtask 2—Coaching

In the same way that the Consolidating subtask focuses on reviewing the time the client has been engaged in therapy, the Coaching subtask focuses on previewing the possible situations and issues the client may encounter when they move on from their therapy.

In recent years the field of coaching has become a profession in its own right as more people recognise their professional careers and personal lives require a closer mentoring and guidance process. This new profession makes us aware of many tasks implemented by competent counsellors in the closing phases of therapy for decades:

- identification of probable troublesome situations
- identification and rehearsal of appropriate strategies to meet such situations

- identification of community and personal resources to assist when such situations arise

Identification of Probable Troublesome Situations

Most clients will leave therapy with a sense of trepidation. They will usually be able to identify areas of possible conflict and regression. It is important that they have the opportunity to do so, as an unexpected bad day or event might otherwise seriously derail their functioning.

Counsellors will already have addressed many of the probable areas of conflict during the therapy sessions but there could be some that result from therapy itself. For example, a woman with poor boundaries who has found her voice and the ability to set limits will often encounter some resistance to her changes and will survive better with awareness of, and inoculation against, this pressure.

A note of caution is appropriate here. Beware the mistake of turning a prediction into a prophecy. When we identify probable troublesome situations, our clients will more than likely assume we have already determined that the situation is inevitable and may feel very vulnerable. It is often better to let the clients identify the situations and, if they overlook any, tactfully add them to the list.

> *When we identify probable troublesome situations our clients will more than likely assume we have already determined that the situation is inevitable and may feel very vulnerable.*

Identification and Rehearsal of Appropriate Strategies to Meet Such Situations

Once the troublesome situations are identified, review the strategies that the client has found successful in the past that can be used or adapted to new situations. If others are needed then introduce them to the client.

Role-playing can be a very beneficial way of rehearsing these anticipated conflict situations. It is important that the client and the counsellor role-play *all* parts in the scenario as this provides a broader appreciation of the issues involved and helps the client prepare for more possible areas of conflict. We look at this in more detail in Chapter 13.

One of the more important strategies clients can use when confronted with disappointment or discouragement is to review their gains and rehearse their positive self talk. It is often beneficial to have their gains and key encouraging phrases written on small wallet-sized cards for easy reference. In a similar fashion we have regularly written appropriate Scripture verses on such cards for our clients to carry with them when they leave therapy.

Identification of Community and Personal Resources to Assist When Situations Arise

In most communities, our clients will find valuable resources to assist them in their ongoing recovery or issue management. Quite often these resources are provided by government bodies or NGOs, such as churches and social clubs. A brief scan of the local and regional government websites will reveal the range of such programs offered in the community. Often the programs on offer will include Meals on Wheels, Alcoholics Anonymous (AA) and Narcotics Anonymous (NA) meetings, refuges, community mental health centres, and volunteer emergency phone services such as Lifeline or Salvo Care-line. Do not ignore the assistance that can be gained by sympathetic and informed medical or allied health practitioners. These agencies need to be identified as resources for those occasions when the counsellor is sick, on vacation or in the event of the counsellor dying.

The most accessible resources, however, are those of a personal nature. These include the client's own family and friends as well as their employment HR departments and health fund ancillary services.

Subtask 3—Celebrating

Fortune, Pearlingi & Rochelle (1992) surveyed clients about their reactions to the termination of counselling and found they most commonly identified a mix of feelings including pride, health, a sense of accomplishment, independence, cooperativeness and calmness. Clients reported feeling alive, agreeable, friendly, "good," healthy, thoughtful, and satisfied. It is important for counsellors to be aware that these positive feelings are those most commonly identified, as they may tend to expect clients to feel more negative emotional reactions to termination. In the same research, the most frequently rated counsellor reaction was pride, both in terms of their clients' growth and their therapeutic skill. With this in mind, there is every reason to celebrate the gains achieved during counselling.

Celebration of the gains made, and the end of the relationship, is important because it allows the client to view the "ending" as a form of "graduation" and something of a significant milestone in his or her life.

Some clients want to do their celebrating during the last session. Both of us have experienced a client arriving for their last session with a cake, drinks, and party poppers. More often though, the last session is more subdued with, perhaps, a card or thank-you note and a good-bye blessing, or most commonly, with a

> *Celebration of the gains made, and the end of the relationship, is important because it allows the client to view the "ending" as a form of "graduation" and something of a significant milestone in his or her life.*

simple "Thank you". Whichever way, within reason, when your client decides to celebrate, it is appropriate to encourage him or her.

Some clients will celebrate with family and friends in their traditional ways, while others will simply write a letter or make an extended journal entry to mark the occasion.

Further Reading

Fortune, A. E., Pearlingi, B., & Rochelle, C. D. (1992). *Reactions to termination of individual treatment.* Social Work, 37, 171-178.

Hunsley, J., Aubry, T. D., Verstervelt, C. M., & Vito, D. (1999). Comparing therapist and client perspectives on reasons for psychotherapy termination. *Psychotherapy,* 36, 380-388.

Joyce, A. S., Piper, W. E., Ogrodniczuk, J. S., & Klein, R. H. (2007). *Termination in psychotherapy: A psychodynamic model of processes and outcomes.* Washington, DC: American Psychological Association.

Zuckerman, A., & Mitchell, C. L. (2004). Psychology interns' perspectives on the forced termination of psychotherapy. *The Clinical Supervisor,* 23, 55-70.

PART 3

Practical Skills Training

CHAPTER 9

The Skills of Connecting

The first task of counselling, as we have discovered, is Connecting. This chapter begins the process of identifying the skills that counsellors need for effectively handling this task. Exercises designed to help trainee counsellors practice these skills are included.

*   *   *   *   *   *   *   *   *

Exercise 1—Establishing Rapport

<u>The first skill for any counsellor beginning the task of Connecting is the ability to establish rapport, or to develop a therapeutic connection, with the other person.</u> The task of Connecting is a much larger process than simply establishing rapport, but nevertheless, this is the first step. Discovering the ingredients of rapport is quite a simple process. The following exercise gives the opportunity to begin the process of discovering the micro-skills associated with establishing rapport.

> Pair up with another person in the training group, preferably someone you are not familiar with, and begin a conversation with him or her. Use as a topic "What I did on the weekend," but make establishing rapport the central purpose of your interaction. After talking together for about five minutes, stop the conversation and process the exercise. Did you feel you were able to begin to establish rapport? What were the micro-skills that contributed?

After you have built a list of the ingredients that contributed to the establishment of rapport, look to the end of this chapter to see some of our suggestions.

Exercise 2—Attending

Another vital set of skills that enable the process of connecting to occur, are the skills of *attending*. Many of these micro-skills have already been identified in the exercise on establishing rapport. However, a number of important points need to be made in relation to attending skills.

Gerard Egan, in *The Skilled Helper* (2010), suggests the acronym SOLER be used as a reminder of the key micro-skills in attending. He uses the acronym to remind of the importance of

S—Facing the client **S**quarely;

O—Having an **O**pen posture;

L—**Le**aning forward to express interest;

E—Maintaining appropriate **E**ye contact; and

R—Having an appropriately **R**elaxed posture.

While this is useful, we are of the belief that too many qualifications need to be made about some of these suggested micro-skills in order to helpfully use them. We prefer our own acronym of SONAR, standing for

S—**S**afe positioning

O—**O**pen posture

N—**N**onverbal warmth

A—**A**ppropriate eye contact

R—**R**elaxed demeanour

Safe positioning draws attention to the importance of how we are positioned in relation to the other person. While it may be useful and appropriate to face someone squarely at times, it is probably more common for counsellor and counselee to be positioned in seats that are at a less-threatening, more oblique angle to one another. In many cultures, too direct a positioning is likely to be perceived as aggressive or threatening and hinder the task of Connecting. Obviously Egan is aware of this and clarifies the point by noting that the central issue is not one of "inches and angles" but of how well the positioning communicates interested involvement. We want to endorse the goal of interested involvement but, from our perspective, the instruction, "Face the client squarely" brings some confusion. Rather, we emphasise the importance of making sure that we are positioned in ways that feel safe to the counselee.

Open posture is a useful reminder that, as part of our attending, we want to convey an openness, a non-defensiveness to the counselee and his or her sharing. We are aware that any closed positioning of our body, perhaps with crossed arms, hunched shoulders, or angled-away seating is likely to communicate negative messages, such as lack of interest rather than interested engagement. We usually prefer to avoid having a table or any other furniture standing as a "block" between counsellor and counselee. In whatever way we position our body, the goal is to communicate interested but non-threatening availability to the person.

Nonverbal warmth reminds us of the importance of the *whole range* of nonverbal cues that communicate to the other person. We draw particular attention to posture (in open posture, above) and, in a moment, eye contact (in appropriate eye contact, below), but the range of nonverbal micro-variables involved in attending is actually much greater. A gentle smile, head nodding in agreement, focused attention, a furrowed brow, a comfortable adjustment in our seating—all of these contribute to the level of interpersonal safety, interest, and warmth, which is so important to therapeutic connection.

Appropriate eye contact reminds us that, while this is vital in Western cultures, we need to be sensitive to the differences that exist in other cultures. Asian cultures tend to be much more deferential in their use of eye contact and, in Australia, Aboriginal culture, in many contexts, sees it as very disrespectful to make direct eye contact. The goal is to communicate "I am interested; I am here for you," and we need to continually monitor that this is the message we are conveying in order to mediate our attending. When we are unsure it is helpful to enquire about cultural norms.

Relaxed demeanour brings everything together—our positioning, our posture, the pace of our speech, the volume and intensity of our communication, our choice of words, the comfortableness of our interaction, and so on. Obviously this is an area we improve with experience and familiarity in the counselling role. Frequently, the beginning counsellor feels quite anxious and all of these variables may show some of this. At this stage it is enough to be reminded that the degree of appropriate comfort in the counsellor will contribute towards communicating an interest and genuine care to the other person.

Exercise 2a—Experimenting with Attending Skills

Pair up with another trainee counsellor and communicate for a couple of minutes while breaking the attending guidelines reflected in the SONAR acronym above. Have one person share a difficult task he or she completed at some time in his or her life while the receiver

- sits too close or too far away;
- attends with a closed posture;
- avoids, as much as possible, any nonverbal warmth cues;
- avoids eye contact or, alternatively, stares;
- tries to look anxious and nervous.

After each exercise, take a few minutes to debrief. How did it feel for the counselee?

Change roles so that each of you has the opportunity to experience these behaviours that interfere with healthy attending.

Having completed the exercise, now try attending to your partner, making use of the micro-skills suggested by the SONAR acronym. Discuss with one another, or as a class, the differences that you are aware of.

Exercise 3—Listening to Nonverbal Information

As we have seen in the chapter on Listening, one of the most important sources of information that we receive from the other person, comes via their non-verbal communication. A significant amount of information comes through eye contact, facial movements, body posture, hand movements, head movements, flushing of cheeks, the glistening of a tear, and so on. In situations where these cues are absent it is a lot easier for people to be confused, or less confident, about the communication: Questions come up, like: Is this person angry with me, or is he or she teasing? Am I being laughed at? And so on.

In this exercise you are asked to communicate in the absence of nonverbal cues.

> Pair up with another trainee. Position your chairs so that they are back to back and seat yourselves so that you are unable to see each other. Now decide who will be first in communicating information. The task of the other person is to listen and understand. To this end, the "listener" can
>
> • ask questions to clarify or draw more information out;
> • but he or she does not contribute any sharing of their own.
>
> Take as a topic: *Lessons I have learned in my life*. Take a few moments for the exercise, each noting personal behaviour, reactions and feelings. Change roles, and do the same for a few minutes. Together as a group, process the experience. What impact does it have when we are deprived of nonverbal information?

Discuss: What are some of the situations we face where nonverbal cues are missing in the communication? Discuss the effects of this absence of nonverbal information.

This exercise is a variation on the previous one, giving you a further opportunity to experiment with communication in the absence of nonverbal cues.

> Pair up with another trainee. Face each other, *but close your eyes as you communicate*. Once again, decide who will be the first communicator and who will be the person with the task of listening and understanding. As above, the "listener" can ask questions to clarify or draw more information out, but he or she does not contribute any sharing of their own. Take as a topic: *Things that I really enjoy*. After a few minutes, change roles and repeat the exercise. Then take time, with your partner, to process your experience—thoughts, feelings, wonderings, awareness, images—anything you notice. Try to summarize how the *absence* of nonverbal information affected communication for you.

Exercise 4—Listening to Emotions

One of the distinctive qualities of a competent listener, as we saw in Chapter 6, is the capacity to hear the *affect*, or emotional state, of the other person. Listening for emotion is a "bread-and-butter skill" for the rest of your counselling life, and of course it is a very important skill in any interpersonal relationship. When we hear the other person's feelings, and respond to him or her, it helps the other person to sense that we are *really* listening, really "tuned in" to him or her.

The purpose of the following exercise is to explore

- how we convey our feelings to others; and
- how we perceive the feelings of other people.

Consider the following list of feeling words:

anxious	apprehensive	angry	afraid	annoyed	bored
confident	calm	confused	disappointed	frustrated	guilty
happy	hostile	hurt	incredulous	irritated	joyful

lonely	loving	mean	outraged	perplexed	rejected
sad	serious	shocked	stern	suspicious	timid
tired	terrified	unmoved	weary	welcoming	woebegone

Pair up with another trainee. Now choose one of the words from the list that you can identify with because of an experience you had. *Without using the feeling word at all*, describe the situation, seeking to convey the emotion associated with it. For example, you might choose *lonely*, because you can recall feelings of loneliness when you first went to boarding school. Spell out your recollection along lines such as, "My stomach wouldn't settle and I was off my food. It just felt like something important was missing, like I was looking for something or someone..." and so on.

Your partner should allow you as much "space" as you need to convey the "picture," not jumping in or interrupting. When you have finished your description, your partner is to try out a response that reflects the emotion, or emotions (because more than one may fit!), he or she is hearing. Your partner may use the template statement, "Sounds like you were feeling..." just to get comfortable with it. If the other person is correct, talk over the elements of your communication that helped him or her identify how you were feeling. If he or she is incorrect, give your partner additional description so he or she can have further practice.

Change roles and repeat the exercise, choosing a different emotion. Continue the exercise, alternating roles and choosing different emotions, until both of you have tried your hand at describing *three* different experiences and conveying the feelings attached to these experiences, *without actually labelling the emotions*. This exercise will give each of you the opportunity to listen for the other person's feeling state, or *affect,* and to practise responding with the generic, "Sounds like you were feeling..."

Exercise 5—Listening on More Than One "Channel"

For this exercise, the training group should be divided into three sub-groups. One class member needs to take the opportunity to share in front of the whole class by describing a situation of current concern, including what he or she tried to do in relation to it, how things have gone, and what his or her beliefs and expectations are in relation to it.

One of the subgroups is given the task of listening to the *content* of the person's sharing, so they can offer feedback about what they have understood from the sharing.

A second subgroup should focus on listening for the *feelings* associated with the topic, so they can offer feedback about what they have heard, while the third group concentrates on listening to *nonverbal communication*, so they can offer feedback about what they noticed and help explore what that aspect might be communicating.

This exercise can be repeated with several volunteers, changing the focus of the groups so that everyone has the opportunity to "listen" to each of the three "channels"—words, feelings, and nonverbal communication.

Exercise 6—Paraphrasing

When we paraphrase what someone has said, we do not repeat it word for word. That is usually thought of as "parroting" and quickly becomes quite off putting to the other person. When we are comfortable at using our own words to "play back" what has been shared, we communicate that we are genuinely listening and this aids in the process of connecting. Of course, paraphrasing involves trying to capture the essence of what is shared, not necessarily every detail.

Example of Parroting

> *Counselee:* I'm really worried about what's happening in my marriage at the moment."
>
> *Counsellor:* You're really worried about what's happening in your marriage at the moment."

Compare this with a paraphrased response.

Example of paraphrasing

> *Counselee:* I'm really worried about what's happening in my marriage at the moment."
>
> *Counsellor:* "Something's not right in your marriage just now and it's really troubling you."

Exercise 6a—Writing out Paraphrase Responses

Try your hand at writing out a paraphrase response to each of these counselee statements. Take time to hear responses from other class members to help you evaluate how you are doing.

1. "I don't feel like I can trust our youth worker any more. A couple of the young people have told me he's been drinking, and last week he was hung over when he came to the youth group."

   ....
   ....
   ....

2. "Yesterday as I was leaving work the boss took me into his office and told me he was really pleased with my efforts

on the last job. He told me he's thinking of giving me a promotion if I keep up the work. I'm so excited!"

....
....
....

3. "John's always been a bit of a pushover. My wife and I have worried a lot about him. But I never thought he'd get involved in using drugs, even less in selling them. But that's what they've told us he's been doing. I don't know how I could have been so blind."

....
....
....

4. "I have had it with my sister! She's just a lazy good-for-nothing! She had a job but got fired because she kept coming late. Now she wants to borrow money from us to pay her bills, and we don't have any to spare."

....
....
....

5. "The only time my father ever spoke to me was when he told me I'd never amount to anything. I haven't seen him for years. No wonder I'm totally over him. I don't want anything to do with him. Yet it must be tough getting a diagnosis of cancer and being told you don't have long to live. I don't know what to do."

....

....

....

6. What if I never finish this degree? What if I fail again? What am I supposed to do then?

....

....

....

Exercise 6b—Practising *Spoken* Paraphrases

Pair up with another member from your training group. Choose who will be the counsellor and who will be the counselee.

The counselee *will role play one of the people suggested in the examples above but extend the issue by making up additional bits of sharing, each one building the situation a bit further.* Each time, make a statement and communicate some information, and then allow room for your counsellor to try his or her hand at paraphrasing what you have said. Make your comments about the same length as the ones above so that your counsellor is not overwhelmed with information to paraphrase. The best practice opportunities will come if the length of each piece of sharing is around two or three sentences long.

The counsellor is to make the effort to put into his or her own words the information that the counselee has shared. If the paraphrase captures the important information, take a moment after each paraphrase to recognise the accuracy before continuing on with the role play. If the paraphrase misses something that is really important, discuss what has been missed before going on with the role play.

Make sure you change roles, so each person has the opportunity to try his or her hand at paraphrasing "on the spot," enabling each one to feel more comfortable in developing this skill.

Exercise 7—Questioning

Asking questions to elicit important information is another vital skill for effective counselling. In some texts these may be called *probes,* although probes can include statements as well as questions. We focus here on questions because they are another "bread-and-butter" skill and there are important elements for us to be aware of.

Counsellors often feel more confident about asking questions—it feels like "familiar territory." We tend to be socialised to be "question askers," so that brings with it the danger that, as counsellors, we can easily slip into overdoing our use of questions.

Relevant guidelines for the use of questions include

1. *A question is only a good counsellor response if it seeks relevant information*, or relates in some useful way to the issue in focus. We are not to ask questions simply to collect information! And we should avoid asking questions purely because we are not sure what else to do!
2. *It is important not to* overwhelm *the counselee with questions*. Too many questions can start to have the feel of an interrogation, so be aware of this danger. Even so, how the question is asked is crucial. A gentle voice tone, slow pace, and interested nonverbal cues will usually take away any sense of interrogation!
3. *Try to ask open questions that encourage the other person to share more*. The best questions will often be "What?" and "How?" questions. These tend to be open questions, in that they cannot be answered by a single word or a couple of

words. An example of an open question would be: *How have you and your wife been getting on lately?*

4. *Try to avoid asking closed questions.* Closed questions, noted directly above, can be answered by one word, or a very limited response. An example of a closed question would be: *Have you been having many arguments lately?* Closed questions are not necessarily a sign of counsellor incompetence; indeed, sometimes they are needed. However, most of the time they contribute less to effective counselling than do open-ended questions.

5. *Try to avoid asking questions that lead the counselee in his or her responses.* An example of a leading question would be: *Have you been feeling angry, or sad, about that?* It is possible that the counselee has not felt either of those emotions but another feeling altogether. By limiting his or her options to these two emotions, we may be leading them in quite unhelpful ways.

6. *Try to avoid asking too many "Why?" questions as they can also add to the sense that this is an interrogation.* "Why?" questions can leave the person feeling stuck, because they don't know "why." It may be that they have come seeking your help in answering that very question.

7. *Be careful to avoid asking multiple questions at the one time.* An example of this might be: *So, do you think he meant the comment to be that hurtful or do you think he was just having a 'bad-hair day', or feeling stressed? Is he usually like that? Is he someone who 'has a go' at others too?* Multiple questions make it harder for the counselee to know which question to respond to.

8. *As a general rule aim at making your questions brief rather than extensive.* Obviously, there are limits to this, but long, rambling questions tend to be less useful in the process of connecting.

Exercise 7a

Try distinguishing Open and Closed Questions from the following list.

	OPEN	CLOSED
What would you like gain from our counselling?		
How many brothers and sisters do you have?		
Have you thought about what you want from counselling?		
What brought you two together in the first place?		
How has the anger disrupted your life so far?		
Do you really want to make changes?		
Why do you think the panic attacks have increased lately?		
Are you able to make the time for this task?		
How has that approach worked for you?		
How do you react—by fighting or withdrawing?		

Exercise 7b

Take the time to try rewriting any closed questions from the list above, turning them into open questions. For example: "How many brothers and sisters do you have?" could be rephrased as "Who are the members of your family?"

Exercise 8— Reflective Responses

The reflective response is another kind of response that is foundational for effective counselling. Like a paraphrase, a reflective response arises out of the effective listening that the counsellor is engaged in. It is an attempt to reflect back to the counselee what you have "heard" in his or her communication. However, the best reflective responses go deeper than a paraphrase, which usually focuses on "feeding back" what is predominantly the 'surface content' of the counselee's sharing. The best reflective response will often reflect back the *affect*, or emotion, contained in the person's communication, which may not actually have been directly mentioned at all.

For example, a ten-year-old boy comes home from football practice, throws his gear on the floor, and declares: "I quit! I'm never going to football practice again!" A *paraphrase* response might be: "You've had enough. You don't want to play football anymore." A *reflective response* might be: "Wow! You're angry about something! What happened?"

Reflective responses often "hear" and reflect back the emotion. They may or may not also reflect the content that has been communicated. Much of this type of counsellor response is included in what Gerard Egan (2010) has called *empathic responding,* or what Thomas Gordon (1970) called *active listening.*

Reflective responses bring several important benefits to the counselling process.

- They further the foundation task of Connecting with the person.
- They assist in the establishment of a warm feeling of connection.
- They contribute to a beneficial "alignment" of understanding in the communication between the counsellor and the counselee.
- They encourage the person to keep sharing, because the counsellor is so clearly "in tune" with them.
- They communicate that the counsellor is genuinely interested and listening *with depth*.
- They encourage ongoing self-exploration by the counselee and, in this way, further the understanding of both counselee and counsellor.
- They make specific use of information "picked up" by the counsellor on "channels" that listen to emotions and other sources of understanding.

Look at the following example of a mother, who has completed one of Dr. Gordon's Parent Effectiveness Training courses and who sets out to use active listening (what we are calling reflective responding) with her son, Danny. Danny, age eight, has been having increasing trouble getting to sleep since he was five years old. He has been settled into his own room for some months now, but he has had even more trouble getting to sleep. The extract is from *PET: Parent Effectiveness Training* (1970). (See also www.gordontraining.com.)

Mother: It's late. Turn out the light and go to sleep.

Danny: I'm not going to sleep.

Mother: You have to, it's late. You'll be tired tomorrow.

Danny: I'm not going to sleep.

Mother (harshly): Turn that light off immediately!

Danny (flatly): I'm never going to sleep.

Mother (I feel like strangling him. I'm so tired, I can't stand this tonight... I go into the kitchen, smoke a cigarette, decide that I'm going in there and try active listening even if it kills me! Enters Danny's room): C'mon, it's late but I'll sit on your bed for a while and rest my feet before I do the dishes. (She takes the book from him, turns off the light, closes the door, and sits on the bed beside him, leaning back against the wall.)

Danny: Gimme that book! Don't turn off the light. Get out of here. I don't want you in here. I'm not going to sleep. I hate you!

Mother: You're feeling angry.

Danny: Yeah, I hate school, and I'll never go back, never!

Mother (He loves school): You're fed up with school.

Danny: It's horrible. I'm not good in school. Don't know anything. I ought to be in second grade. [He's in third.] Math, I don't know it. [He is very good at it.] The teacher must think we're in high school or something.

Mother: Math's pretty hard for you.

Danny: No! It's easy. Just don't feel like doing it.

Mother: Oh.

Danny (sudden shift): I sure like baseball. Much rather play baseball than go to school.

Mother: You really like baseball.

Danny: Do you have to go to college? [Oldest brother will soon enter college and there is much talk about it.]

Mother: No.

Danny: How long do you have to go to school?

Mother: You have to finish school.

Danny: Well, I'm not going to college. Don't have to, right?

Mother: Right.

Danny: Good, I'll play baseball.

Mother: Baseball's really fun.

Danny: Sure is [Completely calmed down, talking comfortably, no anger.] Well, good night.

Mother: Good night.

Danny: Will you sit up with me some more?

Mother: Uh huh.

Danny (pulls up covers which had been kicked off; carefully covers up mother's knees and pats them): Comfortable?

Mother: Yes, thank you.

Danny: You're welcome. [Period of quiet, then Danny starts snorting and sniffing with much exaggerated clearing of throat and nose.] Snort, snort, snort. [Danny does have slight allergy with stuffy nose, but the symptoms are never acute. Mother has never heard Danny snort like this before.]

Mother: Nose bugging you?

Danny: Yeah, sure is. Think I need the stuffy nose medicine?

Mother: Do you think it would help?

Danny: No. (Snort, snort.)

Mother: Nose really bugs you.

Danny: Yeah. (Snort. Sigh of anguish). Oh, I wish you didn't have to breathe through your nose when you sleep.

Mother: (Very surprised at this, tempted to ask where that idea came from): You think you have to breathe through your nose when you sleep?

Danny: I *know* I have to.

Mother: You feel sure about it.

Danny: I know it. Tommy told me, a long time ago. [Much admired friend, two years older.] He said you have to. You can't breathe through your mouth when you sleep.

Mother: You mean you aren't supposed to?

Danny: You just *can't* (snort). Mommy, that's so, isn't it? I mean, you *gotta* breathe through your nose when you sleep, don't you? [Long explanation—many questions from Danny about admired friend. "He wouldn't lie to me."]

Mother (explains that friend is probably trying to help but kids get false information sometimes. Much emphasis from Mother that everyone breathes through their mouth when sleeping.)

Danny (very relieved): Well, good night.

Mother: Good night. [Danny breathing easily through mouth.]

Danny (suddenly): Snort.

Mother: Still scary.

Danny: Uh huh. Mommy, what if I go to sleep breathing through my mouth—and my nose is stuffy—and what if in the middle of the night when I'm sound asleep—what if I closed my mouth?

Mother (realises that he has been afraid to go to sleep for years because he is afraid he might choke to death; thinks, *Oh, my poor baby*): You're afraid you might choke maybe?

Danny: Uh huh. You gotta breathe. [He couldn't say, "I might die."]

Mother (more explaining): It simply couldn't happen. Your mouth would open—just like your heart pumps blood or your eyes blink.

Danny: Are you sure?

Mother: Yes, I'm sure.

Danny: Well, good night.

Mother: Good night, dear. [Kiss. Danny is asleep in minutes.]

This is an excellent example of reflective responding. There are so many places where other responses could have been used but by sticking with reflection of both the content and feelings that she "hears," Danny's mother finally comes to understand what he is really afraid of.

Exercise 8a

Here is portion of a transcript from a counselling session.

- *Partner with someone else* in your training group and decide who will take the role of the counsellor and who will be the counselee.
- Cover the transcript with a blank sheet, so that you can reveal just one comment by the counselee at a time.
- Let the counselee read the first piece of sharing from the transcript. Then, with the rest of the transcript still covered over, let the person playing the counsellor role try giving a reflective response.
- Move the paper down so that you can compare the counsellor's actual response and see how you went.

Continue with this, one piece of sharing at a time, until you come to the point in the exercise where you are asked to change roles, so that the other person has a chance to practise his or her reflective responses.

Of course voice tone, inflection, nonverbal communication, word selection, and a range of micro-components are all important in reflective responding. So do your best to make your reflective responses fit the tone of the counselee at all times. If these micro-components are appropriate, responses that miss the mark will not jar the connection at all.

To help you get "into the flow," ask yourself the following questions:

- What is this person feeling? What is the core message?
- Give yourself time to think. Don't rush your response.

Transcript

Steve: I've really struggled to accept the fact that I may not have much time left. I suppose I have to accept that the doctors are right.

Counsellor: This is really hard for you. Part of you is trying to hold on to hope that the doctors have got it wrong.

Steve: Well, they do make mistakes sometimes. But really I suppose it's just wishful thinking on my part. I need to just get on with it and stop hoping for a miracle.

Counsellor: Yet it isn't that easy to let go of hope. To just quit.

Steve: That's never been my way. I've always hung on to the positive side. When they told us our first child probably wouldn't live, we could have dropped our bundle and given up. Instead, we pulled together and he's married now with two kids of his own!

Counsellor: You've seen hope result in miracles in the past and you don't want to just throw in the towel now.

Steve: That's right. I like to do my best. Giving up feels foreign to me (Sighs). Only, maybe this is different. Maybe I'm just being foolish. Maybe I should accept the fact that I'm dying and get on with things. There's nothing I can do anyway.

Counsellor: Part of you wonders this time if hope is unrealistic. Maybe this time you should just accept the doctor's diagnosis and try to make the best of the time that's left.

Steve: Well, I can't really deny that I'm feeling weaker. Everything is so much harder for me at the moment. I can't just deny that.

Counsellor: There's changes happening and you can't hide from them. You've noticed you're losing your strength.

Steve: Yeah. Well, one thing's for sure, if I am dying there are some things I need to get onto. There's stuff to be done. I can't afford to waste time.

Counsellor: There's a sense of urgency about the time left. It's not like you can just hang around, hoping. There are things to do!

Steve: Yeah. For one thing, I need to make sure our finances are in order... and there'll be a lot of legal stuff to organise. None of that interests me but I need to do it. Funny... I always thought I'd have plenty of time. Now they're saying six months at the most. But most of all there's my wife and the kids... I don't want to leave them yet.

Counsellor: There are important things to get done, but the hardest part is going to be leaving your family... your wife and kids.

[Change roles at this point]

Steve: It's not just the kids! It's the grandchildren too. Charlie's boys are just four and two. We've hardly got to know each other, and now they're going to be without a grandfather. I never knew my grandfather. He died before I was born. It just doesn't seem right.

Counsellor: You never got to know your grandfather and this is almost like some sort of replay. The whole thing seems so unfair.

Steve: Well, it isn't fair. But there doesn't seem much point to playing that tune now. I can tell you I was pretty angry when they gave me the news first time. Why me? I haven't done anything bad to deserve this. I've tried to help people where I could. I'm not a murderer or anything.

Counsellor: It just didn't make any sense. You've tried to live a good life and then, wham, this happens! That hurts.

Steve: It does hurt. I don't know what the Big Plan is, but there's times when I think: this is just a mess! But I try to be strong for the family.

Counsellor: You're not someone who complains easily. But it's really hard not being able to see any purpose in the whole situation. That does get to you at times.

Steve: I don't like to admit it, but I went for a bushwalk when we got back from the last visit to the doctor and I attacked an ants nest with a stick, making them run everywhere. The worst thing is, it felt good!

Counsellor: The frustration and anger just came bubbling out. It was like: Someone or some thing's gotta pay for this!

Steve: Yeah I felt bad later, so I haven't told anyone before, but I thought you might understand. Sometimes it's good to share stuff.

Counsellor: You want to protect the others so you hold stuff in, but it helps to just share with someone else.

Steve: I just don't want to be a burden to Sal and the kids. They've got enough to deal with already. So there's no way they're going to hear me complain too much. If I can help them by sounding positive, I want to do that.

Counsellor: It's important to you to keep trying to protect them as long as you can. That's part of who you are.

Steve: Yeah, I want to make it manageable for them, no matter what.

Reflective responses, as noted by Miller and Rollnick (2002, p.69) often involve something of a guess about the intended communication. The part that we identify as a guess is a reflection that *goes further* than has actually been stated. In this sense it is a guess, but it is not a wild guess, with no substantive foundation. It is a guess that hears on all the relevant listening channels and comes to the conclusion: "This is what you are communicating. And this is the most *useful* part for me to reflect back to you." The counsellor is clearly making a choice much of the time, on the basis of what will be most useful, as to which part to reflect back to the counselee.

Done well, a reflective response can seem as though the counsellor is giving a start to the next piece of sharing by the counselee.

Look at the following extract from a counselling session, again an excellent example of this kind of use of reflective responding. The extract is from *Motivational Interviewing* (Miller & Rollnick, 2002).

Client: I worry sometimes that I may be drinking too much for my own good.

Interviewer: You've been drinking quite a bit.

Client: I don't really feel like it's that much. I can drink a lot and not feel it.

Interviewer: More than most people.

Client: Yes, I can drink most people under the table.

Interviewer: And that's what worries you.

Client: Well, that and how I feel. The next morning I'm usually in bad shape. I feel jittery, and I can't think straight through most of the morning.

Interviewer: And that doesn't seem right to you.

Client: No, I guess not. I haven't thought about it that much, but I don't think it's good to be hung over all the time. And sometimes I have trouble remembering things.

Interviewer: Things that happen while you're drinking.

Client: That too. Sometimes I just have a blank for a few hours.

Interviewer: But that isn't what you meant when you said you have trouble remembering things.

Client: No. Even when I'm not drinking, it seems like I'm forgetting things more often, and I'm not thinking clearly.

Interviewer: And you're wondering if it has something to do with your drinking.

Client: I don't know what else it could be.

Interviewer: You haven't always been like that.

Client: No! It's only the last few years. Maybe I'm just getting older.

Interviewer: It might just be what happens to everybody when they reach forty-five.

Client: No, it's probably my drinking. I don't sleep very well either.

Interviewer: So maybe you're damaging your health and your sleep and your brain by drinking as much as you do.

Client: Mind you, I'm not a drunk. Never was.

Interviewer: You're not that bad off. Still, you're worried.

Client: I don't know about "worried," but I guess I'm thinking about it more.

Interviewer: And wondering if you should do something, so that's why you came here.

Client: I guess so.

Interviewer: You're not sure.

Client: I'm not sure what I want to do about it.

Interviewer: So, if I understand you so far, you think that you have been drinking too much and you've been damaging your health, but you're not sure yet if you want to change that.

Client: Doesn't make much sense, does it?

Interviewer: I can see how you might feel confused at this point.

Exercise 8b

Continue to practise reflective responses by making use of informal practice opportunities, such as engaging with someone over a formal dinner, or at a party, or at work, or in a conversation after church. To the extent that it is appropriate put aside other responses and focus on reflective responses. This may feel a little unnatural and even awkward at first, but if you are doing a good job, you will quickly discover that the other person really enjoys the time. They may even tell you: "It felt like you were really listening."

Exercise 9—Summarising

Summarising responses occur when a counsellor has been listening to the other person for a while, and now feels the need to summarise what he or she understands.

Example: "So, let me see if I understand what you've said. You are worried because you think your son might be starting to mix with the wrong group at school. And you've also noticed that he doesn't seem to want to go to the youth group any more. You've been troubled for a while because his schoolwork has been going down. It's not as good as it used to be. All this is starting to affect your relationship with your wife. You've started noticing that the two of you are arguing a lot more. Have I got that right?"

Summarising responses have a number of specifically useful applications for us. They are appropriate when

- Counselling has been taking place for a while and we want to check that we understand the person's concerns.
- We feel the person is starting to wander or jump around too much, and we want to get some focus again. Summarising can help to bring things back to a main theme.
- We are feeling a bit "lost" and want get clarification as to where to go next.
- The counselee appears to be "stuck," and we want to help him or her move on.
- At the beginning of a session, if we have been making progress on a particular issue that has been in focus.
- Towards the end of a session as a way of pulling together the threads that have been important in the session.

Exercise 9a—Practising Summarising Responses

Pair up with another trainee counsellor from your class and establish who will take the role of counsellor and who will be the counselee. The counselee is to role-play someone with several pressing concerns, and the counsellor will respond, making free use of his or her range of counselling responses—paraphrases, reflective responding, questions, and so on. However, for the purposes of practice, make every third counsellor response a Summarising response. Stop briefly after each summarising response to evaluate the accuracy of the response before continuing on with the next three exchanges. After a number of these, change roles so that each of you has the opportunity to practise these summarising responses.

Suggested Answers for Exercise 1

Ingredients of Rapport

Eye contact

Relaxed-looking eyes

Focused attention

Smiles

Voice tone

Relaxed body position

Body orientation

Distance between

Comfortable chair

Relaxed pace

Hand placements

Hand movements

Nods of agreement

Sitting back

Further Reading

Egan, G. (2010). *Exercises in helping skills: A manual to accompany The Skilled Helper (9th ed.).* Belmont, CA: Brooks/Cole.

Martin, D. G. (2011). *Counselling and therapy skills.* Long Grove, IL: Waveland Press.

Nelson-Jones, R. (2011). *Basic counselling skills: A helper's manual (3rd. Ed.).* London, UK: Sage.

CHAPTER 10

The Skills of Connecting II

Counsellors need a range of skills to handle the varied situations that can emerge in counselling in the Connecting phase. They need to be able to handle situations where the counselee is experiencing strong emotional discharge, so we include, in this chapter, training exercises for the acquisition of grounding and containment skills. Beyond grounding and containment skills, counsellors also need to be able to teach more general calming skills to those who battle against anxiety, stress and other disempowering emotions. In this chapter we include some basic training in teaching diaphragmatic breathing as a calming skill. Finally, counsellors also need skills so that they can assess whether their work is making a difference in the lives of people. The field of counselling requires that we be able to point to some evidence, some data, to validate the usefulness of our interventions. For this reason we also include some basic assessment skills for novitiate counsellors.

* * * * * * * * *

Grounding and Containment Skills

People experiencing a recent crisis, or processing trauma or deep grief from the past, are often susceptible to periods of emotional overload. These are times when they have difficulty feeling in control of their emotions. This is quite different from the situation where someone is discharging emotion as part of a healthy and normal healing experience. Some tears are healing tears and some are damaging tears—clearly indicating a reliving of a trauma, or a time of being emotionally overwhelmed. In this kind of experience a person may curl up and begin weeping, sobbing loudly, obviously caught in "re-living" some traumatic event from the past. These are not healing tears; this is distressing; this is a re-experiencing of a trauma. In a situation like this, the counsellor needs to know how to "ground" the person, how to bring him or her out of the re-living of a past event to the safety of the present. Be aware that there are other ways of grounding people beside the approach we offer here.

Sensory Grounding and Containment

Sensory grounding is taught as a skill for trauma survivors, as a means of helping them bring themselves out of "re-living experiences" such as intrusive memories or "flashbacks." It involves <u>learning how to break free from the *internal* experience by focusing on *external stimuli*</u>, especially "normal," safe, reassuring sensory stimuli. By having them use their senses (usually sight, touch, and hearing) to reconnect them to features of the present external context, this skill serves to disconnect them from the internal stimuli that are triggering their overwhelming emotions.

The need for this skill is relatively rare, unless a counsellor is working regularly with trauma survivors. However, all counsellors should have a working knowledge of sensory grounding, in case it is needed with someone who is dissociating because of intrusive memories from the past.

Exercise—Teaching Sensory Grounding and Containment.

Pair up with another trainee counsellor and decide who will be the "instructor" and who will be the "learner." The learner can role play being distressed and overwhelmed with emotion, curling up and disconnecting from the present context, to provide a "scenario" for the instructor to try out the following kind of protocol.

Handwritten margin notes:
- Look around the room
- Look at themselves (as an adult)
- Feel the floor
- Listen to what is around them

(In a firm, confident voice) "[Person's name], take a deep, slow breath and feel yourself calming down. It's okay. You're safe. That's good. Another deep slow breath. Good. It's okay. You're here with me in the counselling office. That was just a memory. You're not back there any more. You're completely safe.

"Look at the books on the book shelf; what different colours can you see? Look at the pictures on the wall; what can you see there? Feel yourself calming down. Push your feet down hard on the floor. Feel how solid it is... look at your hands. See they're the hands of a grown-up person... you're not little anymore. You're an adult. You're here now with me and you're completely safe. See your fingers. Hear the traffic outside. You're here in the counselling office. That memory was leftover from long ago. You're not there anymore. You're grown up and you will never be hurt like that again. You're safe. You're here. Feel yourself calming down. You're bringing those fears under control. Breathing deeply. Good. That's fine. You're doing well."

<u>Discuss</u> how you went. How did you find it? Did it flow okay?

> *All counsellors should have a working knowledge of sensory grounding...*

Change roles so that each of you has a chance to try grounding someone who has been overwhelmed by their emotions. Here are some important guidelines:

- Begin by asking them to take a deep breath and to feel calmer.
- Avoid touching the person. Even a hand on the person's shoulder may "play into" the flashback, confuse the person, and intensify the terror.

- Speak as firmly and confidently yet caringly as you need to in order to "break in" on their internal experience, helping him or her disconnect from the internal re-experiencing.
- Make sure you use phrases like "you're safe now" and "take a deep breath." <u>Don't be afraid to repeat these often.</u> Repetition of the same sentence or phrase will gradually help him or her connect to what you are saying.

Self-Calming Skills

Diaphragmatic breathing

There is physiological support for the benefit of breathing to the lower parts of the lungs, bordering the area known as the diaphragm. We know that anxious breathing tends to be fearful breathing and tends to be short, rapid, and shallow. Teaching people to breathe to the lower part of their lungs, to their belly or the diaphragm area, is a useful intervention for anyone who is showing signs of becoming emotionally distressed.

Exercise—Teaching Diaphragmatic Breathing

Pair up and decide who will take the role of the teacher and who will be the "pupil." Try to find a comfortable place to sit or, even, to lie down. It is useful to have the learner place their hands on their belly so they can feel that they are breathing to that region. Encourage him or her to *consciously* push the muscles outward a little in that area to make room for the breath to go to the deeper part of the lungs, and to *consciously* pull the muscles of that region in as they exhale.

Different approaches can be used at this point. We suggest you instruct the learner to inhale slowly, smoothly and deeply on a count of about four seconds ("One—two—three—four"), followed by a pause. Then have him or her exhale smoothly ("One—two—three—four") at a similar count. The exhalation should be a complete discharging of the breath, and it is helpful to pause for a couple of seconds before taking the next breath. When you are teaching the skill, count aloud to help the other person develop a gentle, relaxing rhythm. Once someone has learned diaphragmatic breathing, you can instruct him or her to begin that form of breathing as a calming technique if there is any danger that his or her emotions are starting to feel out of control.

Assessment Skills—(Collecting Relevant Data)

i. General Indicators of Progress

Counsellors need to be able to carry out assessments to assist them in learning more about a person's functioning and evaluating whether progress is being made. Within the Incarnational Counselling model *collecting relevant data* is the second important subtask in the Connecting phase.

Behavioural psychology has emphasised for us the value of trying to get a *baseline measure* of a person's problems so that we can document when progress and improvement are occurring and ascertain what is helpful. For this reason it is always valuable to try to assess the frequency, intensity (or severity), and/or duration of a person's problem(s), so we can have some confidence about the effect of our counselling interventions. All counsellors can make good use of these categories, since these three are all Indicators of progress.

Often people seeking help with a problem function with little more discrimination than two positions—"the problem is still there" or "the problem has disappeared" ("I have the problem" or "I am free of the problem"). The trouble with this is that they may actually be making progress but have no sense of that fact, because they are so focused on the *occurrence* of the problem that they are unaware of changes in its frequency, intensity, or duration. If we can show them that the frequency is fewer, or the intensity is lower, or the duration is shorter, then we can help them feel encouraged that they are making progress, even though they may still be experiencing the problem at times.

Frequency

If in the first counselling session, we gather data showing that the "problem," or issue (anger outbursts, panic attacks, times of feeling overwhelmed with grief, number of cigarettes smoked, disturbed sleep, whatever) occurs, say, six times a week, then we have the opportunity to encourage him or her when the frequency drops to lower than that. The person is making progress. The problem is occurring less often!

There will be times when people are able to make a quick *estimate* of the frequency of the "problem," and that is good, but it is even more useful to have the person actually record data for a week or two, so that we have a more objective assessment. We recommend some basic kind of chart drawn up on a sheet or a card, so counselees can record the frequency of the problem behaviour.

Of course some "problems" may not be measurable in terms of *frequency*. An example may be a fairly pervasive depression. The task here is to find a measure that is applicable with this particular client issue. Another measure, rather than frequency, may be needed. For example, we may keep a record of positive feelings during the day, and rate the strength of these. This brings us to *intensity* as another measure of progress.

Intensity

Whether the frequency of the issue in focus reduces or not, the intensity of the problem may lessen. Even if frequency of the problem behaviour is unchanged, say still occurring six times in the week, the person is improving if previously the problem intensity was "8," and now it is only "4" on a "10-point scale." Of course there will also be problems that people seek help with that may not easily be measured on Intensity. An example might be nicotine addiction. It may be hard to measure the Intensity associated with smoking a cigarette although the Intensity of the *desire to smoke* (on a 10-point scale) may be a useful aspect of the assessment.

Duration

Some issues that people struggle with can be usefully measured for *duration*. For example, *how long* did the panic attack last? *How long* before the couple was able to apologise to each other and get over the conflict? *How long* between times of consuming alcohol?

It should be obvious that a person may show no indication of improvement on one indicator, such as frequency, yet be improving on another, such as intensity or duration. On the other hand, improvement may be showing up on every indicator. For the beginning counsellor, being aware of these Indicators of Progress, teaching counselees about them, and making use of them to provide a record of how someone is progressing in counselling is always valuable, because of the potential to guide the nature and direction of the counselling.

By drawing up a card or data sheet, such as the one below, you can easily encourage the counselee to keep a record of the occurrence of the "problem."

	Mon	Tues	Wed	Thurs	Fri	Sat	Sun	Total
Problem occurred (no. of times)								
Antecedent Event?								
Feeling before?								
Intensity of emotion (1-10)								
Duration of problem "experience"								

Figure 7

Exercise 1—Teaching a Client about the Indicators of Progress

Partner with another trainee from the counselling group and decide who will take the role of counsellor and who will be counselee. The counselee can role play someone with an issue that is measurable, such as experiencing panic attacks. In the role play, the counselee should begin with an outline of the problem. The purpose of the exercise is to give the counsellor practice at explaining the Indicators of Progress to the counselee, roughly drawing up a data record sheet to fit the problem, and outlining the homework task of keeping data for the coming week.

Change roles so that both of you have the opportunity to practise explaining the Indicators of Progress and assigning self-monitoring and data recording as a homework task.

ii. Scaling

The development of Scaling as an assessment tool is usually attributed to Solution-Focused Brief Therapy (SFBT) proponents such as de Shazer (1985) and Miller (1997). Scaling usually involves asking a person to rate aspects of his or her functioning on a subjective, made-up-on-the-spot ten-point scale, where "10" represents the best possible and "1" represents the worst possible situation. It can easily be applied to a range of "complaints" that people bring to counselling.

Solution-focused approaches incorporate Scaling in many different ways for all kinds of counselee problems. Because their orientation is focused on looking for *solutions* rather than *analyzing problems*, SFBT counsellors tend to make the "10" on their scale indicate the absence of the problem and the desired outcome of counselling. They tend to use the low score "1" as the measure of "the problem is at its worst." Thus, the scale is always a measure of progress.

Here is a sample excerpt from a counselling session, to give you guidance on how Scaling is used.

Counsellor: So, on a scale of 1 to 10, where 10 represents the happiest and most fulfilled you could be in your relationship, and 1 represents the worst it could possibly be, how would you score your marriage at the moment?

Ralph: Probably between 4 and 5 at the moment.

Counsellor: Well, that's certainly better than last week. You rated it a 2 then. How do you know to rate it between 4 and 5 this week?

Ralph: Well, we haven't argued as much this week, so that's definitely better. On the other hand, we've both been so busy with work, we've had hardly had any pleasant time together either. But I think we both would have been open to doing something nice. We talked a bit about trying to get out for a bike ride this week.

[handwritten annotation: affirmation]

Counsellor: Hey, I'm impressed! You guys are moving. I'm wondering, if you can have your bike ride, will that lift the rating even higher?

Ralph: Well, it will for me. I can't answer for Jo, but I think she'd find it helpful too.

Counsellor: Well, let's see how it goes. I'll check in on how you're rating the relationship next time. Who knows, it may be a 6!

As an on-the-spot assessment technique, Scaling offers a number of potential benefits in counselling.

- It enables the counsellor to get a picture of how the person is viewing progress.
- It enables exploration of the specific actions and other details that have contributed to progress (or regress).
- It enables the counsellor to open up exploration of what needs to change for the score to be elevated to an even higher rating.

Scaling is obviously a subjective measure, but it has strong face validity. It enables the counsellor to assess how the person rates progress on constructs that might otherwise be difficult to measure. Using Scaling, a person can rate the frequency and intensity of feelings like anxiety or depression. It can be used to rate the level of disturbance produced by an *intrusive thought,* or it can serve as a vehicle for establishing the *importance* of a change or a person's level of *hope or confidence* about change he or she wants to make.

Of course counsellors will find that a counselee sometimes struggles to put a number out of 10 on his or her current experience. This may be someone who finds on-the-spot decisions difficult, or someone who is anxious to be precise, so he or she avoids making the commitment of a number on a subjective scale. With someone like this, use a more concrete illustration. Use a ruler or the edge of a book to provide a visual scale, and ask the person to indicate where he or she would position himself or herself between the 1 and the 10. Even if the person is reluctant to give a number, you can easily assign one by visually estimating the point where the person places his or her finger.

Exercise—Practising Introducing Scaling

The purpose of this exercise is to give counsellors practice at explaining Scaling to a counselee while weaving Scaling into their counselling. Pair up with another trainee and role play a counselling session with someone who is depressed. As soon as the counselee has shared a little about the problem, the counsellor is to introduce the concept of Scaling. Explain the idea of the 10-point scale, using something like the following:

Counsellor: So this experience with depression has been affecting you for the past month or so. I'd like to get a bit more of a picture of how it works. Imagine a 10-point scale, where 1 represents the worst the depression has been and 10 represents "I feel great. No depression at all. I'm full of energy and life." Where would you rate the depression today, on a scale like that?

Rob: Today hasn't been quite as bad so it's not right at the bottom. I'd say about a 4.

Counsellor: So on that 10-point scale, what's the worst it's been over the month?

Rob: Well, last week I'd say it was a 1 or 2 most of the time. I had no energy and I was crying a lot. I only made it to work on Tuesday, and even then I came home after morning tea. I just couldn't cope.

digging deeper

Counsellor: So, things are quite a bit better today. You're a 4 today. How do you know it's a 4? How's it different from the worst—when you were a 1 or a 2?

The purpose of the exercise is to practise developing a comfortable "patter" to explain Scaling to the counselee and to begin making use of it, not only as an assessment instrument but as a tool for understanding aspects of the issue and for planning ongoing counselling, homework tasks, and the overall program for change.

iii. Formal Assessment Instruments

It is beyond the scope of this training manual to detail the range of relatively quick but statistically grounded assessment instruments available for use by counsellors. Many, such as the Beck Depression Inventory-II (BDI-II), or the Impact of Events Scale (IES) are available online, or they can be purchased through publishers. There are scales to assess issues as diverse as anxiety in children, obsessive thoughts in adults, the severity of gambling, or even the severity of elective mutism. These scales are more "formal" than Scaling, in that some normative data has been developed for them by having groups of subjects take the test. This has enabled the test developer to work out means and standard deviations on the content of the test for certain populations, or for the normal population. By comparing an individual's score on the test with this normative data, the counsellor is better able to assess the severity of the issue for the person being counselled. It is important to be aware that the strength of any statistical data will vary from one test to another. For this reason, don't just download tests from the Internet without assessing how reliable they are, or without looking into their validity (i.e., whether they are measuring what they purport to be measuring).

As you have opportunity, begin to develop a library of your own assessment instruments, scales that you feel comfortable using and from which you gain useful knowledge.

Exercise—Finding Simple Assessment Tools

Choose three problems or issues that people come into counselling with and undertake some research. Go online or look up catalogues, looking for brief, useful instruments to contribute to the assessment of these issues. Share these with your training group.

Diagnosis and Counselling Themes—(Reflecting on the Person's Issues and Data)

i. Diagnosis

In an introductory training text such as this, we are not able to provide a comprehensive guide to the development of formal diagnostic skills. Focused training courses aimed at familiarising trainees with formal diagnostic categories pick up these skills in much more detail. However, in the Incarnational Counselling model, we see the third subtask of the Connecting phase of counselling as requiring us to spend time *reflecting on the counselee's issues and the data* collected during the initial sessions. At this stage it is perhaps sufficient to alert the trainee to the importance of being able to look at a person's report of distress through the lens of diagnosis. It is important because without some rudimentary awareness of diagnoses, the beginning counsellor could find himself or herself trying to counsel someone whose presenting issues ought to be handled by a medical practitioner, or someone else with specialist training.

However, even beyond the issue of identifying any formal diagnoses, a time of reflection opens up the identification of themes that will become the focus for ongoing counselling. It opens up the importance of beginning to formulate an understanding of what is causing the counselee's distress and what should be the strategy for Incarnational Counselling's second task, Correcting.

In terms of formal diagnostic skills, beginning counsellors are very much "learners." However, even at this stage they need to be able to recognize when a person is suffering from major psychological disorder, so that they can refer to someone with more specialized skills and training. We believe that a number of issues should be referred on, although there may be times when it is appropriate to work with some of these people in collaboration with other specialists, and under close supervision. Diagnoses that normally require referral, or collaborative work, would include:

- Major Depression
- The Schizophrenias
- Bipolar Disorder
- Dissociative Identity Disorder
- Suicidal Clients
- Educational or Developmental Disorders requiring specialist training
- Any diagnoses that have a physical or medical "core"
- Severe Personality Disorders

At the general level it is not that beginning counsellors are unable to contribute in working with people who have these kinds of diagnoses; it is more that additional experience and training is important, and this can only come with further opportunities for training.

ii. Counselling "themes"

Careful reflection on the counselee's report of his or her distress and struggle allows a counsellor to begin listing the kinds of "counselling themes," or issues, that it will be important to try to address in the counselling process. It is impossible here to detail these fully. This reflective process will partially take place in the counselling session but, importantly, it also requires thoughtful deliberation outside the actual counselling session. The questions the counsellor is trying to answer from the person's "story" at this point, as well as from assessment information collected thus far, are

- What is the main issue this person is looking for help with?
- What other issues are important and also need to be addressed?
- What has the person, or other counsellors, tried so far in the way of interventions, and how have these turned out?

These kinds of questions lead the counsellor into formulating a plan for Incarnational Counselling's second task, the task of Correcting.

Selecting Intervention Approaches

Finally, it is important, as part of the process of *reflecting on a counselee's issues and data,* to give thought to the best way to approach helping. This will involve putting the data together into a case formulation so that a plan for counselling can be developed.

Once again, it is beyond the scope of this book to provide detailed training in case formulation. We can think of formulation as the process of developing a provisional explanation for the difficulties and distress currently experienced by the person we are counselling. A case formulation represents our best effort to place a *theoretical* explanation on the development of the person's problems. Of course how we conceptualise will often vary depending on the particular theory of counselling we follow. For example, a counsellor who works from a psychodynamic theory of counselling will formulate the person's issues differently to a counsellor who follows a CBT theoretical approach (see outlines of these theories in Chapter 2).

Formulation is an important part of reflective practice in counselling. A helpful formulation will guide the counsellor in his or her selection of areas to question into, as well as shape the actual questions that are asked. A case formulation will serve as something of a map guiding the counsellor as to the direction to take. It will influence the input of psycho-education as well as the kinds of interventions and techniques the counsellor makes use of. It is always useful if the formulation is written out in some detail, particularly in the early period of counsellor education.

At this stage of training, with students still developing their understanding and familiarity with particular counselling theories, it is enough to note that, regardless of the theory being followed, the following aspects should be considered when formulating your understanding of the person's issues:

- What is the history of the problem or issue?
- What are the symptoms?
- What factors have brought this problem or issue to its present state? Long-term factors? Current factors?
- What currently triggers the occurrence of the problem or issue?
- What is maintaining the problem or issue?
- What other factors do I need to consider (such as cultural, spiritual, or ethical issues)?
- What are short-, medium-, and long-term goals for my counselling with this person?
- What risk factors exist that could work against resolution of the issue?
- What diagnosis would I give for this problem? Are there any recommended treatments of choice for this kind of diagnosis?

Here is a sample case formulation, written predominantly from a CBT framework.

The Case of Kiana

Background History and Presenting Problem

Kiana is a fifty-one-year-old single female, never married. She currently lives with ageing parents, her father with health problems as well as early stage Alzheimer's, and a mother who appears to have no energy so contributes nothing to the running of the house. Kiana works four days a week at a busy service-delivery corporation. She came into treatment some four years ago, on the advice of her doctor who referred her for CBT for depression. Initially she was seen fortnightly, but as progress began to show, sessions were spread out to once a month. This has been the current pattern for the last three years, with the exception of an emotional crisis period last Christmas, the result of emotional depletion and an escalation of work and home pressures.

At intake, Kiana reported that while she had loved her work at first (she has been there five years), the organisation has experienced staff cuts, and the demands of dealing with the public, plus a lack of support from management, had caused her to begin to feel overwhelmed. She usually comes home from work exhausted, only to take on the responsibility of cooking a meal for herself and her parents. She reported that she had left a previous job after fifteen years because the pressure had built considerably, and she had begun to feel that she was unsupported. At that time her depression had first become established, and she was put onto antidepressant medication, which she had continued. She reported that it helped.

Kiana has never been in a long-term dating relationship, but she was active for many years in a bowling league until, about ten years ago, she damaged her shoulder and had to have surgery. This prevented her from continuing the bowling, and she went through some years of rehabilitation. On the positive side, she has never had difficulty making deep friendships, and she has a number of excellent, continuing friendships with caring, supportive people, mostly from her bowling contacts, but also from her previous workplace.

Kiana has one older brother who has been married three times. He lives in a country town so has never been available to help much with his parents. He has two adult children and two teenage children, and Kiana is a much-loved aunt to them, although visits are infrequent. The relationship with her brother is close, although Kiana tends to be caught up in his problems and often gets involved on the phone trying to help him sort through his relationship issues. She does not seek this role and in fact hates getting caught up in it, but he does not seem to understand and regularly "unloads" his problems when they talk.

The crisis at Christmastime was largely precipitated by a breakdown in the relationship between Kiana and her brother over a misunderstanding. The relationship has now been repaired, but at its worst, Kiana rang her psychologist in tears late one night and required a visit to stabilise her functioning. She ended up taking a week off after seeing her doctor and her psychiatrist.

Kiana's initial presentation gave evidence of depressive symptoms. Specifically, she exhibited

- depressed mood, crying, and anxiety about her future;
- the absence of feelings of pleasure;
- a pervasive sense of worthlessness;
- poor sleep; and
- fatigue.

Her initial Depression, Anxiety, Stress Scale (DASS) score produced a raw score of 28 for depression, placing her at the 98th percentile in the Extremely Severe range. Her score on anxiety was 16, placing her around the 95th percentile and in the Severe category. Her score on stress was 25, placing her just below the 95th percentile and in the Moderate category. There were no indications of suicidal thoughts at all. Here is a written case formulation by her psychologist.

Case Formulation

Precipitants: Kiana's depression seemed to arise initially as a consequence of her problems with her shoulder and the subsequent loss of her ability to be in the bowling league. Prior to this she reported that she was always positive and outgoing. This was added to by the long period of physiotherapy and the painful process of rehabilitation. Kiana reported that during these years, she lost a lot of her previous self-confidence that she has never fully regained. In more recent years, the growing pressures at work, where she is excessively responsible, and, consequently, an overused employee, together with the escalating health concerns of her parents, which requires her to take them to medical appointments and care for them, continues to make it difficult for her to "rise above" her depressive experience.

Cross-sectional view of cognitions and behaviours: In recent months Kiana's depression has fluctuated from moderate and coping to tearful reoccurrence of feeling overwhelmed and hopeless. These fluctuations appear to have been directly linked to increased work pressures and her inability to be assertive with management. She tells herself that she "should" be able to cope and that she "must" keep going. She also resists being assertive with people, because she has a history of breaking into tears. Her current manager has used Kiana's times of emotionality to say things like, "It's okay. You've got a lot going on," which has helped her feel some support. However, the busy-ness of the work situation, together with increasing parental demands, has tended to bring about periods of feeling very depressed. Her friends have been a lifeline for her, and she has tried to keep fairly regular outings and contacts going, but there have been times when she has been simply too tired.

Longitudinal view of cognitions and behaviours: Although her early years of coping appeared to be well handled, there are indications now that Kiana has carried some self-doubt issues associated with her lack of any romantic relationship. She has always been an extremely capable worker and appears to have carried the belief that, if she was selfless enough and sacrificial enough, others would see her worth. This pattern of functioning—always doing more than her fair share, and always going the extra mile—has been highly valued by the decent people in her life, but it has also led to her being vulnerable to those who "used" her at work. For many years now she has struggled to see herself as competent and capable, though others around see her that way.

Strengths and Assets: Kiana is actually an extremely competent worker, in part because she pushes herself to be competent and accurate in her work. She is also genuinely compassionate and she has helped many in their time of need.

Working Hypothesis: Kiana's depression was precipitated by her accident and the loss of her social and recreational outlet in bowling. She has had long-term issues with self-doubts, which she has been able to compensate for in her bowling, work, and friendships. However, the loss of the bowling and the growing stress at work has taken two of these supports away, leaving her vulnerable to the depression of recent years.

Treatment Plan

Problem List

- limited physical capacities and opportunities for recreation
- depression and self-doubts
- lack of appropriately assertive behaviours
- overcommitment to the needs of others
- lack of a "lower gear" in her working style

Treatment Goals

- Provide psycho-education on the cognitive "roots" of depression.
- Teach assertive behaviours, practise them, and begin appropriate use of them.
- Teach boundary-setting behaviours and help Kiana implement them at work.
- Develop a weekly plan that includes self-care times.
- Teach relaxation and other stress-reduction techniques.

Plan for Treatment

Liaise with Kiana's GP and her psychiatrist regularly. Begin working initially on helping her identify core beliefs about herself and Negative Automatic Thoughts (NATs) that run in specific situations. Help her to challenge the core beliefs and develop rational, balanced alternatives. Help her to learn to challenge the NATs that run so automatically when she is under pressure.

Thus,

- Treatment will focus initially on cognitive therapy of depression and the implementation of thought-change interventions.
- As this progresses, treatment will move to developing a self-care plan that includes regular times of renewal that will be programmed into the week.
- It will be important to work at teaching boundary-setting and assertiveness skills, so that these can be built into Kiana's functioning.
- A thorough exploration of the availability of community resources to assist with the care of her ageing parents will also be undertaken.

- If needed, processing the option of changing her work situation will be canvassed.

 Exercise—Developing a Case Formulation

Use the subheadings in the case formulation above to guide you in jotting down a case formulation for someone you are currently counselling. If you are still working in triads, developing your basic skills, apply the subheadings to your thinking about your work with your particular counselee. Otherwise apply this to a person you are seeing for counselling in some other context. Since this is not a formal task, simply jot down notes under each subheading rather than write the formulation out as fully as the example above. Let your notes guide you in your ongoing work with your counselee.

What we are emphasising here is the importance of developing a way of reflecting thoughtfully on the client's issues and the data collected, in order to plan the approach to counselling. This is a vital subtask in the Connecting phase of counselling, one that precedes and helps the task of Correcting.

Further Reading

Johnstone, L. and Dallos, R. (Eds). (2006). *Formulation in psychology and psychotherapy.* New York: Routledge.

Seligman, L. (2004). *Diagnosis and treatment planning in counseling (3rd Ed.).* New York, NY: Springer.

CHAPTER 11

The Skills of Correcting I: Correcting Distorted Thinking

Correcting is the second task in counselling. In many ways it is the central task, except that we recognise from research that successful Correcting depends largely on the quality of the counselling relationship. In other words, effective Correcting derives from and is dependent upon the success of the Connecting task. In this chapter we give attention to the skills and interventions involved in effectively Correcting distorted thinking, but our focus is on providing beginning counsellors with a range of intervention tools and examples of their use, rather than providing training opportunities. Developing skilled use of these interventions comes out of understanding what they involve and then trying them out in our counselling.

In the next chapter we focus on skills and techniques involved in Correcting disruptive emotions and Correcting destructive behaviours. Whole books are written with a focus on these kinds of interventions, so the content we offer here represents simply a selection of interventions, ones that we see as especially relevant for the beginning counsellor. Further content and training in each of these areas, for example, through attendance at workshops and seminars as well as personal supervision, will be an essential ongoing focus for all trainee counsellors.

* * * * * * * * *

Subtask 1—Correcting Distorted Thinking

A number of theories of counselling are built around correcting the thinking processes and thought content of distressed people. These approaches are labelled *cognitive theories* because they emphasise the distorted thinking of the client and its role in creating the distress the person is experiencing, and they try to intervene in ways that bring helpful changes to patterns of thinking and to thought content. Here are some of the skills and interventions that we see as useful for the beginning counsellor.

Psycho-Education

With the swing towards brief counselling approaches in the last thirty years, it has become increasingly important to help clients by providing an understanding of their experience that derives from the findings of sound research. The shift away from the counsellor being the all-knowing but distant "expert" to a knowledgeable collaborator who can sometimes contribute helpful information is, by now, well advanced. Whereas in earlier psychoanalytic approaches the counsellor remained aloof and took the role of the "knowledgeable one" who offered to interpret client experience, counsellors now seek to work collegially, adding their expertise to that of the client, wherever this is beneficial.

Obviously, for the *beginning* counsellor there is a limit to the evidence-based knowledge that he or she can bring to help the person understand what they are experiencing. The point of emphasising psycho-education as a cognitive intervention even for novice counsellors is to encourage the beginning counsellor to continually seek to expand his or her knowledge base by reading widely and consulting more-experienced practitioners. Out of this ever-expanding pool of understanding, helpful information, appropriate to the client, can be offered. Such psycho-education could be purely informational, or it might assist a helpful formulation of the person's current struggles.

Both of us recall times when, in the beginning phase of our training as counsellors, we were confronted with a client whose issues were new to us. At the urging of supervisors we headed off to university libraries (this was the pre-Internet era!) and scoured journal articles and books to give us a knowledge base for working with the particular client. And out of that foundation knowledge we sought to share information that we deemed appropriate in providing a different perspective, or helpful new understandings, for our clients.

> *For the beginning counsellor, intervening via psycho-education increases the risk that he or she could slip into talking too much.*

For the beginning counsellor, intervening via psycho-education increases the risk that he or she could slip into talking too much, so this needs to be monitored under supervision. Psycho-education is valuable and takes a crucial place in most brief counselling approaches, but it must never become an excuse for the counsellor to "show off" his or her knowledge, nor should it override or diminish the importance of taking the time to listen and carefully explore the person's experience before deciding on the appropriateness of an intervention. Determining whether some aspect of psycho-education is justified is a crucial part of the subtask, *Reflecting on the issue and the data,* in the *Connecting* phase of counselling. The two crucial growth aspects of this for the counsellor are to continue to work at reading, undertaking supervision, and attending workshops to constantly expand the knowledge base in areas of counselling, and also to constantly work at doing a better job of sharing appropriate knowledge in helpful ways with individual clients.

Assets that are more and more widely used in helpful psycho-education include the use of analogies and metaphors to help clients "get a feel" for what is being communicated about their struggle. Additionally, the drawing of explanatory diagrams, and the use of a white-board in depicting some aspect of the problem or the path to solutions is increasingly being used. We encourage counsellors to develop and incorporate these intervention tools into their counselling whenever they offer the possibility of being helpful to clients.

Normalising

Often people seeking counselling help have no clear understanding of the nature of their problem and whether it is something others also experience. They wonder if they are different from everyone else and may even fear that their symptoms indicate the onset of some serious mental illness. Their question is: "Am I normal, or is there something seriously wrong with me?"

A client shared that she was the primary carer for her elderly mother in the last few years of her mother's life. In the process of doing her best for her mother, she was, on many occasions, yelled at and told she was stupid by a younger sister, who had something of a reputation for being aggressive and bullying. This experience left the client feeling as though she had "failed her mother" at times because she felt so intimidated by her younger sister that there were times when she avoided doing what she felt her mother needed. In the period after her mother's death the client reported difficulties sleeping. She had dreams about, and replayed in her mind, scenes in which she had been screamed at to the point where she felt completely controlled. She reported being unable to stop the "replays." She became aware that she was avoiding people and worried she must be "going crazy." A simple intervention aimed at explaining the "normal" symptoms experienced by people who have gone through a trauma turned out to be very helpful. She was able to put aside much of the fear that she was "going mad" and in counselling was able to learn some simple techniques to help her regain a sense of "being in control."

There will be many occasions when, out of his or her experience and understanding of human behaviour, the counsellor is able to provide a new perspective that helps the client by reassuring him or her that the experience is within the normal range of human reactions.

Of course there are important guidelines to follow if we are intervening by "normalising" the person's experience.

First, we need to avoid rushing to "normalise." We need to make the space to listen carefully and make sure our intervention is appropriate. Done badly and insensitively, normalising could convey a sense that we think the issue is a trivial one; we could project a dismissive, insensitive-to-the-person's-distress kind of attitude that would not be helpful or offer reassurance at all, but add to the person's self-doubts. This would be a complete misuse of normalising as an intervention. <u>Always make sure you take the time to hear the person's distress and respond with empathic sensitivity before making use of any normalising.</u>

Secondly, there will be many times when the person's experience is not "normal" but indicates an underlying issue of depression, anxiety, or something else that needs an approach other than normalising.

A client who went through a traumatising experience as a five-year-old, such that, in adulthood, he felt his life was constricted to living "in a box," was not reporting normal symptoms. The intensity of his symptoms was way beyond normal experience. Other interventions were necessary to help him begin regaining a greater measure of freedom.

Finally, even when normalising is appropriate, it is more likely to be a start to the healing process, rather than a sufficient intervention on its own. This needs to be kept in mind. That said, there are times when it is entirely appropriate to use normalising because of its capacity to adjust distorted thinking, lifting unrealistic worries from the client and helping him or her begin the healing journey.

Self-Disclosure

Self-disclosure, or counsellor self-sharing, is often listed as a basic counselling skill in counselling training books and manuals (Egan 2010). There are approaches to counselling that would eschew any counsellor self-disclosure at all because of the capacity for it to change the nature of the relationship. In truth, having the counsellor share information or perspective from his or her life does carry the potential for it to change aspects of the counsellor-client relationship. Such sharing, introduced insensitively, has the potential to take the relationship to a more intimate level that could be unhelpful, or even threatening, for some clients. However, done sensitively and purposefully, it clearly also has the potential to offer a different perspective to clients, enabling them to begin to adjust their thinking about their issue(s).

Given the mix of possibilities it is vital that counsellors are judicious in their use and application of counsellor self-sharing. While we encourage trainee counsellors to develop this as an intervention skill, we offer the following guidelines in its use.

- *Counsellor self-disclosure should be used infrequently.* If a counsellor finds himself or herself sharing personal experience regularly, something is wrong.
- *Self-disclosure must be directly relevant to the issue in focus for the counselee.* It is never appropriate for the counsellor to share his or her life experience unless it connects quite directly with the experience of the client. Self-disclosure is not an invitation for the counsellor to indulge the desire to shift focus from the counselee's issue.

- *Any counsellor self-disclosure should be purposeful.* For the most part it should seek to enable the client to reflect helpfully, and more expansively, on his or her experience by comparing it with the counsellor's experience. A helpful self-disclosure will usually enable the client to explore his or her experience in the light of someone else's (the counsellor's) lived experience.

- *For the reason just mentioned, a helpful self-disclosure should always connect back directly to the client and his or her issue.* This will normally be achieved by having the counsellor, at the end of the self-disclosure, make the link back to the client by asking questions such as, "Is that the sort of thing you have been experiencing?" or "Does that make sense in terms of your experience?"
- *The best counsellor self-disclosures will encourage client exploration, not offer answers or advice.* If the self-disclosure communicates the message, "So that's how I overcame the problem," it is likely to also carry the unspoken and unhelpful message, "And you should be able to do the same."
- *Counsellors need to keep any self-disclosure moderately short.* We recognise that, since a self-disclosure often contains some narrative, it will require some description. However, the goal is to keep this description to the minimum necessary—perhaps a few paragraphs. To take longer increases the risk of shifting attention from the client's issue by introducing counsellor content.

Discovering Client Strengths

People seeking counselling help frequently see themselves "at the mercy" of their problem. They have usually tried lots of ways to overcome the distress associated with their particular situation and have come to the place where they feel desperate, with no confidence at all in their ability to resolve the problem. As part of the overall approach to helping clients make changes to thinking that is contributing to the maintenance of the problem, it is often useful for the counsellor to find ways to sensitively "feedback" the strengths and resources that they see in the client. Done well, this can help clients regain a sense of self-efficacy and hope.

Joan was a client in her early seventies who was referred by her husband and adult children because they were worried about her increasing use of alcohol and her inability to cut back on her drinking. She acknowledged she had tried to stop the drinking but didn't seem able. She cared about her family and her marriage and knew they were worried about her.

In the course of collecting some history, it emerged that, as a sixteen-year-old, Joan had come down from the country to live in Sydney and to train for a career in nursing. She had found accommodation in a hostel that was less than ideal. There were some difficult people living there, most of them much older, and the conditions were sparse. She often had little money left for her food. Even so, she was able to support herself during her training by doing some part-time work, and she completed her qualifications and worked as a nurse for many years. She provided a history that spoke of perseverance, courage and the ability to make wise decisions. As aspects of these qualities were shared with Joan in the course of her counselling, she began to feel as though she had the strength to break free from her growing dependence on alcohol.

Joan entered a live-in rehabilitation program at a large hospital and, over the course of several weeks, was able to make use of the program and break free. Interestingly, she was one of only three members who finished

> *Taking note of client strengths and finding ways to helpfully feed this information back can make a significant difference to someone who has lost hope...*

the course, while seven others dropped out along the way. Asked how she was able to make it through and get free of her alcohol dependency, she explained, "Well, I reminded myself that I had done lots of harder things than this in the past."

Taking note of client strengths and finding ways to helpfully feed this information back can make a significant difference to someone who has lost hope and who thinks he or she can never overcome his or her problems. A number of different theories of counselling make use of this intervention as a way of helping to correct distorted thinking. Solution-Focused Counselling (O'Connell and Palmer 2003) gives considerable emphasis to the value of this, as does Narrative Counselling (Payne, 2006). Motivational Interviewing (Miller and Rollnick, 2002; Heather and Stockwell, Editors, 2004) includes affirmations, or the identifying of strengths and resources, as one of its four primary counsellor skills.

Of course there are important considerations to take into account in identifying and "offering" your observation about client strengths and resources to people in counselling. Once again, it is important the counsellor does not rush into this as an intervention. Clients need to feel that the counsellor has "heard" their pain and distress; any pre-emptive move by the counsellor to identify positives could be taken as merely evidence that the counsellor has *not* listened and does *not* realise how distressing the situation is. Done badly, identifying client strengths runs the risk of appearing to be just an example of the counsellor "jollying the client along"—figuratively patting his or her head and conveying: "There, there, it's not that bad." Nothing could be calculated to be less helpful to a client.

So timing and attunement to the client's state are vital aspects of sharing client's strengths with the person. Carried out well, this intervention has been compared to the process of building a campfire, where tiny twigs and bits of bark are first placed, and this is gradually built upon and expanded as the fire catches. Bombarding a distressed client with "large logs of affirmation" simply risks completely "snuffing the fire of connection out" (Gerald Monk in Monk, Winslade, Crocket, & Epston, 1997).

However, handled with an appropriate degree of attunement to the client's state and needs, the sharing of observed or noted client resources has the potential to make a significant difference to his or her thinking, at its best returning a sense of hope to someone who has been in danger of losing hope.

Challenging Irrational Beliefs

Part of the distorted thinking for many clients involves the presence of one or more unexamined irrational beliefs, by which they try to live. Perhaps the person who has done most to alert us to this is Albert Ellis who, in his writing on Rational Emotive Therapy (RET), built several lists of the irrational beliefs he found to be most frequent in people (Ellis, 1977). It is useful in helping people correct distortions in their thinking to look through these lists, which are readily available in the Internet.

The most common of these irrational beliefs are those attached to a person's sense of self, their view of others, or their attitude towards the world. One of the most common irrational self-beliefs is that of "the perfectionist." He or she tends to live out of an unexamined belief that could be paraphrased something along the lines of "I must always be thoroughly competent, adequate, and successful in everything I do, otherwise it's terrible and I am a failure" (or some similar conclusion). It is clear that we can divide such a belief into at least two parts: the belief and the conclusion. How do we go about helping people change so they no longer live under the irrational belief or the condemning conclusion?

Ellis suggests clients be taught to

- Challenge such beliefs by asking themselves strongly, not timidly, questions like: Who says? Where did that belief come from? Is it one of the Ten Commandments? Does it derive from some such authoritative source, or have I just taken it onboard as a result of my childhood? Was it laid on me by my parents, either directly or indirectly? If so, did they live by it and, if they did, how did it work for them?

  This kind of "testing" of the belief is the starting place for "poking holes in" and disarming its authority. Ellis argues that a rational challenging of any such core beliefs, can begin a helpful shift in thought distortions that are producing distress in someone's life.

Christians are not immune to perfectionistic thinking. Indeed, sometimes they are more prone to adopt such beliefs because of their strong desire to honour God with their life. A recent client struggling with this belief found himself unable to get university assignments in on time because they were never as good as they "should be." He was in danger of failing. Some history taking made it clear that his parents, both high achievers and committed Christians, had unknowingly reinforced this perfectionistic demand for him by praising him for academic performance over the years, while holding back in their affirmation of a brother who was not so gifted academically. Together we challenged the belief by asking if Jesus had required this of people in his teachings. We looked briefly at Jesus's words, "Be perfect, even as your heavenly Father is perfect" in order to note that it was not a call to perfect performance but a call to pursue the maturity and wholeness that God exemplifies. We also noted that the gospel is completely grounded on the assumption of our *inability* to be sinlessly perfect. If it were possible for us to reach that perfect standard, there would be no need for Jesus's sacrifice on our behalf. And so on.

- *Ellis suggests we work at helping people change demands to preferences.* As noted above, the irrational belief can be divided into the belief and the conclusion. The belief, as stated, is a demand—"I must..." There is no flexibility possible with the word "must"—no margin or "wriggle room" at all. Words like "must," "should," and "ought" are uncompromising. They are demands!
- If we were to change this demand to a preference, it might be expressed as *I would prefer it if I was always thoroughly competent, adequate and successful in everything I do...* or *I would like it if...*, or even, *It would be nice if...* It can be helpful to completely rewrite the original belief as a preference rather than a demand, and then have the client repeat it aloud a few times to get the feeling of holding the belief as a preference rather than a demand.
- *Ellis also encourages the rewording of the original (irrational) conclusion so that it is a rational conclusion.* The conclusion in the original statement is *otherwise it's terrible and I am a failure.* The task here is to challenge this conclusion. *Would it prove that I am a failure if I got something wrong? Do "successful" people get everything "right" all the time?*, and so on. When this aspect is reworded, we might have a conclusion like... *the truth is doing something imperfectly does not make me a failure and it is also true that it is possible to live a very fulfilling and worthwhile life, even if I sometimes get things wrong or make a mistake.*
- It is our practice to write out the full version of the alternate rational belief on a white card or sheet of paper so clients can take it with them and rehearse it every day. Using the above example, the full revision of the belief might look something like this: "It would be nice if I was always thoroughly competent, adequate, and successful in everything I did, but the truth is, that's not possible. It's also true that making

a mistake in something does not make me a failure, it just makes me a normal human being. And it's also true that I can live a very fulfilling and rich life, even if I make a mistake sometimes."

In working with clients to help them change distorted thinking, it is helpful to try to get them to identify the core beliefs that have driven their life over the years, so that these can be rationally examined. Using the model above, we can then help them make changes to the core belief so that it is no longer irrational.

A recent client came up with the following:

- I have to be working hard in order to be worthwhile or I am letting God and myself down.
- I must always carry the responsibility for what happens or I am not fulfilling my duty as a Christian.
- It is wrong (sinful) to spend money on myself.
- I have to have affirmation from everyone or I will have failed in my witness and will feel terrible.

Each of these distorted beliefs, and others like them, required challenging in order to weaken their influence in the client's life.

Finally, it needs to be noted that Ellis wrote and functioned quite aggressively from an atheistic stance most of the time, so there will be a need to put aside any aspects in his writings that do not sit comfortably with the counsellor's or client's beliefs as a Christian. Even so, there is much of value in Ellis's approach to challenging irrational beliefs, and we encourage counsellors to look into his work in order to glean that which is useful.

Replacing Negative Thinking Patterns with Alternative Balanced Thoughts

The work of Albert Ellis has been taken further by many theorists and practitioners, and has developed into Cognitive-Behavioural Therapy (CBT) or counselling. Perhaps the best known of these is Aaron Beck and his followers (Beck and Beck, 2011). Beck realised that many people find themselves caught in a spider's web of negative thinking patterns. They live with an excessive flow of negative thoughts that attach to their view of themselves, their situations and their future. In CBT, practitioners seek to help people identify these patterns of negative thinking and take them through a process of learning to replace negative patterns of thought with alternative, balanced thoughts as an effective way of modulating the emotional distress caused by the negative patterns.

The most common starting approach in counselling is to work through some specific situations in the client's life and, using a Thought Record, identify the flow of negative thoughts and the consequent emotional distress, then work to produce some alternative, balanced thoughts for the person to run, in order to alter the outcome. The Thought Record is usually a grid or table used in this training process, to help the client begin to get a feel for altering his or her pattern of negative thinking. Many writers and clinicians have developed their own variation of the basic grid.

Activating Event (Situation)	Beliefs (Negative automatic thoughts)	Consequences (Emotions experienced) (Scale of 1-10)	Disputing thoughts (Alternative, balanced thoughts)	Emotion change (Scale of 1-10)

Figure 8 - Thought Record Example

The first step in using the thought record is to have the client describe a situation in which he or she has been troubled by negative thinking. Just a word or two is used in the first column to identify the situation.

The second step is to proceed by jumping past Column 2 and going to Column 3 to fill in the emotions and/or physical symptoms experienced by the person, as well as the strength of these on a 1-10 scale where 10 represents "Could not have been more intense" and 1 represents "no real strength at all."

The third step is to go back to the Column 2 and ask: "What thoughts/beliefs/pictures were running through my mind to produce the feelings and outcomes already identified in Column 3?" The task now is to write out as many of these thoughts as possible into Column 2.

The fourth step is to go to Column 4 and have the client address the question: "What *alternative*, balanced, rational thoughts could I have run in my mind about the situation?" Again, write out as many as you can.

Finally, consider Column 5 and ask: "If I run the alternative, balanced thoughts, what emotions or other symptoms do *they* generate, and how would I rate the strength (on the 1 to 10 scale) of these?" Sometimes a completely different outcome is produced but often clients will find that the emotion remains much the same, while the intensity reduces considerably.

Here is an example of the use of this kind of thought record to help someone cope better with anxiety. The client was a minister in mid-life, who had come to doubt his capacity to preach and carry out his duties well, despite the evidence that his church was stable and his parishioners were generally happy with his ministry.

Activating Event (Situation)	Beliefs (Negative automatic thoughts)	Consequences (Emotions experienced) (Scale of 1-10)	Disputing thoughts (Alternative, balanced thoughts)	Emotion change (Scale of 1-10)
Preaching on Sunday morning	—"What if people see my nervousness?" —"What if I forget what I have to say, or people find it boring?" —"The minister down the road is doing really well and his church is growing. I'm not as good as him." —"How will I handle it if someone criticises me at the door on the way out?"	Anxiety 8 Low confidence 3 Nausea and upset stomach 7	—"If I take a few slow breaths before I start, I won't feel so nervous." —"I have the sermon fully written out, so I don't really have to worry about forgetting." —"It's not helpful to compare myself. God just wants me to do my best." —"People generally give me positive feedback, so I don't need to worry too much about being criticised."	Anxiety 5 Moderately confident 6 Free from nausea

Figure 9—Client Thought Record

It is useful for trainee counsellors to work at creating a Thought Record that they can become confident in using and then try out as an instrument for helping people alter ingrained patterns of dysfunctional or negative thinking.

Disconnecting from Unhelpful Thinking

Over the last thirty years or so, Acceptance and Commitment Theory (ACT) has been developed as another approach to helping people break free from the influence of distorted thinking (Hayes and Smith 2005; Harris and Hayes 2009). It is beyond the scope of our work here to go into a description of ACT in any detail. However, it is certainly worth the counsellor's while to look at gaining further understanding and skills from this variation to traditional CBT.

In part ACT builds from the observation that challenging thoughts and working to free ourselves from their influence, often seems to have the paradoxical effect of increasing their influence. The theory notes that if someone forbids us to think of, for example, "a little red train engine," we are automatically thrown into thinking of the forbidden item. A stance of opposition can often increase the potency of the forbidden thought.

With this as a starting point, ACT encourages people *not* to try to stop a thought or thoughts but to disconnect from these by taking the position of *noticing* them, or *becoming aware* of them, rather than engaging them. In ACT, practicing "staying on the platform" rather than "getting on board the thought train," is used as an intervention to help people learn to "live with," rather than "fight against" certain thoughts. This process of disconnecting from the impact of thoughts is labelled *cognitive defusion*, and is the opposite of *cognitive fusion*, which involves our being immersed in our thoughts and, in a sense, living under their control.

There is much psycho-education in ACT, including an understanding of the nature of our brain's functioning, reassessment of what thoughts are as one way of diminishing their potency in our lives, and ways of learning to tolerate the suffering our thoughts produce.

ACT encourages clients to learn *mindfulness*, which can be helpfully thought of as *learning to be attuned, acceptingly, to our experience in the present moment* rather than living excessively in regret for the past or fear of the future. It recognises that our thinking tends to take us into excessive rumination about past or future experiences and events, and this interferes with our capacity to enjoy the present. Learning ways of re-dressing this imbalance is one of the goals of this approach. Finally, if our thinking is "taken off the pedestal," in the sense that we are no longer giving excessive influence to thoughts as the guide for our living, ACT seeks to provide people with a new foundation for living. It reminds people that values or "what is really important to us" are a much richer and more stable guide for shaping our lives. Thus, ACT takes people into working out core values and encouraging them to live out of these values, rather than allowing their behaviour to be shaped excessively by thoughts and feelings, particularly if these contradict deeply held values. There is much here that synergises with our Christian faith.

There is much more that could be said about ACT as an approach to helping people disconnect from the distress of excessive introspection. For the beginning counsellor, it offers another way of helping people, not to escape from distressing thoughts but to expand their capacity to live with such thoughts without being "ruled" by them.

The Acceptance in ACT, thus, involves learning to accept and be at peace with formerly distressing thoughts, while the Commitment in ACT involves identifying our deepest values and committing to live by them rather than by our thinking and feelings. In many ways it fits with the Serenity Prayer of the Alcoholics Anonymous movement: "Lord, grant me the Serenity to accept the things I cannot change, the Courage to change the things I can, and the Wisdom to know the difference".

Further Reading

Backus, W. & Chapian, M. (2000). *Telling yourself the truth*. Minneapolis: Bethany.

Beck, J. & Beck, A. (2011). *Cognitive behaviour therapy, (2nd Ed.): Basics and beyond.* New York: Guildford Press.

Cormier, S., Nurius, P. S. & Osborn, C. (2009). *Interviewing and change strategies for helpers.* Belmont, CA: Brooks Cole.

Ellis, A. (1977). *Handbook of rational-emotive therapy.* New York: Springer.

CHAPTER 12

The Skills of Correcting II: Correcting Disruptive Emotions

While thinking, feelings, and behaviour are all dimensions of human functioning that we can easily conceptualise as separate and distinct, we need to remember that, in truth, they all interrelate simply because people function as an integrated whole. So each of these areas affects the functioning of the other areas. Any attempt to intervene in one area will probably necessitate working with the other areas in some measure as well.

In the previous chapter we looked at a range of skills and interventions that have value for the beginning counsellor in helping those who struggle because of distorted patterns of thinking. Here we take up the task of looking at more options available to the counsellor who wants to intervene helpfully with those distressed by emotions that disrupt their ability to get on with their lives.

However, it will quickly become obvious that some of these interventions could also be included in the chapter on Correcting Thinking or, perhaps, the chapter on Correcting Behaviour, such is the degree of overlap and the experiential interaction of thoughts, emotions and behaviour!

* * * * * * * * *

Subtask 2—Correcting Disruptive Emotions

In human functioning it is true that we exercise less *direct* control in the area of our emotional functioning than we do in our thinking or our behaviour. We are aware that it is not at all helpful to say to a person who is in tears, *Don't be sad; be happy*! The absence of any capacity to simply change our emotions at will is the reason that most people seeking the help of a counsellor tend to speak of *emotional* distress when asked what they are seeking help for. Clients will speak of struggling with depression, anxiety, fears, anger, confusion, loneliness, lack of confidence, jealousy, and so on. Our emotional functioning has the capacity to immobilise us and disrupt our ability to function in effective and healthy ways.

Our emotions are good. They are a gift from God. The whole canon of Scripture demonstrates clearly that God is a God of emotion. We see in the life of Jesus someone who integrated a healthy range of emotional functioning, not allowing his emotion to over-control or direct his behaviour, but expressing his feelings readily before others. Jesus rejoices (Luke 10:21), weeps (John 11:35), is angered (Matthew 23; Mark 3:5), and feels compassion (Matthew 14:14). Feelings are clearly affirmed as a gift from the Creator.

There are times when we meet a client who has been so damaged by life that he or she seems to have found a way to largely disconnect from his or her emotions. Psychoactive medications are often useful here in "turning down" the intensity of emotion, but there are people who prefer to avoid these medications because they don't want to lose their capacity to feel. Feelings add so much colour and joy to life that we are reluctant to block them completely. Blocking feelings might be helpful in some respects, but it may also have unexpected costs as a method for managing disruptive emotions. In people who have internalised or in some other way "shut down" their emotions, researchers have often found a correlation between this defensive pattern and increased physical problems, largely resulting from lower rates of the production of antibodies in the immune system (Kennedy-Moore & Watson, 1999; Lovallo, 2005). Learning to integrate our emotions and manage our feeling responses seems a better alternative. How can we go about helping people with this as counsellors?

Helping People Manage Disruptive Emotions

Often clients are concerned that they have lost control of their emotions. At this point the first task is likely to be that of assisting them to feel a measure of control once more. We looked at some primary skills for the counsellor – grounding and containment – in Chapter 10. Containment is initially a counsellor skill or capacity that we seek to also develop in the client, while grounding is an intervention that we seek to train clients to implement. Here we consider additional skills and interventions that the counsellor seeks to bring to the client so that he or she begins to feel more in control.

Physical Exercise

We would be remiss to omit identifying the value of exercise as an intervention directed at helping someone manage disruptive emotion. Physical activity serves to "burn up" the stress chemicals, such as adrenaline and cortisol, associated with strong emotion, while releasing endorphins and enkephalins. People readily report feeling more "chilled out" or "mellow," when they have played a strenuous game or taken themselves out of the house and been active. While it would be natural to include exercise in the section on managing destructive behaviours, it is such an important intervention helping people who struggle with depression, anxiety, anger, and the range of difficult emotions that we are compelled to mention it here (Lovallo, 1999).

Journaling

Often clients find it helpful to journal their experience, including their emotions, from one week to the next, while they participate in counselling. This will vary from one person to another, but where clients are open to it and where they find some benefit in externalising their feelings in a personal journal, it can be a most helpful intervention. If we have a client who is able to make good use of journaling, we usually try to have him or her bring the material to counselling sessions so we can further process it.

It is not unusual for clients to want the counsellor to read their journal. While this is not a problem, we usually prefer to encourage the client to *read the contents to us*, rather than simply have us read it. Of course there will be the occasional client whose journal content is so emotionally potent he or she cannot manage to read it aloud, and in this case, we would read it ourselves. However, a significant benefit of having the client read it out aloud for us is that it becomes *another* method of ventilation. Writing it for themselves tends to be helpful, and then reading it out serves as a second discharge. Often because of the nonverbal signals, we can see which part of the content is most difficult or most potent in our clients' experience. We see them hesitate, we hear their voice begin to choke, we see the intense emotion, the tears—and it provides help for us in understanding what the clients are going through and where our focus may need to be. The alternative in which we read the content ourselves loses all that additional information and introduces possible "contamination" because we are now reading and understanding through our own filters. So we encourage the client wherever possible, even if this is difficult for him or her.

> *Often clients find it helpful to journal their experience, including their emotions... while they participate in counselling.*

When journaling is helpful, we tend to see that clients are able to contain their emotion better in their normal day-to-day experience.

Self-Calming Skills

In Chapter 10 we looked at teaching clients diaphragmatic breathing as an intervention. Relaxation training is another important skill for helping clients calm themselves.

Progressive Muscle Relaxation

Progressive muscle relaxation is widely used as an intervention aimed at helping people manage emotions such as stress, anxiety, and confusion. There are two common variations—relaxing muscles from a "standing start" and relaxing muscles by first tensing and then relaxing. Both approaches are fine, although the use of tensing does perhaps assist people more in becoming aware of what muscle tension feels like and how this feels different from relaxation.

The approach we use most involves making use of seven major muscle groups:

- the person's dominant hand and arm, right up to the shoulder
- the other hand and arm
- the person's dominant foot and leg, right up to the thighs and buttocks
- the other foot and leg
- the front of the torso, including belly and chest muscles
- the back of the torso
- neck and head muscles

We usually teach this skill by having clients rate their current level of stress, muscle tension, or anxiety on a Subjective Unit of Discomfort Scale (a SUD scale), giving themselves a rating between 0 and 100. We define 100 as "Could not be more anxious; totally stressed, tense or anxious" and 0 as "The degree of stress, tension and anxiety you feel a few seconds before drifting into peaceful sleep." Because we all need a measure of arousal and muscle tension for normal functioning, we set a score of 35 as "The degree of muscle tension necessary for normal functioning."

After having clients rate their current levels, we work through the muscle groups in the order above. Using a "tense-relax" process, we usually get clients to tense their dominant hand and arm by squeezing their hand into a tight fist so that they can feel the tension right up into their shoulder and hold this for around five seconds. We then have them relax this, with instructions like: *Now relax all those muscles. Just let your hand and arm become limp and loose and floppy. No tightness or tension at all. Just completely relaxed. Relax your fingers and hand; relax your wrist and forearm and around your elbow; relax your upper arm right up to your shoulder, so that the whole of the hand and arm has no tension at all. Completely relaxed. That's good.* We usually do each specific muscle group twice.

Next we move to the other hand and arm and repeat the process, encouraging them to try to keep the dominant hand and arm as relaxed as possible, even while they tense and relax the other hand and arm.

With the dominant foot and leg it is important to get tension by pointing the toes *inward and up*. It is possible to get tension here by pointing the toes down but this is not the approach to use because of the danger of cramping up the calf muscle and causing a lot of pain. We have them point their toes inward and upward and instruct them to hold that for about five seconds, noticing what it feels like for the muscles to be tensed, before taking them through a sequence of relaxation instructions. We have them follow the instructions: *Now, relax your toes and your foot, letting the muscles become loose and flaccid, no tension at all; relax the muscles around your ankle and your calf up to your knee; relax you upper leg, right up to your thigh and buttocks, just letting the chair (floor) support you; no muscle tension at all. Just allow your muscles to completely let go. Feel yourself experiencing a calm, peaceful state and enjoy taking control of your muscles and relaxing them. Keep relaxing even more for the next minute or so, just enjoying the experience.*

Follow this by tensing and relaxing the other foot and leg.

We teach clients to get muscle tension in the front of their torso simply by tensing stomach muscles as tightly as they can and holding that for some five seconds or so. The instructions for relaxing are something like: *Now, just let those muscles relax. Letting go in your stomach area and up through your chest. Breathing easily and naturally, no tightness or tension in the muscles at all. Just let yourself feel calm and peaceful, completely relaxed and safe.*

We teach clients to get tension in the back of their torso by pulling their shoulders back towards each other for a brief period. This can be quite painful so it is best not to have them hold it for more than a few seconds. The instructions are then given to relax the muscles in their lower back and right up to their shoulders, and to notice what this feels like and to enjoy the control they have over the muscles of their body.

The final muscle group includes their neck and head. Here we get them to tense neck muscles by counter-posing the muscles in the back of their neck against those in the front, and feeling the tension. We get them to tense head muscles simply by scrunching all the muscles of their face and head so that they feel the tightness. Instructions for relaxing take them through relaxing their neck muscles, relaxing their lower jaw, relaxing the muscles around their mouth and nose, relaxing muscles around their ears and across their foreheads and relaxing all the muscles right across their scalp.

In order to make sure they are gaining benefit from the exercise, we ask clients to do another rating on the SUD scale, just to ensure that they are actually relaxing their muscles.

The purpose of progressive muscle relaxation is to teach clients a technique for shedding muscle tension, which has been accumulated because of tension, stress or anxiety during their day. It is very helpful in re-connecting clients to a sense of their own self-efficacy, as they see that they can make a difference to their sense of stress. We encourage them to practise once a day, explaining that it is a simple skill and that they will improve quite quickly with a little practice. We talk of the unity of our being, and explain that if we physically relax, there is a likelihood that we will concurrently let go of some of the worries and distressing emotion that we might otherwise accumulate.

Breath-Focused Relaxation

People who struggle with anxiety, whether this is a general feature of their functioning, or whether this is related to specific situations (such as speaking in front of people) can benefit from other ways of calming themselves. There are a number of ways of learning how to relax, and research evidence does not indicate that any single method is better than another. One of these other methods is usually called breath-focused relaxation because it enables people to bring anxiety under control by focusing on breathing.

Here is a sample script that you could use as you practise teaching someone the skill of breath-focused relaxation. Work with another trainee counsellor at this stage of your training. This script assumes the other person is a Christian. The script is drawn from *Unloading the Overload* (Powell and Barker, 1998). If your client is not a Christian, simply leave out the second paragraph.

"I want you now to take a moment to get yourself comfortable. You may sit in a chair, feet firmly and comfortably on the floor in front of you, or you may want to lie on a carpet or on a bed. Just make sure that you are as comfortable as possible. You may want to remove contact lenses or glasses, if you wear them. You may want to loosen a belt or a tie, or make some other adjustment—just as long as you feel comfortable.

Now close your eyes and take a moment to think about your breathing. Scripture records that in the beginning God breathed into mankind the breath of life. Your breath is a gift from God, given into your hands so that you might live. What a wonderful gift it is—taking air into your body and miraculously making use of that part of it, the oxygen, which your body needs, then expelling the rest. A natural, effortless process, that goes on whether you are thinking about it or not thinking about it. This is indeed a gift to praise God for! No wonder the psalmist says 'Let everything that has breath, praise God!' Take a moment to praise God for the gift of your breath (30 seconds of silence).

Now we're going to make use of your breath-gift to help your body relax. You will be in charge. Your breath has been given as a gift by God to you. I want you now to slow your breathing down just a little, and as you do, let your body relax and enjoy that feeling of relaxation, of letting go of anxiety and stress. Just slowing your breathing a little and relaxing as you do. Take a moment now to slow your breathing down and feel that pleasant feeling of relaxing. Go ahead, now (30 seconds).

And as you breathe more slowly, I want you also to breathe that little bit more deeply, allowing yourself to relax even more. Breathe just a little more slowly and deeply, letting yourself relax and enjoying the feeling of using your breath-gift to be kind to your body. Continue to breathe more slowly and deeply (30 seconds).

And as you breathe more deeply and slowly, I want you now to make your breathing as smooth as possible. Make it such a smooth, gentle, unforced action that it feels as if your body does it without you. Such a smooth, even, relaxed action that all the jerkiness is gone—your chest just rising and falling smoothly as you breathe in and out. So smooth that it almost seems as though the change from breathing out to breathing in is unnoticeable, and the change from breathing in to breathing out is unnoticeable. Smooth and regular, slow and deep. It might help you to think of your breathing as being like the long, flat arc of a swing, as it moves slowly and perfectly evenly, back and forth to the rhythm of your breathing. Smooth as lamb's wool or downy feathers.

Keep on breathing smoothly and deeply and slowly. And now take a moment to review the various muscle groups in your body, making sure they are relaxed. Make sure your toes and feet, your ankles, your calf muscles, your knees, your upper legs, right on up to your thighs and buttocks are relaxed, with all the tension gone. Make sure your stomach muscles and your back muscles are relaxed. Just let all the tightness and tension go from them and enjoy the feeling of relaxation. Relax your fingers and hands, your lower arms, elbows and upper arms, right up into your shoulders. Relax your neck and scalp muscles, relax your face muscles—the muscles around your eyes and across your forehead, the muscles in your cheeks and around your mouth and chin. Allow your whole body to relax more and more and enjoy the feeling of being relaxed, free from anxiety and tension, safe and secure, warm and calm inside (30 seconds).

And while you continue to breathe slowly and deeply and smoothly, I want you to notice just how good your control over your body is. I want you to notice that in your hands there is the slightest increase in warmth, almost so slight that you find it hard to notice, so slight that you may not be able to detect it. But you may be able to just notice that slight increase in warmth. There is nothing magic about it at all.

When you relax you open the blood passages up so that your blood can flow more easily and fully—and it tends to produce a warmth in your fingers and hands. You are being kind to your body when you relax like this. You're making its work easier. Now continue to enjoy your control over your body for a moment longer as you continue to relax (30 seconds).

In just a moment I'm going to count back from ten to one, to give you an opportunity to re-orient yourself from your relaxed state. When I get to five I want you to wiggle your fingers and toes just a little. When I get to one, open your eyes and reorient yourself. You'll feel pleasantly relaxed but fully alert, ready to go with any task that you have for the rest of the day. Okay? Ten... nine... eight... seven... six... five... wiggle your fingers and toes a little, that's good... four... three... two... and one! Open your eyes and reorient yourself. Squeeze your hands into fists and then let them go. You may want to stretch a little. That's right. Allow yourself to adjust to the external environment again.

By practising this process you will be able to learn to relax quite quickly, simply by controlling your breathing rate. You will be able to use this to calm yourself and take control back from anxiety and tension. You can use this just before you go into any situation you think will be stressful. Remember the key to success is practice. If you practise faithfully once or twice a day for ten or fifteen minutes, you will certainly be able to notice an improvement in your handling of anxiety and stress in a few weeks. You will feel calmer, more in control, and more relaxed simply by focusing on your breathing—making it slower, deeper and smoother".

We encourage students to practise memorising this kind of script so they can use it to teach relaxation to someone who battles with anxiety or stress. If you are teaching relaxation to someone, you need to take him or her through a few practice sessions. Feel free to create a spoken copy using this script so that any counselee can take it with him or her and practise daily sessions. The skill has application for anyone who, from time to time, finds his or her emotions threatening to become overwhelming.

Mindfulness

Mindfulness can be defined as "focused attention to here-and-now experience in an accepting manner." Some Christians can be a little anxious about the term mindfulness and its association with Buddhist philosophy. For these reasons we are not particularly keen on the term "mindfulness," but we affirm the value of helping people work to re-establish their skill in learning to focus in an accepting manner on their present experience. We align ourselves clearly with those who separate this technique from any Buddhist association, but we accept the research evidence that says it has value for people who battle to manage their emotional functioning.

If we ask ourselves, "At what life stage are humans most in touch with the present?," we will inevitably conclude that it is when we are young children. A healthy young child runs around playing chasings, or becomes engrossed in play with a toy, without thinking about *yesterday* ("Mummy was upset at me yesterday; I hope she still likes me!") or *tomorrow* ("I hope Daddy has remembered to pay the car registration, otherwise the police might arrest us"!).

However, as we grow and our brains develop, we begin to cultivate the capacity to imagine ourselves in the past and the future. This is a most helpful capacity. It enables us to evaluate, learn from past experience, make judgment calls, predict, sense potential danger, anticipate opportunities, and so on. The trouble is that this capacity can start to become excessive. We can over-think situations and find ourselves living excessively in our minds, regretting the past, or worrying about tomorrow.

Jesus offers us important direction when he instructs us to focus on giving priority in our life to God and his kingdom. In Matthew 6:34 we are instructed, "Therefore, do not worry about tomorrow, for tomorrow will worry about itself. Each day has enough trouble of its own." We would not be doing harm to this teaching to draw from it the wisdom to learn again the skill of focusing our attention on the present context, rather than living "in our mind" and worrying about the future.

> *We can over-think situations and find ourselves living excessively in our minds, regretting the past, or worrying about tomorrow.*

So, mindfulness involves relearning to give focused attention to the present—a skill we had as children but lost touch with as we grew and started to project ourselves excessively into the past and future. The value of regaining this skill is that it enables us to disconnect from the worry thoughts and anxious feelings that threaten to otherwise rampage through our lives (Harris & Hayes, 2009; Hayes & Smith, 2005).

Sentence Stems

The use of sentence stems as an intervention is well described in Ecker and Hulley's *Depth-Oriented Brief Therapy* (1996). Originally called Depth-Oriented Brief Therapy or DOBT, they have since come to call their approach Coherence Therapy. The sentence stem intervention is a good example of the overlap between correcting cognitions, emotional responses, and behaviour patterns.

There are times when a client struggles with an emotional/behavioural symptom or set of symptoms but they have no understanding of why they react this way. As counsellors we suspect that some disruptive emotional construct holds the client in a "stuck" position in terms of his or her functioning in regard to this problem. A construct, in this case, we take to be a *construction of reality* that exists perhaps out of the person's conscious awareness, so that if we were to ask: "What is the belief or understanding that makes it so important for you to continue with this pattern of emotional/behavioural response?," the person could quite truthfully say, "I have no idea. I just don't know." What we need in such cases is a way of helping the person to become aware of the "emotional truth" (Ecker & Hulley, 1996) underlying their stuckness. The use of a sentence stem is one way of trying to access this out-of-conscious-awareness cognitive/emotional/behavioural content.

Ecker and Hulley suggest that often the construction of reality that holds the disruptive emotional response in place will simply "bubble up" in the person if we can provide the right stimulus. If what bubbles up for the person is, in truth, holding the symptoms or symptoms in place, it will resonate emotionally. There will be a kind of "aha" moment for them and the client will recognise that it is "emotionally true" for them. Ecker and Hulley's suggestion is that, in this kind of situation, we frame a sentence stem that seeks to tap into an unrecognised, unconsciously held construction of reality. To do this they suggest we offer a sentence stem that links with the *unconscious necessity of the symptom,* rather than the consciously held *desire to get rid of* the symptom. We ask clients to simply relax and allow themselves to finish a sentence stem that we, as the counsellor, offer them. The idea is that we offer a sentence stem that is paradoxical or counterintuitive to their surface understanding of wanting to get rid of the symptom. Our instruction might be something like, "Please repeat this sentence stem after me and finish it, without trying to edit at all, with whatever comes to mind for you." We then offer a sentence stem such as, "This symptom has served me well in that..." We might run this sentence stem several times, encouraging the client to stay with it and just see what bubbles up into their awareness. Or we might use something like, "When I am finally free from this symptom, the trouble with that will be..." Of course we will not be surprised if early responses tend to be accompanied by some client puzzlement and statements such as, "It hasn't served me well at all. I hate it. I just want to get rid of it." The appropriate counsellor response to such a statement is obviously something like, "I understand exactly what you're saying but please stay with it a few more times in order to see if any other responses come to mind." We then run the sentence stem a few more times, possibly reworking our words a little to see if any unconsciously held response comes up.

One client came to our clinic because, as a Christian, he was troubled by a pattern of behaviour that had developed in his marriage. His wife tended to visit her mother a few times a year, away in the countryside. During the last several times she had gone away, the client found himself going on a drinking binge at a nearby pub. Through the Saturday he drank himself to the point of being quite inebriated and then spent Sunday morning not going to church, but allowing himself time to sober up before his wife came home. When we explored some history, he shared that he had been converted out of a heavy drinking background some years back. The return of this behaviour troubled him because he did not understand why he felt compelled to do it, as it clashed with his position as a leader in his church congregation.

After some further exploration of history, he was asked to simply relax and repeat some sentence stems, just allowing whatever came to mind to "bubble up." The sentence stem was something like, "This pattern of binge drinking serves me well in that..." At first he looked a bit puzzled and responded with statements such as, "I really want to get rid of it." This was affirmed: "I know you do. But just stay with the process and don't edit anything. See if any other awarenesses come up for you."

We continued on, and after a few more sentence stems, he responded, "I don't want to lose touch with 'real guys.'" He was asked if that "felt true" and he nodded. "It really does," he said, looking a bit surprised. We continued on and he came up with, "I don't want to feel completely controlled by my wife."

We took the time to consider these statements, but there was little need. These were moments that had tapped into some *fear* of losing a part of his identity, a deep fear of being controlled, and he was able to acknowledge that these unconscious fears had been "driving" the production of the symptom of binge drinking. We talked about other ways he could avoid losing his identity as "a real Aussie bloke" and ways he could avoid being "over-controlled" by his wife. We wrote the statements out on a white card for him to read over each day, just to keep the new awareness of what the symptom meant and what the out-of-conscious-awareness emotion was that lay behind the production of the symptom and then finished the session.

He got up to go, and just before he walked out of the door, he suddenly turned and said quite energetically, "And another thing—I don't want to be completely controlled by my mother!" It was suggested he add that to the white card too when he got home, and he left.

At the next session he spoke of how dramatic it had been for him to discover that an out-of-awareness fear was causing the behaviour. He had not had a chance to see if the symptom was still a problem, but he felt confident he could handle things differently now. He was going to connect up with some of his Christian mates and go dirt-bike riding next time his wife was away. And he had already spoken to his wife about feeling that he wanted to be more involved in decision making. He was surprised that she seemed happy about that.

This client's experience serves as an example of the fact that there are times when unconscious emotions can produce symptoms that leave us confused. It also serves as an example of the use of sentence stems as an intervention aimed at revealing some emotional construct that is producing a symptom and holding it in place.

Trial Sentences

Another technique that has value in trying to "unearth" an emotional construct that is holding a distressing symptom in place is the use of trial sentences. Like sentence stems, trial sentences are useful in trying to tap into the unconscious mind. They have a place when, in the process of counselling, we begin to suspect a link between unconscious emotions and distressing symptoms, or when we want to check out a connection between surface behaviours and unconscious motivations.

When we make use of a trial sentence, we preface it by saying something like, "Please try saying this out loud. It may or may not fit with your experience. We're just trying it out to see if it resonates for you." Then we craft a sentence that fits with something we have begun to suspect.

In a recent session with a couple, the husband complained about what he described as his wife's "lack of trust." They had been married less than a year, and he reported being very content in the marriage and that he loved his wife. However, they had had a number of arguments because she kept questioning him about his behaviour. She wanted to know everywhere he had been, what he had been doing when he missed her phone call, why he hadn't accounted for everything he had spent, and so on. He was upset that she kept taking his phone and checking his phone messages, and he felt she was "like a private detective."

Both shared some of their history. The behaviours had become worse shortly after they were married. As the wife shared, she reported that her father, whom she loved dearly, had been unfaithful in his marriage, and she had come to learn of this quite recently. To heighten her distress, her father had been someone people everywhere had trusted and seen as a "genuine Christian."

At this point we offered a trial sentence to see if it resonated for her at all. She was asked to repeat something like, "My father's unfaithfulness hurt me so much that part of me is terrified my husband will turn out to be unfaithful." Even as she started to repeat the sentence, it was evident that it connected with her at a deep level. Tears welled up as she said, "It's true. I never realised it, but that's why I do it. I'm scared you'll betray me. I'm so sorry." Using a trial sentence such as this can help to bring unconscious emotional constructions into *conscious* awareness and, thus, demystify a distressing behaviour.

Of course it is important that we adequately explain that trial sentences can also "miss the mark," and it is important that we genuinely allow for this to occur, freely giving permission to the client to say, "No, I don't think that's it," or "No that doesn't seem to fit." In our explanation, and in our use of this intervention and the use of sentence stems, it is important that we keep in mind that the intervention is simply a trial to see if something emerges from unconscious mind that carries experiential authenticity for the client.

Finally, while we do not have the freedom or space to consider a fuller range of interventions aimed at helping people with difficulties in emotion regulation, we would point to the model and the range of resources included in Linehan's book *Dialectic-Behavioural Treatment of Borderline Personality Disorder* (1993), and her skills-training manual (1993). Although the books are designed for working with clients whose issues go beyond the skill-level of novitiate counsellors, there are many helpful worksheets that could be adapted to clients with disruptive emotions, especially from the skills training manual.

Further Reading

Ecker, B., & Hulley, L. (1996). *Depth-oriented brief therapy.* San Francisco: Jossey-Bass.

Kabat-Zinn, J. (2012). *Mindfulness for beginners.* Boulder, CO: Sounds True Inc.

Linehan, M. (1993). *Cognitive behavioural treatment of borderline personality disorder.* New York: The Guilford Press.

Linehan, M. (1993). *Skills-training manual for cognitive-behavioural treatment of borderline personality disorder.* New York: The Guilford Press.

Powell, C. J., & Barker, G. A. (1998). *Unloading the overload: Stress management for christians.* Sydney: Strand.

Siegel, R. (2011). *The mindfulness solution.* New York: Guilford Press.

Williams, M., & Penman, D. (2011). *Mindfulness: An eight-week plan for finding peace in a frantic world.* New York: Rodale Inc.

CHAPTER 13

The Skills of Correcting III: Correcting Destructive Behaviours

Once again, at the outset we emphasise the interrelationship and overlap that occurs between and among thoughts, feelings, and behaviours. This is especially obvious in the fact that Cognitive Behaviour Therapy (CBT) specifically combines an emphasis on both cognitions and behaviour change. So we need to stay mindful that when we speak of behaviour change, we are inevitably overlapping cognitive and emotion change. Not surprisingly, it is often a moot point as to whether the change is primarily a cognitive or behavioural one.

Even so, this chapter looks to give particular focus to the counsellor's role in helping people change destructive behaviours and the skills they might use. Of course along with other debilitating behaviours, a focus on behaviour brings in the whole counselling field of addictions, a realm that seems set to increase as more people are caught up in the pressures of life and the enticements increasingly on offer in Western society. While we are not able to give extended attention to addictions here, we encourage beginning counsellors looking for help in this area to acquaint themselves with Motivational Interviewing (Miller and Rollnick, 2002) for further help in working with such client issues. Here we seek to address just a few of the basic skills and interventions available for the beginning counsellor.

* * * * * * * *

Correcting Destructive Behaviours

Self-Monitoring

It is always useful to have a way of assessing aspects of any problem behaviour. Self-monitoring enables the counsellor to establish a baseline regarding the destructive behaviour, obtaining a measure of how often it occurs, how severe or intense aspects of it are, what the duration of the behaviour is, and any other useful elements. A range of factors useful for understanding how the behaviour functions in the client's life can be easily included in a Self-Monitoring Record.

Here is an example taken from work with a client who was looking for help in overcoming an addiction to online pornography.

Month and Date	Prayed? Y or N	Acted Out? Y or N	Trigger?	Emotion Before	Temptation Intensity (1-10)	Action Taken?	Time Spent?
1 May							
2							
3							
4							
5							
6							
7							

Figure 10—Self-Monitoring Record

(Note that the example above is limited to data for seven days, whereas in practice we usually create a record that includes thirty days [a full month] in the left-hand column).

Having a client fill out a Self-Monitoring Record helps get a picture of the pervasiveness of the problem behaviour. However, it does more than that. It also serves as an intervention that usually begins the process of bringing change (Antony & Roemer 2011). It is not unusual for someone who begins to monitor an aspect of behaviour, particularly one he or she wants to change, to find the behaviour begins to reduce in some way, although this is not always a change that sustains for long.

In Chapter 10 we learned that in assessing a behaviour, the most important measures are frequency, intensity, and duration. You will notice that each of these aspects of the behaviour is assessed in the Self-Monitoring Record above. The column labelled "Acted Out?" provides a record of the *frequency* or number of times a behaviour occurs although, depending on the specific behaviour, the recording process may need to be adjusted. For example, we may need to provide specific instructions on how to record the data if more than one viewing on the Internet occurs in a single day. If we were recording a different behaviour, such as the number of cigarettes smoked in the day, we might need to adjust the columns to enable this to be recorded.

The Self-Monitoring Record also records the *intensity* of the temptation to view pornography, making use of a subjective scale that goes from 1 (hardly any temptation at all) to 10 (extremely intense temptation; could not be stronger). Finally, the particular sheet also records the *duration* of the behaviour in the last column. It might also be useful to collect data on the time when the behaviour occurs.

When drawing up your own self-monitoring record, it is important to think through what data you want to record. You may find yourself adjusting the sheet as data starts to be collected and you begin to think of aspects that might be valuable to understand. Perhaps a useful guideline, though, is to keep the sheet as simple and user friendly as possible to maximise the likelihood the client will fill it out. If you have an ongoing record, you will be able to see any changes that occur in the behaviour and also tease out any patterns (such as "the weekends seem to be a more difficult time for you") that are influencing the performance of the behaviour. Remember of course that improvement in any of the three indicators of progress—frequency, intensity, or duration—signals positive progress and has the potential to give hope to someone who has previously felt quite defeated.

We usually think of making use of a self-recorded intervention like this for four or five weeks so we have a reasonable bank of data. And we are likely to ask the client to fill out another record every now and then beyond that in order to check that change continues to happen in a positive direction.

One last point. When we have clients *self-recording* the occurrence of behaviours, we are aware of the possibility that they may have deliberately or unintentionally distorted the data. Our normal assumption is that people are honest, but we keep this possibility in mind so that we look to check the data for reliability in whatever way we can.

Behaviour Rehearsal and Role Playing

When working with someone battling an addiction, much of the focus is naturally on reducing or removing an undesired behaviour. However, it would be naïve to think that removal of behaviours is the counsellor's only concern. Even when we are looking to help someone overcome an addiction, we always need to give attention to *building in new behaviours*. And anyone who has worked with people struggling with long-held patterns of behaviour will be aware how difficult it is for someone to make changes like this, removing a behaviour and replacing it with something else, when all he or she has is an explanation of the new behaviour the client is to try out. It is so much easier if he or she has had the chance to practise the new behaviour in the safety of the counselling room, with someone who can coach the desired response. In some contexts, what we are calling behaviour rehearsal might be thought of as coaching.

One client seen at our clinic was Chad, a fifteen-year-old boy who, unfortunately, suffered from grand mal epilepsy. Although medication helped control the seizures, every now and then he would still experience one at school. Not surprisingly, a small group of students were just cruel. They teased and humiliated him, subjecting him to a reign of abuse, taking pleasure in their bullying. They called him names—the usual "spazzo" and other brutal labels. They followed him around the schoolyard, kicked his bag when he put it down, and did everything they could to get him to react. School was torture for him much of the time.

Though he had tried his best to control his reactions, he tended to explode with frustration under the relentless victimising. At such times he would scream and swear, chase students around the grounds, throw anything he could lay hands on at them, and generally escalate to an out-of-control pattern of behaviour. Teachers and parents had referred him to see if something could be done to help him.

Obviously the school had a problem, but it was Chad who needed help first. The first session detailed what was happening. In behavioural terms it was clear that the little group of bullies were being reinforced by the "game of uproar" that broke out when Chad reacted.

The first intervention was to teach Chad what we called "big deal therapy." The aim was that whatever happened, he was to just say "big deal" to himself as matter-of-factly as possible, and try to not show any emotion or outward reaction at all. It was explained that we were working with a kind of slot machine model. People play slot machines because, every now and then, they get a "payoff" of some kind—flashing lights indicating a win or some such thing. If the slot machine breaks down so that *it never pays off again,* the player will lose interest and find something else to do. He understood the analogy and agreed to try it out.

In the counselling room we rehearsed the behaviour using role plays. First we reversed roles, so that the counsellor played Chad while he took the part of the bullies. He was allowed to poke the counsellor and make use of all the names he had been called. Initially, each time he tried to get a reaction, the counsellor responded by saying quietly, in a flat, emotionless voice, "Big deal." After demonstrating this for a while, the procedure changed so that the counsellor now simply said "Big deal" to himself, and just to let him know it was being said internally, the counsellor nodded each time. We did this for a number of practices while Chad quite enjoyed being the antagonist, poking away and "getting in the counsellor's face" with rude comments.

Then the roles were changed. Now the counsellor called him names and tried to ridicule him while Chad spoke out loud, responding with a flat, emotionless, "Big deal… big deal… big deal," to every attempted provocation. We then shifted to his doing this silently in his thoughts (including the head-nod cue that had been used). At this point he felt he was sufficiently ready to try it out. Chad did brilliantly. Over the next few weeks he responded to every provocation by "big dealing" his reactions away, even when they escalated in the first week. By week three he reported the bullying had virtually stopped.

This is a helpful example of the use of role playing in counselling to develop a skill aimed at making a change in the behaviour of a client. The goal was to help Chad find a different behaviour response to his usual out-of-control anger reaction, one that would stop reinforcing the behaviour of the other kids. By rehearsing the new behaviour in the counselling session, he was able to build his confidence to the point where he could implement the changed behaviour and, to his great relief, discover that it worked.

Behaviour rehearsal and the implementation of role-playing is not an intervention that can always be used. However, where it can be used, it is often a most helpful "tool" enabling the development of a new behaviour or pattern of behaviours. It has application in a range of areas, including learning to cope with the anxiety of making phone calls, developing the capacity to speak assertively, learning conversation skills, and so on.

Behavioural Experiments

Another useful intervention involves asking people to try out a "behaviour experiment" in order to see what they can learn. There are many books containing helpful descriptions of the purpose and structure of such "experiments" (e.g., Westbrook, Kennerley, & Kirk, 2007). We like to emphasise the importance of giving an explanatory framework on the front end. We usually say something like the following: "Here's what I'd like to suggest. How about if, between now and next time we meet, you try out an experiment. In other words I'm asking you if you would be willing to become a bit of a scientist—they're the people who run experiments. I suppose we could ask: Why do scientists run experiments? Well, it's pretty simple. They run experiments in order to make observations, and they make observations in order to draw conclusions about what works and what is important and so on. So that's the kind of task I'm setting out for you. Run an experiment, make some observations, and let's see what we can learn from it. Does that sound okay?"

The "experiment" needs to be a behaviour that opens up the possibility of producing a shift in an area of need for the client. Clearly there will be aspects of both cognitive *and* behavioural change involved, and the outcome will hopefully include an emotional shift as well, from distress to a sense of improved hope, confidence, or well-being. Often the new behaviour, the "experimental behaviour," might have some logical connection to the problem that has brought the person in to counselling, but it may not.

For example, someone who is highly anxious about starting a conversation with anyone, after some behaviour rehearsal on conversation skills, might be asked to use his or her new skills to begin a conversation with someone on the train or bus this week, in order to make observations after the experiment, and see what he or she can learn.

On the other hand, someone with a pattern of anger outbursts in reaction to his or her spouse might try out walking three times around the room when he or she feels anger rise, before he or she says or does anything. There is no direct logic to this latter intervention other than it breaks in on the previous destructive pattern of behaviour and allows for the person to choose differently.

Behavioural experiments can be of two different kinds. Sometimes it may be helpful to prepare for an *observation* task, while at other times it may be useful to consider a more active *exposure* intervention. At one point a mother brought her seven-year-old daughter, Carla, who had an excessive fear of dogs, to our clinic. The girl was so terrified of dogs that she would scream and hide behind her mother if she even *saw* a dog on the streets, even if it was on the other side of the street and not attending to her at all.

After organising the intervention, Carla was invited to *observe*, from a safe spot, what the counsellor did when he patted and spent time with the friendly Labrador next-door to their home. We spent time talking in a detailed way about how the dog was approached, what movements were made by the counsellor and the dog, the speed of the movements, the way the counsellor spoke, and so on. This gave her a reservoir of understandings about dogs and interacting with them that she had previously lacked. We talked about the importance of slow movements of the hand, and the value of a gentle voice tone and saying, "Good dog," and other reassuring comments. We talked about the way dogs sometimes move their heads quickly, snapping at a fly or something, even barking if they heard or saw something, and that this is just dog behaviour and not something dangerous. The interaction was helpful for her and seemed to reassure her.

Of course further progress required moving to an active *exposure* task. The following week we went back to the dog while she stood perhaps ten feet away, and her mother and the counsellor patted it once more, slowly encouraging her to move closer. She was able to respond and so was slowly faded in to the point where she stood with the counsellor and her mother, holding nervously on to her mother's hand while we patted the dog. At this point the counsellor faded himself out, moving slowly back a foot or so at a time, while the mother continued. Next, Carla very nervously allowed her mother to take *her* hand and help her pat the dog a little. Finally her mother removed her hand and encouraged Carla to pat the dog on her own. At the end of our time there, Carla was beaming at her display of courage and reported that she was not so frightened of dogs.

We thoroughly talked through everything that had been accomplished and debriefed. This whole process of behavioural intervention took just less than an hour. Carla's mother was given the task of furthering the experiment, taking her to a pet shop to engage with some puppies and looking for other ways to promote the changed thinking about dogs and the changed *behaviour* in response to the presence of a dog. Carla did fine, and her previously phobic reactions were eliminated.

Usually a behavioural experiment like this requires some initial explanation, perhaps the teaching and practising of some new skill for the person, such as relaxation, and then the exposure to a situation where the skill can be implemented and a new pattern of response developed. In the example above, the behavioural experiments, from the initial observation task onward were worked out with Carla, her mother, and the counsellor. It is vital that any such tasks be collaboratively worked out with adult clients. If they are simply imposed by the counsellor, there is a much greater chance that they will not be implemented and so fail to be helpful.

> *Exposure tasks are really always behavioural experiments, although they usually involve changes in thinking.*

Exposure tasks are really always *behavioural* experiments, although they usually involve changes in thinking. They are frequently used with people battling anxiety in specific situations. Thus, people fearful of having a panic attack in a supermarket are often taught to implement relaxation strategies or some other cognitive/emotion-regulation skill, and encouraged to expose themselves to the feared situation. It is always important that the person is fully prepared and supported in the running of the behaviour experiment, and that the task, in collaboration with the client, is broken down into graduated and manageable steps.

Thus, a lift-phobic client who needed to be able to get to the top floors of a high-rise building in the city in order to take up a new job was first helped by *in-session* relaxation training, including imaginal rehearsal (i.e., imagining herself getting into a lift while staying as relaxed as possible). When she reported feeling ready, we moved together to a four-storey building where there were lifts, and with her "coach" by her side and by implementing her relaxation response, we did some runs up and down, getting off at various floors. When she was ready, she proceeded to do some runs up and down on her own. The whole process was debriefed, and she was left with the task of doing further behavioural runs with her husband in high-rise office blocks in the city. She reported that she still felt some anxiety but was able to travel in elevators from then on.

Between-Session Tasks

Finally, it is important that counsellors make use of the time between counselling sessions by prescribing between-session tasks, so that active change is encouraged in the other 167 hours of the week. Although our emphasis in this chapter is on the changing of behaviour, it is once again obvious that the changes will often include cognitive changes and, as a result, hopefully emotional changes also.

Different theories of counselling lend themselves to tasks that fit with the particular emphasis of that theory. Thus, cognitive practitioners tend to set tasks that involve monitoring cognitions or implementing cognitive change techniques. Constructivist counsellors, such as solution-focused or narrative, often ask people to act "as if" something is different as an experiment, trying to move people away from their usual and problematic constructions of reality. Behavioural theorists tend to ask clients to try out a specific behaviour change.

Often the focus of the between-sessions task is the practising, or implementation, of a skill or an intervention that has been practised or discussed in the counselling room. The range of such tasks is quite huge and is limited only by the ingenuity and creative capacity of both counsellor and client. Specific tasks need to be designed so they fit the area of behaviour change that clients need help with.

De Shazer's generic task for the end of the first marriage counselling session, for example, goes along these lines: "Between now and the next time we meet, I would like you to observe and make a note of the things you would not like to lose from your current marriage, so that you can report on them for me at the next session. Make a list and bring it along with you." This is a most useful task in that it deliberately shifts the client's orientation from what is wrong in the marriage to recalling positives. It also moves the focus from the past (normally full of hurts) to the future (where positives can be built on).

Between-session tasks can include such homework tasks as reading to increase understanding of a problem area; keeping a chart or record (such as the Self-Monitoring Record above) on emotions, thoughts and behaviours; undertaking an activity such a pleasant event; practising a communication skill such as making requests or being assertive in a situation; challenging negative thoughts and replacing them with rational alternatives; practising relaxation or mindfulness or listening to relaxing music; starting a realistic exercise program; and so on.

> One of the most common deficit-areas in terms of client behaviours exists when clients are unsure about their ability to hold a conversation.

When progress is already occurring in terms of changes to destructive behaviours, the most common task is to ask clients to "Do more of what's already working."

Conversation Skills

One of the most common deficit areas in terms of client behaviour exists when clients are unsure about their ability to hold a conversation. Often this relates to clients who struggle with anxiety or, perhaps, with a range of personal insecurities. These insecurities are likely to show up in their avoidance of social interaction. With clients who lack this skill, we teach them how to have a conversation.

Understanding the various elements that make up a conversation can provide clients with a template.

Elements of a Conversation

1. *Introduction*—People take the initiative in introducing themselves. If the person is new, it's likely to be, "Hi, my name's Donna. I don't think we've been introduced." There are other possible variations.
2. *Usually someone asks a question:* "Are you new in the area?" "Are there other folks that you know already? Who?" By far, the majority of conversations start with someone asking a question.
   A variation: Occasionally a conversation begins when someone shares something of themselves, instead of asking a question. An example of this kind of start to a conversation might be: "Wow, what a week it's been. On Monday I found out I'd been nominated for..." Even so, this approach is considerably less common than the one that starts by someone asking a question.
3. *Follow-up questions are asked.* These follow-up questions are drawn from the sharing of the other person. Normally a limited number of follow-up questions occur before the other person asks a question back. If he or she doesn't do this naturally, we can take the lead and begin sharing some of our week, so that it flows back and forth rather than becoming an interrogation.
4. *Finish*—We have a number of conventions for finishing a conversation. They are all aimed at reassuring the other person that they are fine and we have enjoyed being with them. Statements like, "Wow! Look at the time. I'd better get moving. It's been good talking to you."

Important Aspects

1. Listen for *"Free Information"* when the other person is responding to a question. Free information is any content

that he or she includes that goes beyond a strict answer to the question. For example, if you asked if the person was new and he or she answered, "Yes. We've just moved down from interstate. We were living on a farm in Western Australia, but my husband had to come to Sydney to get work. He was retrenched from the railways over in the west." This answer has free information about living in Western Australia, living on a farm, working for the railways, being retrenched, and so on. The good thing about free information is that you can ask more questions about any aspect of it at any time, if the conversation starts to flag. (For example, "Oh, by the way, you said you came from Western Australia. How did you find living over there?" It is always safe to ask about free information.)

2. The other side of free information of course is that, when you share with the other person, you need to *self-disclose* some material. This is your gift of free information to him or her! It helps with flow because now he or she has areas to follow-up on with additional questions.

3. Try to share in "paragraphs" when you are self-disclosing, not in "sentences" (too short), or "chapters" (too much information). Sometimes it might be a few paragraphs, but too much of your material could make the conversation seem one-sided.

By teaching this kind of format to clients, and then undertaking a behaviour rehearsal by having practice conversations in session, you enhance the capacity of clients to be able to incorporate this vital piece of behaviour into their skill set.

Further Reading

Antony, M. M., & Roemer, L. (2011). *Behavior therapy.* Washington, DC: American Psychological Association.

Linehan, M. (1993). *Skills-Training manual for cognitive behavioural treatment of borderline personality disorder.* New York: The Guilford Press.

Skinner, B. F. (1938). *The behaviour of organisms: An experimental analysis.* New York: Appleton-Century.

CHAPTER 14

The Skills of Concluding  a make-out session

Not surprisingly, the greatest work in any counselling experience involves the middle stage of Correcting. However, although much shorter, it is important to be aware of the specific issues associated with concluding counselling and to have some perspective on the tasks and skills associated with this phase of counselling.

* * * * * * * *

Knowing When to ~~Conclude~~ Cuddle

The final stage of counselling, Concluding, presupposes that we have some way to determine the right time for counselling to finish. Of course there is no objective test that gives us the "magic answer" regarding the right time to finish counselling. This does not mean, however, that we are left with no "markers" to guide us.

Clearly, one such marker is the counsellor's own sense of whether the client is ready to finish. However, another marker, even more important, is the client's perspective. The decision to finish usually comes out of a conversation, perhaps brief, triggered by one of the two parties. Often there is some objective evidence to support the decision, such as a marked improvement on some measure of symptoms, although this is not always available. Often the process is prefigured to some extent because counselling sessions have started to be held further apart. If someone was seen weekly or fortnightly and they have made good progress, sessions often get booked at three-week intervals or a month apart, so there is a growing awareness, often directly addressed, that we are "heading towards the finish line." Quite often a "thirty thousand-mile checkup," a session two or three months later, is booked on the understanding that it will be the final session if healthy progress is still continuing.

Commonly, at some point, the counsellor raises the issue directly, with a statement such as: "You've done some great work over these past few months. You've rated these last three months the best you've gone for years. I guess I'm wondering where you're at in relation to the thought of finishing up. You're the one whose thoughts count most."

Obviously raising the question like this suggest the counsellor thinks it may be time to finish, and that is true. However, the quality of the counsellor's voice tone and the assurance that you want to give primacy to the client's thoughts usually means there is no awkwardness. Most often a plan for moving towards concluding is mutually worked out with no real difficulty, although there may be a bit of flexibility needed to start with. Most of the time, once the decision is made, the Concluding phase only involves one session, although it can be a longer process, requiring a few sessions. Again, it is best to be guided by clients.

> *Most often a plan for moving towards concluding is mutually worked out.*

Once the decision is made that the work of counselling is now coming to an end, the questions arise: What should we include in these last sessions? What is the content of this Concluding phase of counselling?

In Chapter 8 we identified our three subtasks as Consolidating, Coaching, and Celebrating. Here we focus more directly on the skills relevant to these subtasks and look at their appropriate use with clients. It is important to note that while we separate out Consolidation and Coaching, these two aspects tend to be carried out concurrently rather than in any chronological order.

Subtask 1—Consolidating

As we noted in Chapter 8, when we reach the point of actively working towards finishing counselling, the first important task is to take time to consolidate the gains made by the client.

- *Summarising*

The consolidation subtask has some specific goals. Obviously an important part of it, as the label implies, is to help the client consolidate the gains made by taking time to clarify *what* has changed and what the client has done to contribute to these changes and, then, summarising these. Is the client aware of changes to previous patterns of thinking? Has he or she let go of some irrational belief (such as the belief he or she must do everything perfectly) and is the client now functioning with a much healthier, rational attitude? Has the client learned some ways of modulating or regulating previously disruptive emotions? What are the changes that have been made, and how were they made? Has the client broken some previously held destructive pattern of behaviour? Again, what has he or she done, and how was it done?

Clearly this part of consolidation is not limited to the input of the client, although that is probably the best starting place. However, the opportunity to summarise the changes made and the client's contribution to this provides great scope for counsellors to affirm the competencies, courage, and work of the client.

This whole process of consolidation, or fixing aspects of progress in the client's mind, may be relatively short or it may actually spin out over more than one session. In order to highlight client "work," it is useful to find a way to write this out. Some counsellors like to put summary points on a white card, or a wallet-sized card, for the client to carry with him or her. Some clients like to make brief notes in their smartphone or tablet. Other counsellors simply give a verbal summary, emphasising the important steps in client progress. Sometimes a counsellor writes a summary letter, or sends an e-mail, to their client. Any action that strengthens the client's sense of self-efficacy is a valuable contribution to the ongoing growth of the client. Of course it needs to be noted that all such affirmations from the counsellor need to be genuine. In appendix C we offer a sample letter.

Subtask 2—Coaching

As client and counsellor begin this part of the counselling journey, there will inevitably be the need to undertake some coaching on the part of the counsellor. In this context, coaching is seen as drawing out and emphasising skills, capacities, and resources that will be helpful as the client moves into his or her future *sans* regular counselling sessions.

 • *Predicting and preparing for lapses*

Often client and counsellor will try to look ahead and foresee difficult situations and contexts for the client. Part of the work of coaching will involve preparing the client as to how he or she will cope at such a time. What are the skills that will need to be used? What resources can the client make use of in order to cope? Much of this work can be thought of as coaching in order to avoid relapses or, better still, coaching in order to prepare the client to handle normal lapses without allowing these to turn into *relapses*, a full-blown return of the problem that brought him or her into counselling in the first place.

> *Lapses are common, not rare. They are reasonably normal and the counsellor needs to prepare the person*

Some sensitivity is needed at this stage. Sometimes beginning counsellors worry that if they even speak of the possibility of the problem "making a comeback," they will undermine the client's confidence. They are afraid that the client who has made good progress and who is now confident about his or her capacity to cope with the future will suddenly think, *Why are you bringing this possibility up? Do you* expect *me to fail?* In reality, this will be an unlikely occurrence. However, as part of responsible client care, we believe it is incumbent upon the counsellor to raise these possibilities, if only to "normalise" them in the client's mind so that he or she does not overreact and plunge into despair. Lapses are common, not rare. They are reasonably normal, and the counsellor needs to prepare the person, not necessarily for it to happen but to highlight what actions to take *if* it happens. This is all part of what we think of as relapse-prevention coaching.

Usually, the possibility of the problem returning can be introduced by a statement like: "What I think we should do for a little while here is try to anticipate any future situations where the problem might return. The purpose is just to prepare for that, so you've got a good sense of what you are going to do at that time. Hopefully you won't find this necessary at all, but if the problem does try to return, you'll know what you are going to do because we rehearsed it here."

Coaching then proceeds by talking through possible scenarios and planning or, possibly, rehearsing steps to take in terms of self-talk, behaviours, checking back over resources, or whatever would be helpful and appropriate.

- *Networks of support*

As part of this coaching/consolidating phase we usually take a little time to consider networks of support the client has or that need to be built up for the client. At this point the counsellor may take the time to talk over relationships the client already has, highlighting the value of maintaining those that offer physical, emotional, and spiritual support. This may be a time when client and counsellor look together at how such a network could be broadened, or how it might be rebuilt if a major support person were to move. The possibility of a one-off "refresher" counselling session may also be mentioned as an option if the client needs this.

Assuming the client is a Christian, we will want to highlight the important of guarding his or her relationship with Jesus. We will want to review what he or she is already doing, and how the client can guard that which is helpful and grow that which is still a bit shaky. We will want to encourage the client to continue on with his or her study and devotional reading of Scripture, and maintaining and deepening his or her life of prayer and involvement in the Christian community.

Subtask 3—Celebrating

The third subtask in Concluding involves looking at ways the client can celebrate the gains he or she has made. Already mentioned, we try to pull together a summary of genuine affirmations deriving from the client's work and what we have learned of his or her discipline, creativity, courage, determination over the course of counselling, and so on. All of this is directed towards celebrating not only achievements accomplished but celebrating the specific capacities evidenced in the client in making these achievements.

- *The who and how of celebration*

We usually take time to explore who else knows of the changes the client has made, and how any such people might be invited into a "celebration by friends." If the client is a family-oriented person, how could his or her spouse and/or children be included in the celebration of their progress? Would it be appropriate to have a meal out, or a party (big or little) at home? Would it be appropriate to think of making a speech, letting others know more specifically what has been accomplished? Would it be useful to think of inviting others to speak on what they have noticed in the way of positive changes in functioning? All of these and many other variations are possibilities.

The purpose of this celebration phase is to emphasise the effort and achievement made by the client. In our fast-paced world, it is sad but true that often our most significant moments of growth get lost because of the next bit of life "coming down the pike." We want clients to savour their growth.

Finally, if the client is a committed Christian, we want to consider with the client how we might express appropriate thanks to God. Some clients will be happy to say a prayer of thanks or to invite the counsellor to do so. Others sometimes suggest something a bit more significant. We never push this, but we like to open up the possibility by asking if it would be appropriate. It sometimes adds a moving moment to the process of concluding.

Further Reading

Fortune, A. E., Pearlingi, B., & Rochelle C. D. (1992). *Reactions to termination of individual treatment*. Social Work, 37, 171–8.

Hunsley, J., Aubry, T. D., Verstervelt, C. M., & Vito, D. (1999). *Comparing therapist and client perspectives on reasons for psychotherapy termination*. Psychotherapy, 36, 380–8.

PART 4

Integrating Spiritual Resources

Just to be absolutely clear, incorporating spiritual resources does not free us from the hard work of growing in our theoretical understandings and practical skills as they apply to counselling. We must always remain committed to personal and professional development if we are to be responsible counsellors.

Even so, the counsellor who works from an Incarnational Counselling model will be open to integrating spiritual resources where this is requested by the counselee. He or she will also consider sensitively offering these where they are deemed appropriate. Thus we are open to integrating the use of prayer, Scripture, Holy Communion, times of repentance-confession-absolution, anointing with oil, revelation from God, times of meditation, worship, journaling, special "services" such as planning a memorial time for someone grieving over a stillborn child, acts of reconciliation, and so on. Obviously this is not an exhaustive list. And certainly not all of these would necessarily be appropriate for in-session work, although they might be incorporated into counselling as post-session tasks. Over the years in our work, counselees have requested and made helpful use of one or more of these interventions as part of their healing journey. Although it is not our common practice, there have also been times when we have felt led to offer the use of one or more of these spiritual resources, as an aid to the healing process. The availability of these spiritual resources in the work of a Christian counsellor marks a distinction that we bring which would not be offered by a secular counsellor.

Unfortunately, it seems to be part of our human condition that when something is helpful, we are tempted to turn it into a "technique." In the training of counsellors, we see these resources as having significant transformative potential for people we counsel, but we are at pains to avoid turning them into techniques that can be routinely, and perhaps, mindlessly, applied in counselling. In these next chapters we aim to discuss the appropriate integration of such resources, with a focus on the when and how, and with sensitivity to God leading in this process.

One of the important considerations that we emphasise in training and in the application of such resources is the awareness that none of these are "magic bullets." This is not to say God does not use them—at times in quite dramatic ways—to bring about an experiential shift in the life of the counselee. But we do not want to set up false expectations for the counselee, and we do not want to encourage a superstitious kind of dependence upon these by a counsellor who is unable to think of anything else to do. We have a strong commitment, both in our training and in our own practice, to avoiding the "routine-ising" of the use of spiritual resources. However, where their inclusion is the outcome of a client-sensitive, thoughtful, and indeed prayerful assessment of the need, we have no hesitation in making use of them.

When we seek to counsel people as representatives of the God who heals (Psalm 103:2–3: "Praise the Lord, O my soul, and forget not all his benefits—who forgives all your sins and heals all your diseases"), we are aware that our capacity to be helpful depends entirely on his presence with us. This is inherent in our incarnational perspective in that we see our usefulness as ultimately dependent upon him. As Christian counsellors, we seek to acknowledge the presence of Jesus and use the spiritual resources that God has given us, in ways that are sensitive to the needs of the counselee. Since it is not possible for us to instruct here on how to make helpful use of all of the interventions that fall under the heading Spiritual Resources, Part 4 looks only at guidelines for the integration of three of these—prayer, the use of Scripture, and the involvement of times of repentance-confession-absolution. We also look at the sensitive topic of how we hear God in the counselling process.

CHAPTER 15

Using Prayer in Counselling

"I pray—not because I lack confidence but because I am realistic about what I am able to do and confident about what God is able to do". (Levy, D., 2011)

Christians pray. As counsellors, operating out of a Christian worldview, it would be unusual if we did not make use of this as a spiritual resource at some level in our work with people. However, there is plenty of room for misunderstanding and misapplication of prayer as an intervention. This chapter seeks to lay down some useful guidelines for effective integration by Christian counsellors.

* * * * * * * * *

Any reflection on the use of prayer in counselling needs to begin with a call for Christian counsellors to work at developing their personal prayer life, quite apart from counselling. Without turning this call into a legalism, or a "should," or, indeed, any source for self-recrimination, it is good to remind ourselves that the Master was a man of prayer. The truth is, Jesus's prayer life is very challenging. There were times when he prayed all night! In Luke 6:12–13 we read: "One of those days Jesus went out to a mountainside to pray, and spent the night praying to God. When morning came, he called his disciples to him and chose twelve of them." We note in Luke 5:16 that prayer was a regular practice for him: "But Jesus often withdrew to lonely places and prayed." It was not an occasional action—he *often* withdrew to pray. It is apparent that he received guidance from his times of prayer, that in some sense it helped him recalibrate his life and make decisions regarding what he should do and where he should go.

For example, Mark 1:35 tells us, "Very early in the morning, while it was still dark, Jesus got up, left the house, and went off to a solitary place, where he prayed." When the disciples came to report that people were seeking him in the town of Capernaum, where he had spent the previous evening healing, he tells them that his priorities lie elsewhere. It seems that he receives direction as he spends time in communion with his Father.

The disciples saw this dimension of his life and were drawn to it. It is interesting that nowhere do we have them requesting Jesus to teach them to do miracles, or to speak with great power, but we *do* have a record of them coming to him to ask him to teach them how to pray (Luke 11:1). Prayer is foundational in the life of Christians.

> *There is encouragement for us, as Christians involved in counselling, to develop our prayer lives.*

So there is encouragement for us, as Christians who are involved in counselling, to develop our prayer lives. Obviously, if nowhere else, we would find it helpful to pray for people we are seeking to help, asking God for grace upon them, and interceding for his blessing in their lives as they go through difficulties. It is also apparent that it would be valuable to seek his wisdom for ourselves in our counselling with people.

All this is to emphasise that, whether prayer is ever integrated directly into the counselling session, it is available as a personal resource for us in counselling. And Scripture gives us plenty of encouragement to develop disciplines of personal prayer.

However, prayer can also be directly incorporated into counselling. On occasions it might be used, *with the counselee's approval*, in a brief moment of praising God and thanking him for his evident goodness in the progress that the counselee is making, or because of an answer to prayer that he or she has received. One very distressed solo mother with a teenage son who was battling quite deep depression came to our clinic. She shared that the previous evening she had had the thought that it might help his depression lift if he could spend time with her brother's family overseas. Early that morning, quite "out of the blue," a phone call came from her brother in the United Kingdom, wondering if her son would like to come over for a visit and spend some time. It seemed very appropriate for the two of us to stop and briefly give thanks to God for what was clearly for her a profound moment of grace.

At other times we might pray prayers of supplication, seeking God's help and guidance. Prayers of intercession where God's help is specifically sought on behalf of a situation or need, often for someone else, abound in Scripture. These might legitimately be incorporated at times into counselling. Prayers, such as David's famous prayer in Psalm 51, are clearly times of confession and seeking forgiveness, and these will be appropriate sometimes in counselling. Prayers of benediction occur widely, especially in the epistles of Paul. There will be times when these kinds of prayer, and others, may be appropriately incorporated, significantly heightening the potential for personal growth, and for positive change, in the experience of the counselee.

What Kinds of Prayer Might We Incorporate into Counselling?

- *Prayers of Praise and Thanksgiving*

In Incarnational Counselling we emphasize that the counselling work is directed at *the healing* needs of the counselee, and that this will come primarily out of a relational experience that fosters *growth* for the person. This growth focus will derive from the presenting needs of the client—we are not advocates for the imposition of a one-size-fits-all curriculum of growth! As in the example of the teenage boy above, there may be times when we are struck by encouraging evidence of change and growth taking place so that it seems appropriate, even natural, if the client is a Christian and is open to this, to pause the counselling process and to give praise and thanks to God for the changes we are seeing.

For the most part, such times will generally be fairly brief, rather than long. It may be that the person is experiencing significant improvement in the levels of distress that brought them into counselling, or they are reporting a significant shift in their external circumstances or their internal experiencing. While we would not want to turn these into *routine* moments for thanksgiving or praise to God, we see it as completely legitimate for the counsellor, committed to the foundation proposition that healing belongs to God, to stop the flow of the session for a moment in order to acknowledge God's goodness at work in the person's life. In these situations, it may be appropriate for either the counsellor or the counselee or both to offer a brief prayer of thanks acknowledging God's active involvement.

- *Supplication and Intercession*

Again, while we avoid *routine-ising* prayer, we recognise that there are times when it is abundantly clear that prayers of supplication and intercession are appropriate. In the book of Psalms, David and others regularly cry out for God's assistance in situations where they need help. Obviously this is an area for personal prayer before we spend time in the counselling session and after the session. However, such prayers may also be built into the actual counselling, as long as we do not make this formal or ritualistic. Our preference is always to be open to the

> *Our preference is always to be open to the leading of the Spirit of God in terms of our use of prayer.*

leading of the Spirit of God in terms of our use of prayer. We note that Jesus did not routinely go into times of prayer when he was engaged in healing work, although there is certainly evidence of his praying openly at times (for example, John 11:41–42). So we want trainees to be open to the value of this in counselling and to seek the leading of God's Spirit with regard to appropriateness.

- *Deliverance*

We do not normally involve ourselves in what has come to be known as deliverance ministry—taking authority in the name of Jesus and binding spiritual forces that are afflicting people. Part of our caution is that we have worked with counselees who have had quite insensitive and unhelpful deliverance ministry "waged" at them by people, and we have seen the emotional damage that this can do. We have also worked with counselees who, in avoiding the need for change, would *prefer* to see their issues as "attacks from the enemy," rather than face more confronting truths and acknowledge personal responsibility. For these reasons we take a cautious approach to deliverance.

In our counselling, praying for deliverance for someone is quite rare, and we have learned to refer people to others who have demonstrated a sound track record in this area of ministry, rather than carry it out ourselves. There are boundary issues here for us. We tend to see deliverance ministry as part of a specific prayer ministry, rather than part of counselling or the practice of clinical psychology. We are wary of people who see the work of Satan everywhere while failing to acknowledge personal responsibility. We are cautious about any approach that sees *every* problem as a spiritual problem.

Having acknowledged the above, our general position with regard to deliverance is that we acknowledge the reality of the spiritual dimension in people and the possibility that someone may be experiencing spiritual oppression. As a result both of us have, at times, with the permission of the person, found ourselves taking time to pray for a counselee, binding the power of oppressive spirits in the name of Jesus. Our approach at such a time is that we prefer to "underplay" the moment, rather than dramatise it. We simply take authority in the name of Jesus and bind any spirits that might be oppressing the person and interfering with their capacity to make the changes they need to make. Then we move on to working on underlying issues that the person still needs to address and grow through. Again, our preference is to refer the person for prayer ministry to someone we have developed confidence in.

A quite unusual experience that occurred many years ago started with the Holy Spirit "enlivening" a passage of Scripture in an early morning devotional time. The counsellor, on this occasion, was struck by this verse: "We demolish arguments and every pretension that sets itself up against the knowledge of God, and we take captive every thought to bring it into obedience to Christ" (2 Corinthians 10:4–5). The first thought attached to this verse was that this was very cognitive-behavioural! But beyond that, the awareness registered that he did not really know what a "pretension" was! The impact was sufficiently strong that the verse was written out in his journal before finishing the devotional time.

At work that morning a distressed phone call came in from a minister. He was in tears, so he was slotted into the only spot available—lunchtime! From the outset his "story" was very unusual. He had a large church and carried a lot of stress. As a way of "escape" from the constant pressure he had begun to spend time developing a fantasy life about one of the leading female tennis players of that time. It was not a sexual fantasy, he assured, but it was to do with her life away from the pressure. He imagined she had a beautiful getaway place, and he spent time fantasising about how she relaxed, and so on. He read articles about her in magazines and filled out details in the fantasy. The distress came out of the fact that this "escape fantasy" had now taken over his thinking to the point where his mind was completely preoccupied by it. He shared that he could not concentrate on sermon preparation or church work. He could not even give appropriate attention to his wife and family. Aspects of the fantasy preoccupied him when he was talking to people. He couldn't seem to break free!

As he shared, the first thing that came to mind was that this was a spiritual problem and the verse from the morning's reading came back to mind. It registered quite strongly that this oppressing spirit was a "pretension" seeking to take the place of God! After asking him for his thoughts on the problem, the counsellor shared that God had actually prepared him for this in his devotions that morning and went on to talk through the idea that he was experiencing spiritual oppression, having opened himself to it by not submitting his thoughts in obedience to Christ. What had seemed a harmless fantasy had now become an entry point for some kind of spiritual oppression. The minister gave eager assent. Yes, that was exactly what it seemed like!

With his agreement, there was a time of prayer and he confessed his sin, renounced it, and asked for forgiveness. He recommitted his life to God, particularly submitting his thinking. In the authority of Jesus, the counsellor was able to bind the spiritual "pretender" and command it to cease its oppression. It was all pleasingly undramatic. The session finished and both were standing at the reception desk as the news on the hour was broadcast. Suddenly a news item about this particular tennis player winning a tournament registered for the two of them. There was a moment of confusion and shock. What was this? Some kind of spiritual counterattack or a confirmation of freedom and healing? The client smiled. "It's okay," he said.

The experience was unusual enough for it to be followed up, and over the next few months he was able to report that, in the aftermath of the session, he was free from the obsessive focus on the tennis player.

Incidents like this are extremely rare in our experience, and it would be a mistake to turn them into the "bread and butter" work of counselling. Nevertheless, they reinforce the fact that there can be occasions when necessity may demand that we incorporate deliverance prayer into our counselling. However, as we have stated, our general position is that a better context for deliverance is in the midst of an experienced prayer team, where proper guidelines and joint wisdom can operate.

- *Inner Healing*

Prayer can be also used for inner healing, when we become aware of the emotional wounds that someone has suffered. Once again, this is not an area that we normally incorporate into our counselling, preferring to refer the person to a prayer room ministry or to someone we have come to know and trust. We do not refer to people unless we have come to trust their sensitivity and godliness. And as we have intimated, for us such referrals are more the exception than the rule.

We do not see this kind of prayer ministry as the answer to every problem, yet we have had people find significant release as a result of such prayer. A recent client found herself freed from panic attacks for a period of a month after inner healing prayer with a team, though the panic attacks had been occurring daily prior to the prayer time. An easy mistake to slip into is to assume that the problem is now dealt with, and that no further growth is needed. In truth, her pattern of anxious overreacting still needed further work. However, the period free from panic attacks gave her encouragement that God is involved and she is now making further progress.

- *Physical Healing*

While we would not normally see counselling as the place for prayers for physical healing, there have been times when God has stirred us to pray for this. If this occurs, it is likely to be in a time of prayer at the end of a counselling session. One of us was moved to pray for a keyboard player who had severe RSI to the point where he had been unable to play for more than a year. During a brief prayer for healing, at the end of a session which had been focused on his depression, he reported feeling a warmth go down his arm, and he was subsequently able to start playing at church again. The experience was sufficiently intriguing to merit follow-up and, at three months followup, the healing was stable and he was teaching pupils again as well as playing at church. Not surprisingly, the depression had also lifted.

- *Seeking Guidance*

It is always appropriate to seek God for guidance, both for us as counsellors in our work with people, but also for guidance for the person struggling with the need for direction in his or her life. When we pray for a counselee, seeking guidance in their life, it is almost certain that this will be in a prayer at the end of a counselling session.

How Should We Pray?

Incarnational counselling is not formulaic. We are completely committed to the importance of a vital, personal relationship with God, and this clearly involves developing a life of prayer, but beyond praying for counselees in our personal prayer times, we resist any move to include prayer of any kind as a *routine* part of counselling. During most counselling sessions we do not directly or openly pray with people. However, we do seek to be open to the leading of God's Spirit with regard to the need of the person, the request of a client, the appropriateness of an open prayer time as an intervention, or in response to a direct leading.

Having said that, we both have had counselees who have asked for prayer at the start of every session. We are open to responding to this but prefer to have the person himself or herself lead. We have had people spontaneously pray for us at the end of a session, something we are always open to! Most of the time when we have incorporated open prayer into a counselling session, it has been at the end, and we have been simply asking for God's presence with the person and God's help as he or she works through the issues of growth that confront the person.

It is also valuable to pray quietly in your spirit during counselling sessions, even though no attention is drawn to this and it is certainly not announced. This practice keeps us helpfully focused on God as the source of our wisdom, rather than on our own skills.

What General Guidelines Are There for the Conduct of a Prayer Time?

As Christians incorporating prayer into our counselling, we look to follow a few helpful guidelines. These are not legalisms, and there have been times for each of us when we have not followed them. Nevertheless, they serve as useful parameters most of the time.

- Obviously, introducing open prayer into a counselling session will always require the assent of the counselee. This is a non-negotiable. If you feel prompted to include specific prayer in the session, make sure you ask your client if this would be okay.
- Don't rush. If incorporating prayer is a significant moment in the midst of a session, take time to talk through the purpose and to prepare.

- Don't trivialise the moment. It is important to be clear about what you are transacting here. Perhaps even consider kneeling.
- Don't *routine-ise* prayer. Seek God's leading as to when and how, if you are incorporating a time of open prayer.
- During the session, try to give the lead in praying to the other person as much as possible. As often as possible try to take a support role. In our experience it is normally a more significant moment if the person can take the lead and use his or her own words in formulating a prayer.
- Use familiar language, and don't allow yourself to slip into any special "prayer voice."

Finally, keep in mind that it will never be wrong to pray for people *before* counselling, silently *during* counselling, and *after* counselling! Whether or not we feel free to pray aloud with someone in counselling, we need to encourage ourselves in developing these disciplines.

Further Reading

Gubi, P. M. (2008). *Prayer in counselling and psychotherapy.* Philadelphia, PA: Jessica Kingsley Publishers.

Levy, D., & Kilpatrick, J. (2011). *Gray matter: A neurosurgeon discovers the power of prayer.* Carol Stream, IL: Tyndale.

VanZant, J. C. (2010). *Prayer in counselling: The practitioner's handbook.* Bloomington, IN: WestBow Press.

CHAPTER 16

Using Scripture in Counselling

Christian counsellors also incorporate the use of Scripture as a resource in their counselling. Scripture has the potential to be a significant aid to people in trouble. However, as is true for other interventions, it is important that we use Scripture in ways that are sensitive to the person's situation and need, rather than routinely or in a way that trivialises the Word of God. This chapter sets out some of the practical guidelines you might make use of as you seek to integrate Scripture into your counselling.

* * * * * * * *

The possibility of bringing God's Word into the practice of counselling can easily convey the impression that this is a one-size-fits-all practice—you just get a Bible down from the shelf, or you pick up the weighty Bible from the table and find the verse that will "fix" the person's problem! Nothing could be further from the truth, and any approach like this would be wrong. However, there are a number of ways Scripture might be helpfully built into counselling.

Ways of Bringing Scripture into Counselling

Incarnational Scripture

First, we should remind ourselves that, as followers of Jesus, we carry the presence of God and the Word of God in our being. If we are truly dependent on God in our counselling, we don't need to feel pressured to *always* open the Bible. If we are living the presence of God, he will speak to people through our very presence at times. While we hold to the highest view of the Bible, seeing it as the inspired Word of God, sufficient for life and practice, we do not worship it, nor do we limit the Living Word to the type on printed pages. The Living Word is ultimately the person of Jesus, who presences himself with us by the Holy Spirit and who is active even beyond the written Word. So, although we may not have a verse of Scripture in our mouth, if we come into counselling with a vital relationship with Jesus, and we are open to his presence, we can function as incarnated "narrations" of the presence of God. Our smile, our manner can speak the word of God to another. We hold this to be a simple truth, yet not one that produces pride. Rather, it reminds us that we are completely dependent on him for healing involvement with others.

Paraphrased Scripture

If we are living out of a healthy relationship with Jesus and regularly spend time reading his Word, it is quite likely that we will at times speak out paraphrased biblical truths in our counselling. Perhaps the most important thing in being aware of this is to make sure that we do give priority time to allowing the Word of God to take shape in us, spending time in studying, meditating, and memorising Scripture. This is *more* than Bible knowledge; this is to do with how we apply the Word of God to our own personal growth.

Using Scripture helpfully with counselees requires us to be diligent Bible students ourselves. As *we* take Scripture seriously, reading and soaking in God's Word on a regular basis for our own lives, we will gradually accumulate a reservoir of passages and references and verses that are potentially helpful for people going through difficult situations in their lives. Whether or not we make use of any of these in a counselling session will largely depend on how the Spirit prompts us.

If we have developed a personal grounding in Scripture, there will be times when we share clear truths from the Word of God with a counselee without directly opening a Bible or even mentioning that this is a biblical truth. We may simply speak a paraphrase in the course of our normal counselling. For example, a counsellor might say: "Every marriage that is healthy and growing has to show the characteristics of love between the two people. How do you show your love to each other?" In a statement like this, the counsellor has not opened the Bible, nor has he or she mentioned that the call to show our love in actions is a truth from 1 Corinthians 13 and other parts of Scripture. The counsellor has simply paraphrased the truth in his or her own words as seemed appropriate to the situation with the couple in counselling.

Direct Use of the Bible

Of course there will be times when we *do* refer directly to Scripture in counselling, for many different situations and needs. Scripture passages can "speak" to the deep needs of people in all kinds of situations.

- When someone is in grief, the Bible may bring comfort (e.g., Psalm 23: "The Lord is my Shepherd, I shall not want..."). A person going through grief may find reassurance in this and similar passages.
- When someone is contemplating a choice or action that would break a clear command of God in his Word. Such a situation may be one when it is appropriate to look together at a Scripture passage for the purpose of challenging the person (e.g., Job 22:21 NRSV. "Agree with God and be at peace; in this way good will come to you"). A verse like this calls us back to being on God's "page" rather than simply going our own way.

- When someone is operating with a confused or incorrect understanding about something and Scripture has a clear word on the issue. At such a time, Scripture may provide the relevant corrective instruction or information (e.g., Ephesians 4: 26–27: "Be angry but do not sin; do not let the sun go down on your anger"). People sometimes grow up with the sense that anger is sin. While we need to be "slow to anger" (James 1:19), this verse in Ephesians makes it clear that anger is not, in and of itself, sin. Thus, it may have a corrective function.
- When someone is avoiding a step of growth that God calls him or her to, it may be appropriate to direct the person to a specific passage or teaching. In this case we may be making use of God's Word as a resource for spiritual development. For example, we might assign the task of reading The Parable of the Prodigal Son (Luke 15) each day for a week in order to have the counselee rethink his or her understanding of the character of God.

How Should We Use Scripture?

As with prayer, it is possible that we can turn any use of Scripture in counselling into a relatively meaningless ritual, unless we are actively engaged in spending time studying and allowing the Word to shape our own lives. As a corrective to this, we are careful not to use the Bible in a *routine* way in counselling, whether that is by opening it in the session or quoting verses. We always have a copy of the Scriptures available, and we *do* open it with counselees from time to time, but this is not our normal practice. There are quite a few books that list verses or passages of Scripture, such as, "Do not be anxious about anything, but in everything, by prayer and petition, with

> *We are careful not to use the Bible in a routine way in counselling.*

thanksgiving, present your requests to God. And the peace of God, which transcends all understanding, will guard your hearts and your minds in Christ Jesus" (Philippians 4:6–7) for anxiety. We recognise that lists of verses can be very helpful, especially for someone who does not have a good grasp of the Bible. So it is sometimes useful to provide a counselee with something like this, or a single verse, for his or her own study or meditation.

However, as counsellors, we believe the most appropriate biblical verses or passages will be those that God *stirs into life* out of our own study and reading. Sometimes, because we are carrying a client's issues in our heart, Scripture lights up, and it occurs to us: "That passage is very relevant for..." Rather than get too excited, we would caution counsellors to ask God whether or not the verses are for personal edification and understanding, or whether they are to be shared with the client. The important thing is not to jump to conclusions without praying for wisdom. The same caution that we suggested with regard to prayer applies here; the Word of God is not to be used as a "magic bullet."

That said, we have developed a number of guidelines for the use of Scripture in our counselling.

- We try to *involve the counselee actively* if we are referring directly to a Scripture passage. Provided there is no problem with their reading, it is always best to have people read the passage for themselves out loud, rather than reading it to them. That way they engage the content. If we read the section *to* them, this increases the possibility that they will be disengaged, or less impacted.
- We ask counselees what *they* see as the relevant teaching for them in the verse or passage. It is always necessary to *check the application* that they take from the passage. Ask directly: "What do you get from that passage? What is its relevance

for you?" Make sure that the person accurately understands the biblical instruction that you want them to see. If we fail to check their understanding, it can sometimes happen that they take a very unusual "lesson" from the passage.
- As we noted above, Scripture can also be used as a source for valuable homework assignments. On occasion we have asked counselees to read through Philippians every day for a week, leaving themselves open to whatever God would say to them through his Word. Once again, it is very important to check what they have gained from an exercise like this at the next appointment, rather than assume that all will be well. Counselees who struggle for self-worth can sometimes find condemnation where we may only see positive encouragement and affirmation!
- Finally, it is important that Scripture is used as a resource in ways that fit with good counselling practice. Bringing the teachings of the Bible directly into the counselling context is never an excuse for moralising or preaching! Its use needs to be *relevant* and potentially helpful for the person being counselled. And of course it should only be used when the counselee is open to its use!

An example of the Holy Spirit activating a Scripture passage occurred for one of us one day in pondering Jesus's encounter with Nicodemus, recorded in John 3. The thought came: "This is a really interesting passage for psychologists and counsellors. It's probably the best record we have of Jesus in a counselling-type situation." While it's true that there are a number of wonderful accounts of Jesus interacting with people, such as the woman at the well, they are not necessarily accounts of people coming to Jesus, seeking help with a problem. However, clearly Nicodemus *has* a problem and he has come seeking help. He wants Jesus's wisdom in helping him sort something out!

Another thought occurred: The trouble is we never find out what Nicodemus's problem is! The interaction starts, as so many counselling interactions do, with Nicodemus "feeling his way" and even perhaps flattering Jesus a bit! "Master, we know that you are a teacher come from God, because no-one could do the miracles that you do, unless God is with him." (Yes, we can both recall counselees who have started with that kind of introduction!). Interestingly, Jesus doesn't even stop to ask what is troubling Nicodemus! He launches directly into "I tell you the truth, no-one can see the kingdom of God unless he is born again."

Further reflection posed a question: "Why didn't Jesus even give time to hear what was troubling Nicodemus? Why jump in so suddenly?" And then a final thought: "Perhaps the *actual* problem didn't really matter. Perhaps Jesus's answer is the *generic* answer, no matter what the problem is! Perhaps no matter what is troubling a person, the answer is always the need for new birth!" After all, birth is the very first step in the normal process of growth! And ongoing-new-birth-ness *is* growth.

In the aftermath, as this thought settled within, the following session took place: A Christian who was struggling in his marriage came in for counselling. He and his wife had been seen from time to time over a number of years, and here he was sitting down once more, talking of the struggles to get his marriage working the way he wanted. On this occasion some inner prompting seemed to say: *Hang it all. Why not?* "Jake [not his real name]," I heard myself say, "you know what the problem is, don't you?" Not surprisingly, he looked a bit mystified. I went on: "You need to be born again." There was a moment of silence and he asked hesitantly: "What do you mean?"

I went on to explain that we often hope that a little bit of tinkering will fix things. We don't really want to have to change too radically. Part of us doesn't want to undertake the dramatic growth we need.

We would prefer to undergo a bit of tweaking, a slight adjustment, a spot of finessing here or there, maybe try out a new communication technique or read another chapter of a "recommended book." I explained that the reality is that we need a transformative event, an experiential shift, a radical makeover—we need to recognise that our current way of doing things is broken, that we are broken, and we need to be new-birthed! We spent quite a bit of time talking about what that might mean for him in his relationship with his wife and how he might go about opening himself to the Spirit's involvement in that process. At the end of the session, as he was leaving, he shook my hand and said, "That's the most important session we've ever had."

I need to report that, in the aftermath, he dramatically changed his approach to his wife and his marriage, and very quickly their marriage was blossoming. In different circles our paths have crossed from time to time, and something has changed. I think something in him got "new-birthed" and, as a result, their marriage has been "new-birthed"!

It is appropriate to remind us all here that there is always a temptation to turn an intervention like this into a "technique." We need to guard against this. Although it was dramatically significant for Jake and his marriage, it would not be appropriate to turn "new-birth therapy" into a routine therapy approach with clients. It was appropriate for him in that moment. And that is enough. The way I see it this was simply a moment when, out of time spent soaking in the Word of God for my life as a disciple of Jesus, the Spirit was able to activate a biblical concept appropriately, and transformingly, for this person.

"Psalm Therapy"

It is worth reminding ourselves that many of the psalms, written by David and others, are simply prayers as Scripture. The interesting thing is that the psalms often seem to resonate very helpfully with people going through life difficulties. Distressed people often "find themselves" in the psalms—they identify with the emotions expressed by the writers in their times of difficulty. For this reason, it is often helpful to set the reading through the book of Psalms as a homework task, requesting the client to just be open to what God would want to say to him or her in the process.

> *Distressed people often "find themselves" in the psalms...*

In addition to regular reading from the Psalms, it is often helpful to have clients write out their own psalm or psalms. In this sense we make use of "psalm therapy" as a kind of journaling, in which clients pour out their hearts in writing before God, expressing their struggles and seeking his help.

Noticeably, in many of the psalms, writers' emotions shift quite significantly as they pour out their hurts and struggles before God. For example, in Psalm 52, David starts writing out of strong anger at the actions of Doeg, the Edomite, whose betrayal led to the slaughter of eighty-five priests in the town of Nob. The anger is palpable; sarcasm drips from his opening words. "Why do you boast of evil, you mighty man?" He works his way to "You love every harmful word, O you deceitful tongue!" and looks forward to Doeg being disgraced before people.

At verse 8, suddenly the tone shifts completely, the emotion is different. Somehow the anger has dissipated and David is now feeling reassured and more peaceful, and he expresses this in his words. "But I am like an olive tree flourishing in the house of God; I trust in God's unfailing love forever and ever." His prayer becomes personal, shifting from third person to first person. He is communicating directly with God. "I will trust you forever and ever for what you have done; in your name I will hope, for your name is good. I will praise you in the presence of your saints." External circumstances have not changed, but David has come to a place of renewed hope as he has spent time in God's presence and ventilated his emotion.

There are clients who will find it helpful to journal their own "psalms," pouring out their emotions before God and seeking his help. And for many of them, the likely outcome is that they will feel a deeper level of peace as they discharge emotion in writing. For many there will be a renewal of hope, as in David's experience.

Once again, the warning: Avoid turning psalm therapy into a routine counselling intervention. But by all means, feel free to incorporate it into counselling if your client is open to this and if it seems potentially helpful.

Finally...

Be confident about this! Activated by the Spirit of God, the Word of God has transformative power! It has the potential to produce significant experiential changes to perspectives that otherwise are producing bleak, confused, lost or discouraged experiences in the lives of counselees.

Further Reading

McMinn, M. (1996). *Psychology, theology and spirituality in Christian counselling.* Carol Stream, IL: Tyndale.

Wimberly, E. P. (1994). *Using Scripture in pastoral counselling.* Nashville, TN: Abingdon Press.

CHAPTER 17

Confession and Forgiveness in Counselling

"Of private confession I am heartily in favour... for it is a cure without equal for distressed consciences." (Martin Luther)

"Emotions can create health or cause disease. And spiritual health affects emotional health. Laughter and joy are known to restore and encourage health, while bitterness and resentment promote disease. Forgiveness has well-documented health benefits" (Levy, 2011).

* * * * * * * * *

The field of secular psychology is beginning to realise that forgiveness is incredibly valuable in helping people caught up in despair in their lives. Robert Enright, professor of educational psychology at the University of Wisconsin, and Richard Fitzgibbons, psychiatrist, wrote the seminal work in this area in their book *Helping Clients Forgive* (2000). Their work has shown the pivotal importance of forgiveness in helping people resolve anger over past betrayal and hurts; in restoring fractured relationships; in overcoming the legacy of depression, anxiety disorders, and other emotional disturbances; and in bringing people back to peace of mind. Recognising the therapeutic importance of this area, *The Journal of Psychology and Christianity* for Spring 2001 (Vol. 20) published several articles on forgiveness. The truth is that secular psychology has little to contribute to the person overwhelmed with guilt because of his or her life choices and actions, apart from some "fairy floss" intervention directed at trying to get people to not feel guilty! When someone is genuinely guilty, only appropriating forgiveness helps!

Where this is especially important is in those times when people come for counselling out of a guilty conscience because of some wrong that they have done. At such times it is appropriate as part of the counselling process, and provided they are open to this, to take them through steps of repentance, confession, and asking God for forgiveness. If this is sought, the most important guideline is not to rush the process. We do disservice to our counselees when, by inadequate preparation, we tend to trivialise this extraordinary means of grace that God has provided.

When we are burdened with sin, Scripture invites us to come before God in repentance. The call to renounce sinful behaviour and to repent of it, turning away from it and turning back to God, marked the beginning of the ministry of Jesus. Mark records Jesus's first sermon, given as he walked on the shores of Galilee, as this message: "The time has come! The kingdom of God is near! Repent, and believe the good news!" (Mark 1:15).

Repentance is preparatory to God's action in forgiving us. We are assured that, "If we confess our sins, God is faithful and just and will forgive our sins and cleanse us from all unrighteousness" (1 John 1:9). Central to our Christian understanding is the truth that, in his death on the cross, Jesus took the judgment and penalty of our sin, making forgiveness freely available to whomever commits their life to following and serving Him. These are glorious truths to be able to share with anyone who is truly repentant!

Two Important Dimensions to Forgiveness

Of course it is important to be aware that there are biblical instructions that pertain to the receiving of forgiveness. The first is that, in order to avail ourselves of God's already-purchased gift of forgiveness, we need *first* to forgive others who have wronged us. Passages such as Jesus's teaching about The Unforgiving Servant (Matthew 18:23–35) make it clear that our own forgiveness is riding on our being willing to forgive others. Where the issue of seeking forgiveness is central in the counselling context, we take time to make this teaching clear.

1. Forgiving Those Who Have Wronged Us

Obviously the starting place in any counselling that has a focus on forgiving others will be to take time to empathically hear the story of the suffering that the counselee has experienced. This cannot be rushed. When the time is right we move on to some spiritual education, so that there is a framework for further intervention.

> *The starting place in any counselling that has a focus on forgiving others will be to empathically hear the story of the suffering...*

We teach what forgiveness is not!

If someone has been deeply wronged by others, it is not always a simple thing to have them come to a position of extending forgiveness to the other person. Many people have a misunderstanding of what it means to forgive. This needs to be processed and clarified for them. We teach that

- *Extending forgiveness does not mean having to tell the other person, "I have forgiven you."* Often people are not safe and to make a declaration like this to some people could invite further abuse or ridicule. At its essence, extending forgiveness to someone else is a transaction between the person doing the forgiving and God. King David was right when he addressed God in Psalm 51:4: "Against you, you only have I sinned and done that which is evil in your eyes." We teach counselees that the business of extending forgiveness is centrally transacted between themselves and God, and the decision to share it with the person is a completely different issue.

- *Extending forgiveness does* not *mean "It doesn't matter..."* The hurt or wrong done to a person *does* matter. It mattered enough in God's eyes for it to need dealing with—through the death of Jesus. We need to help people see that forgiving another person is not taking the position that the wrong is unimportant. We teach counselees that extending forgiveness is quite a separate matter.
- *Extending forgiveness does* not *mean "Now I have to resume contact with the person who has wronged me."* Forgiving someone is a separate issue from whether or not we now have to speak to the person who abused us in the past. The decision to renew contact is a separate choice with people altogether, to be guided by how wise that would be. For example, Is the person safe to talk to? We teach counselees that it is entirely possible to forgive someone, and choose *never* to renew contact!
- *Extending forgiveness does not mean* "Now I will forget..." We tend to tie forgiving and forgetting together, because we see in Scripture that when God forgives he forgets (for example, Jeremiah 31:34). However, as humans we function differently and have a very efficient hippocampal system! We still remember, even though we may have sincerely extended forgiveness. Our memory is triggered by little reminders, something we see as we walk down the street, an allusion from a TV show or a book, a smell, a sound, a visual cue. We teach people that these are not indicators that they have failed to forgive properly. Rather they are indicators that they are *normal* people! We teach that, when the memory is triggered *two* prayers are appropriate. The first is a prayer of thanksgiving: "Thank you, Lord, at least I'm normal." The second is a brief prayer, reaffirming the forgiveness we

have previously extended. "Lord, I continue to reaffirm the forgiveness I have extended to that person and I trust you to work it out for me."

Helping people understand what it means to forgive another requires that we teach them that this *does* mean, "Lord, I give up the desire for revenge, and I ask for you to do good in this person's life." Not surprisingly, that is a huge call for most people who have been wronged. Asking God to bless someone who has wronged them? No wonder we need to go slowly here!

A counselee who attended our clinic had suffered severe trauma through abusive parents. Processing the trauma, we came to a point where extending forgiveness was the appropriate next step, but she was blocked. She could, and did, forgive other abusive people from her life, but she refused to countenance forgiving her parents. Each time the need was put before her she said, "No, I can't!" Finally, it seemed that God was prompting me (Cliff) with the instruction, "Beg her." Not really knowing what to do with that, I tried to sidestep it for a while but it wouldn't go away. How do you beg a counselee? Not wanting to miss out on what God was doing, I finally dropped to my knees before her and said, "Please forgive your parents." I was almost bowled over when she responded, fairly matter-of-factly, "All right." We went ahead with a time of prayer in which she extended forgiveness to her parents.

The next week when she returned, something was different. She shared that on the way home on the bus, she was overwhelmed with what she described as "wave after wave of joy." As she walked to her home she passed by her church and saw the minister. She had never been baptised by immersion so she asked if he would baptise her on the Sunday and this was done. Not long after this the counselling work was done and she moved on. But, in the grace of God, some years later word came of her transformed life, her marriage, and her involvement in ministry. Extending forgiveness has this kind of potential to free people from their past in remarkable ways.

Why should we forgive those who have wronged us?

- We do it in obedience to God. Jesus modelled forgiving others in his words from the Cross and he asks us to follow him and to forgive those who have sinned against us. "For if you forgive others their trespasses, your heavenly Father will also forgive you; but if you do not forgive others, neither will your heavenly Father forgive your trespasses" (Matthew 6:14–15 NRSV).
- We do it because we *need* to. As is obvious in the verses above, our forgiveness is tied to whether we forgive others or not.

How do we incorporate a time of extending forgiveness into our counselling?

We teach counsellors to follow these steps:

1. Prepare. This is not to be rushed. Talk through everything that needs to be addressed. Go through the teaching about forgiveness, taking the time to answer any questions. Explain how the prayer time will be conducted.
2. Conduct the prayer time, as much as possible guiding, yet allowing the person to speak to God in their own words. We usually encourage clients to begin by acknowledging before God, the sin and hurt that has been experienced. For example: "Father, you know what was done to me and how it has wounded me over the years. I acknowledge before you that [person's name] sinned against me by [...]. Thank you that you understand my suffering."

3. Help the person to actively express forgiveness before God. For example: "Father, I choose to forgive [person's name]. I no longer want to see him or her suffer for what he or she did to me. I no longer want revenge. In your strength I pray, instead, for you to bless this person."
4. The counsellor's role is simply to support through the prayer time, so that it becomes a free-flowing time of prayer, with the counselee expressing his or her heart before God and the counsellor supporting and affirming.
5. Finally, the counsellor needs to give post-forgiveness instructions. These will include guidance on
    - How to live now that they have spiritually cut free from the other person's actions.
    - How to handle the reactions and memories, which will still be triggered at times since this is "normal."

2. Seeking Forgiveness for Ourselves

Counselling with someone who carries a burden of guilt and who seeks the restoration of internal peace requires the same kind of preparation. The starting place is to "hear the story," taking time and avoiding any tendency to rush. This needs

- *A time of preparation* when the counselee shares what he or she has done, is guilty over, who has been wronged, and so on. This flows into
- *A time of confession,* asking for forgiveness. It should not "gloss over" sinful actions but should aim to label them honestly, repenting of them, and asking God for forgiveness through Jesus. This opens the way for
- *The granting of absolution* by the counsellor. "If you forgive anyone's sins they are forgiven; if you retain anyone's sins they are retained" (John 20:22). This is a privileged moment for both the counsellor and the counselee. We usually say

something like: "I want you to look at me because I want to say something important to you. I'm no-one special, just a fellow disciple of Jesus. But right now I'm speaking God's word to you. 'In the name of Jesus Christ your sins are forgiven.'" This is often quite an emotional moment for the counselee.

- *It is important to provide post-forgiveness instruction to the person.* We usually alert clients to the likelihood of continued moments when they might feel condemned. We encourage them to take hold of Romans 8: 1: "There is, therefore, no condemnation for those who are in Christ Jesus." The teaching point here is that, if they *do* feel condemnation, it is not coming from God! It could be Satan trying to stop them from living in their new freedom, or it could be their own heart. Either way, God's verdict is the one that counts and they are encouraged to hold to it. (1 John 3: 20: "If our hearts condemn us God is greater than our hearts...")
- Finally, we encourage them *to live as a forgiven person* and to guard themselves in their spirit, so that they do not slip back into sinful practices. We ask them: "How will you be different as you go home, now that you are forgiven?" "How will you be different with your spouse/child/fellow workers now that you have received forgiveness?" and so on.

Once again, we emphasise the importance of using the time well, rather than rushing or trivialising it. We do not go through this kind of intervention for every sin, but really only for the situation where someone is carrying some major condemnation because of sinful behaviour. We would probably not go through a process as comprehensive as this with someone who is struggling with an addiction, though seeking forgiveness is still appropriate.

> *We emphasise the importance of using the time well, rather than rushing or trivialising it.*

Additional Important Notes

- If it is possible for restitution to be made for the wrong committed, this should be considered. There may be times when the person's wrong involves criminal conduct and, quite apart from the ministry of forgiveness, it is appropriate for the person to be encouraged to turn themselves in to the police. This will certainly require preparation if it is relevant.
- Finally, we need to make sure that confession is appropriate. Sometimes people with a very anxious, punitive personality believe they have committed a sin, when they haven't. Some people carry guilt because they think they have committed the Unpardonable Sin. Guilt in these cases is "false guilt" and doesn't need confession and absolution! Psycho-education, other biblical instructions, and a range of other helpful counselling interventions are more appropriate.

Further Reading

Enright, R., & Fitzgibbon, R. (2000). *Helping clients forgive.* Washington, DC: American Psychological Association.

Levy, D., & Kilpatrick, J. (2011). *Gray matter: A neurosurgeon discovers the power of prayer.* Carol Stream, IL: Tyndale.

McCullough, M. E., Pargament, K. I., & Thoreson, C. (Eds). (2000). *Forgiveness: Theory, research and practice.* New York: Guilford Press.

Fisher, P. C. (2006). "The link between posttraumatic growth and forgiveness: An intuitive truth". In L. G. Calhoun & R. G. Tedeschi, (Eds.), *Handbook of posttraumatic growth: Research and practice* (pp. 311-333). Mahwah, NJ: Erlbaum.

CHAPTER 18

Hearing God

Perhaps no area of being "open to the Holy Spirit" has been viewed with so much hesitation (and criticism!) as the area of receiving personal revelation. We affirm the importance of being conservative and cautious because of the danger of misunderstanding and misusing this "means of grace." However, in being true to Scripture and out of personal experience, we dare not omit it in training people to counsel with an incarnational understanding.

* * * * * * * * *

Is it possible that, as a Christian counsellor, I might actually "hear" God, or receive direct revelation from God, in the process of seeking to help people? Our answer is an unequivocal yes. As we noted in the chapter on Listening, we believe that, as Christian counsellors, our "God channel" is one of the eight "channels" that we need to tune in to.

But first, it is important to clarify what is meant by *revelation*. The Macquarie Dictionary offers the following meaning for revelation in relation to religious issues: *God's disclosure of himself and of his will to his creatures.* An instance of revelation is *a disclosure by God of something that would otherwise* not *have been known by the recipient.* Sometimes this is called a "word of knowledge," the spiritual gift referred to in 1 Corinthians 12:8. There are many examples of this in Scripture. Of course, it raises a question.

1. How Does God Speak?

It is clear from Scripture that God speaks in varied ways. Job 33:14–15 (NRSV) is a truth from the lips of Elihu: "For God speaks in one way, and in two, though people do not perceive it. In a dream, in a vision of the night, when deep sleep falls on mortals, while they slumber on their beds, then he opens their ears, and terrifies them with warnings, that he may turn them aside from their deeds..." Here, Elihu identifies three ways that God speaks—in dreams, in visions at night, and in an audible voice that frightens.

However, the range of possibilities goes a lot further. In Matthew 2 there are a number of different ways that God gives revelation. He speaks to the Magi through a sign, the appearance of the star in the East. He speaks through prophets in Scripture, identifying the birthplace of Jesus as being Bethlehem. He speaks to the wise men by a dream, warning them not to return to Herod. An angel of the Lord speaks to Joseph in a dream warning him to flee to Egypt with the young Jesus, and an angel tells him in a dream when to return. Finally, all in this single chapter, Joseph is told in a dream (we don't know if this was by an angel) to move to Galilee.

So, without analysing very far at all, we discover examples in Scripture where God speaks, specifically through Scripture, by direct words, dreams, visions, signs, prophetic people, and angels. And in sober reflection on common human experience, we might add, God speaks also through miracles, preachers, books, songs, music, impressions in our spirit, audible voices, circumstances, TV programs, phone calls, small group members—and many other possibilities! We are told that, as his sheep, we will hear his voice (John 10:3–4, 27).

> *Many Christians have misunderstood (and misused!) the issue of personal revelation in ministry and counselling.*

With good reason, there are those who are very cautious about this whole area of "hearing God." As noted above, many Christians have misunderstood (and misused!) the issue of personal revelation in ministry and counselling, to place "words" on people that were not of God, and these have sometimes been potentially damaging to the recipient. We share the concern that people having counselling should not be subjected to hurtful experiences at the hands of people who believe they have a "prophetic gifting." And we want to affirm that God speaks most directly, and frequently through his Word, enlivened by the Holy Spirit. However, we also want to acknowledge that direct personal revelation *does* occur, if we are open to his Spirit and, used sensitively, it has the capacity to lead to significant "breakthroughs." Still, the counsellor who wants to grow in his or her capacity to hear God has, first of all, to be a person of the Word, committed to disciplined study of Scripture. Additionally, as we noticed in the chapter on *Important Counsellor Qualities*, he or she needs to be a person who gives continuing attention to vital relationship with Jesus. Of course, all of this raises another question.

2. Why Might God Need to Speak to Us, as Counsellors?

Acts 16:6–10 gives us some guidance on this. In this passage, in the space of a few verses we have three clear references to God's in-breaking, with revelation for his disciples. The first indication we have is in verse 6: "having been kept by the Holy Spirit from preaching the word in the province of Asia." The clear implication here is that Paul and his companions were planning to preach in the province of Asia. They were on a missionary journey, and the people of this province needed to hear the Gospel, so they planned to take the opportunity to preach there. However, God had another purpose and another place in mind, so they continued their journey.

Imagine for a moment that the *only* revelation they had was from the Scriptures. In that case they would have known that the clear call throughout the OT was for the Gentiles also to hear the word. Acting on that direction, they would have preached in the province of Asia. But that was *not* what God wanted at this time. The Holy Spirit *had* to break in by special revelation: It was as though God, through the Holy Spirit, said: "I have another task for you!"

Next we read in verse 7, "When they came to the border of Mysia, they tried to enter Bithynia but the Spirit of Jesus would not allow them to." It seems that, once again, they were held back from taking the Gospel where they planned to, by an act of direct revelation. The only way God can direct them to where he wants at this point is by direct revelation, described here as through "the Spirit of Jesus." Without this personal leading, they would again be serving God, with pure motives, *but in the wrong place!*

We are not told exactly how they received their instructions from God on either of these occasions. It seems unlikely that these were visions, since the next revelation is a vision, and is specified as one. Perhaps they were just impressions in their spirit, received by one or other of the party. But clearly Paul, Silas, Luke, etc. are open to this kind of direct guidance, and they take notice.

The consummation of their guidance comes in the form of a *vision* given to Paul in Troas: "During the night Paul had a vision of a man from Macedonia standing and begging him: 'Come over to Macedonia and help us!'" (verse 9). God's plan is now evident. The Gospel is to move into Europe!

Without the in-breaking of God's instruction via direct, personal revelation, the missionary party would have missed this moment. Sometimes God needs to give direct revelation to his servants because he has a specific purpose in mind for this moment. And, without direct leading on this, even with the best and purest motives in the world, we will not be carrying out his intention for this moment but will be engaged in something else!

For exactly the same reason, as counsellors, we need to be alert to the voice of God when working with people. There may be occasions when our intended intervention or way of seeking to help, is *not* what God wants! There will be times when he wants to reveal something to us that goes beyond our knowledge, but will open the way for significant healing. If we are not open to his direct revelation, we could miss his purpose for this person at this moment.

Donohue

On one occasion, in the midst of counselling a client suffering from a dissociative disorder, we were processing some of her earlier distressing memories. There was much that was difficult for her to recall, much that was intensely painful for her to talk about. As she shared her voice faltered and came to a halt. She sat silently before me. At that moment the word "Donohue" popped into my mind. The experience was unusual in that the word was not something that made any sense to me, and it had no connection to anything in my current experience, or in our counselling. Nevertheless, the presence of the word seemed insistent, such that I felt I had to do something with it. Quite hesitantly I said something like: "Jill [not her name], I don't know if this means anything to you, but I have this word *Donohue* that has just been stirred in my mind. Does that mean anything to you?" She began to weep immediately and, when the tears stopped flowing and she was able to explain, she recalled that she had watched an episode of a Phil Donohue show in the past, which focused on "sibling rivalry." It had fascinated her as it dramatically opened her to the awareness of how her parents had played up the issue of differences and favouritism between her and her siblings. The revelation enabled us to move into a new area that led to much more healing release for her.

This kind of experience is not a common one, but it does illustrate the importance of being open to the "God channel." It seems that on this occasion, in the process of healing for Jill, God wanted the issue of sibling rivalry to be processed. It was not something that would have been introduced without his intervention, nor was it something she would have brought up at that moment, but it was God's agenda for that moment, and both of us recognised that. God prompted this part of the counselling process by the word *Donohue*.

3. Revelation, Interpretation, and Application

In the process of training Christian counsellors, we teach students to be very careful with anything they believe could be a revelation. It is important not to rush anywhere with revelation. If we are in a counselling context, remember we are bound to stay sensitive to our client's situation. Much harm has been done in churches, and in counselling, by people who thought they had a prophetic gift and subsequently went around "laying prophecies" on people (e.g., "God wants you to know you will be married by this time next year").

We emphasise the distinction between revelation, interpretation, and application.

- *Revelation* is the actual word, or picture, or impression that you receive. As already noted, some people label this a "word of knowledge," as referred to in 1 Corinthians 12: 8.
- *Interpretation* is what the revelation *means*. A revelation may be accurate, but its *interpretation*, or meaning, may be unclear.
- *Application* is what we are supposed to do with the revelation and/or interpretation—how we are to apply it. It may be that God wants us to share it with a client at the moment we receive it. However it may also be that we have been given this revelation, but it is not something to share *at this time,*

or it is not something we are to share *at all*. It may be that the revelation is given simply for our personal edification, so that we will know that God is in control of events.

Be aware that we can make mistakes at any one of these points. Our "revelation" may not be accurate. There have been occasions when I have shared what I believed might be a "word from God" only to have the client shake their head and graciously assure me that it didn't mean anything to them. They were not being avoidant. It was just that I was mis-hearing. There was some "static" in my spiritual receptors. The important thing about such moments is that we need to be sensitive to the client, and not presumptuous in our sharing. If we feel that we may have a word from God, we usually preface our sharing with, "I'm not sure if this means anything to you but..." and we then go on to share the picture or word. When something like this is shared in a gentle, somewhat hesitant voice tone, it is not difficult for the client to graciously deny its relevance if it is *not* accurate. The mistake we need to avoid is to think too highly of ourselves and "dump" things on people. Of course, if it is accurate, their response will tell us, and we can then work with the relevant issue, knowing God has "brought it to the table." We can be confident that he wants to further the healing in this area.

If you believe you have a revelation from God, ask God if it is to be shared, or if it is just for yourself. If you believe it is to be shared, ask him if it is to be shared now, or at some future time.

We can also make mistakes in interpretation. An interesting example of this occurs in Acts 21:10–11. Here, Paul is on his way to Jerusalem for the last time. The prophet, Agabus, takes Paul's belt and dramatises Paul's impending capture in Jerusalem by wrapping it around his own hands and feet, saying: "The Holy Spirit says this: 'In this way the Jews of Jerusalem will bind the owner of this belt and will hand him over to the Gentiles.'"

The *revelation* to Agabus was accurate, in that Paul was to be captured. However, aspects of the *interpretation* seem to have been inaccurate. According to the account in Acts 21:30–36, Paul was bound by the Romans, *not the Jews* (verse 33), and it was not the Jews who handed him over to the Gentiles but, rather, the Gentiles who *rescued* him from the Jews. It seems most likely that these details in Agabus's *interpretation* of what he saw or heard, were "contaminated" somehow by the "imperfectness" of the human instrument. In this situation it was not anything of consequence. But the case serves to make us aware that, if Agabus could make an error in the details of interpretation, *we* need to be humble, sensitive, and err on the cautious side, rather than be presumptuous in our sharing and interpretation of revelation.

> We need to be humble, sensitive, and err on the cautious side, rather than be presumptuous in our sharing and interpretation of revelation.

The "Bubble of Pain"

On one occasion away from home, I (Cliff) was asked if I would meet with a distressed person. Because of the circumstances, it was extremely unlikely I would have an opportunity to see this woman more than this one occasion. When she began she told me that much of her life (she was in her fifties at a guess) she had been distressed by what she called a "bubble of pain." It was located just below her ribcage in her midriff region. Medical examinations had indicated that there was nothing physically wrong. Of late it had been very distressing.

When I asked her what she thought the cause of the pain was, she replied, "I don't know." In the normal process of counselling, I would have taken time to gather some life history and begun to consider the possibilities behind this symptom, drawing on her life experiences. But beyond this occasion we would not have any other opportunities to meet.

Unsure what else to do, and aware of the constraints of time, I suggested that we ask God for his wisdom, and she agreed. After asking God, we sat silently for a little while, during which time I had a fleeting picture of a little baby crying. Great man of faith that I am (!), I did what I usually do in these situations. Instead of risking myself, I asked her if *she* had received any revelation! When she answered no, I knew I would now have to share what I had seen. So I told her simply of the picture. As she listened she broke down and began to weep. A logical *interpretation* came to mind: *Oh, no, she must have had a little baby that died.*

When her tears finally began to ease, I asked her about the baby. "It was me," she said. Apparently her parents had been quite poor and had found it difficult to cope with a number of small mouths to feed. To reduce the pressure they gave her up, and she, alone of all their children, had been placed in an orphanage soon after her birth. At the age of two she was finally adopted by a nurse working at the institution. In later years she was told by this nurse that she had cried almost nonstop, for the first eighteen months of her life. What does a counsellor do in this situation? My faith was strengthened by the revelation that had just been confirmed, and since we had little time, I simply prayed for God to completely release her from the distress of the "bubble of pain." She felt some shift but reported that complete release did not occur at that time. However, she phoned me some time later to tell me that the process had been completed in another dramatic moment of healing, when she was on her own at home. She had enough medical knowledge to know that her blood pressure went incredibly high before she experienced waves of release and peace and, finally, the "bubble of pain" was healed.

This experience can teach us something. It is worth noting that my initial *interpretation*, which I never had to share, was simply wide of the mark. I reasoned, building on past experiences in counselling grieving women who had had a child die, that she had lost a child. The revelation was of God, but my *interpretation* was faulty, being the product of my own reasoning. Fortunately, in this case, my interpretation wasn't needed. It is wise not to rush anywhere with your interpretation of any direct revelation. As a general rule, if you share the revelation, and if it *is* accurate, let your client tell you what it is about. The processing involved in their sharing will be part of their healing.

4. How Will I Recognise God's Voice?

Many people have written with wisdom suggesting the indicators of God's voice. Something that was very helpful to me came from Virkler and Virkler's book *How to hear God's voice* (2005). They offer the following guidelines:

- *"God's voice in our hearts sounds like a flow of spontaneous thoughts."* In other words, revelation from God is often a flow of thought that does not fit logically, or sequentially, with our normal, linear thought. Usually when we are thinking, our thoughts flow in a reasonably logical, connected sequence. But we have all had the experience of something just *"popping into"* our minds, such that we think "Where did that come from?" Perhaps it was a thought about someone we haven't seen for ages, and when we phone them, they are in need of our prayer or support. Probably much of this happens and we "tune it out," because we are not monitoring that channel—we don't really have any expectation that God might speak to us!
- *Still yourself before God.* Increasing sensitivity to the voice of God will come directly out of quality relationship time, spent with his Word and in his presence.

• *Journal.* Many people, desiring to learn to discern God's voice, have found it helpful to keep a record of any revelation they believe God is giving. Caution is needed but there is both encouragement and learning for us here.

Again, we need to take care. Satan can also "drop thoughts" into our awareness. We need to subject any such thought to the test of Scripture routinely, and we need to be sensitive in our sharing and/or application.

Peter Lord, in *Hearing God* (2011), suggests the following helpful guidelines:

- If God speaks to you about sin in your life, he will be *specific* about what it is you need to do.
- Your self-worth is never attacked by God.
- God's voice will be merciful within you, insofar as it relates to the sins of others.
- God's voice is an encouraging voice.
- God's voice brings peace.
- God's voice brings hope.
- God's voice produces gratitude in your heart.

If the voice we think we hear within contrasts with these guidelines, we do well to be suspicious of it!

Conclusion

When God brings revelation, it is exciting and stimulating, both for the counsellor and the counselee. We can be confident that God is involved in the healing that this person is seeking, and we can proceed with confidence in his leading. However, it is important to be aware that a moment of revelation, as was the case with the "bubble of pain," is rarely a complete healing, or resolution of the issues.

It seems to produce a breakthrough in a specific area, but, rather than the *finish*, it seems more often to be an important next step. In our experience, the need for further changes in thinking, feeling and patterns of behaviour (the hard work of change and growth) go on. People are not instantly and completely "sanctified." So give praise to God for any revelation that occurs, but in your counselling continue to assess, wisely, the need for continuing change, and the need for this to be grounded in the person's life over time.

There are people who see what we would call "prayer ministries" as the only needed approach for counsellors to use. The approach of such people is to rely predominantly on a prayer process that seeks direct revelation from God, and they seek to use this, often as the sole means of bringing the person to healing. We do not find ourselves in line with this approach. While we recognise the appropriateness of prayer ministry at times as the "treatment of choice," obviously, given our training as psychologists and counsellors, we do not support the *exclusivity* of this perspective. We acknowledge the usefulness of prayer ministry (under appropriate training and safeguards), but do not see it as the "only approach needed" as some Christians espouse. Rather, we see direct revelation from God as one of the unique "means of grace" available to Christian counsellors, and we seek to be open to it and to train our students to listen for God's wisdom as they counsel. But we seek to integrate this as one dimension in the overall process, which we have labelled Incarnational Counselling, rather than seeing it as the whole process.

Further Reading

Lord, P. (2011). *Hearing God: An easy-to-follow, step-by-step guide to two-way communication with God*. Bloomington, Minnesota: Chosen Books.

Shirer, P. C. (2011). *Discerning the voice of God.* Chicago, IL: Moody Publications.

Virkler, M., Virkler, P. (2005). *How to hear God's voice.* Shippensburg, PA: Destiny Image.

Willard, D. (2012). *Hearing God.* Downer's Grove, IL: Intervarsity Press.

PART 5

Leaving the Woe, Embracing the Go!

There is a famous World War II photograph depicting a wounded soldier, whose eyes are bandaged, lighting a cigarette for a fellow wounded soldier whose *hands* are heavily bandaged. In this image we see that experiencing the "woe" is not necessarily the end of the story. As the image shows, even two wounded persons can move forward and embrace the "go" when their will and resources are shared and they move together.

A counsellor can heed the several parallels presented within this image:

- All parties within a therapeutic relationship are wounded persons. To deny this truth would be a dangerous position to take. Unless counsellors recognise their own failings and fragilities they will be vulnerable to offering an impoverished experience to their clients who are seeking a fellow traveller on their healing journey. Therapists who fail to recognise their own issues also run the danger that the "healthy" therapist will create a divide between himself or herself and the "unhealthy" client, thereby voiding any empathic responses.
- Embracing the "go" will usually necessitate both therapist and client, utilising their strengths. In our image, both soldiers' strengths have been severely limited. The blind man becomes the handless man's hands, and in turn, he becomes the blind man's eyes. In the therapeutic process a therapist needs to find and utilise their client's strengths. Once the therapy has concluded, it will be those strengths that have been utilised and developed that will enable the client to continue their journey.
- There will also be a need for risk and stepping into unknown territory. It is unlikely that either soldier had experienced this situation prior to what was depicted in the photograph. It took trust on both their parts to get that cigarette lit. The

blind man trusted that the directions given and his actions were sufficient, while the handless man trusted that the blind man could hold the lit match in place while moving his lips and cigarette towards the flame. Therapists need to know their limitations but sometimes a situation arises when, to move clients forward, new strategies and techniques need to be accessed and attempted. Your client will forgive you if whatever you attempt does not work, but they will also benefit wonderfully when you sensitively step into the unknown, trusting God to work!

A final thought. The goal of being an *incarnational* counsellor is, for any follower of Christ, both a present and existing reality and, at the same time, an aspirational goal. However poorly we bring the presence of Christ into counselling, if we are genuine disciples we *do* bring his presence. Incarnationality simply *is*! This is above and beyond skills and theoretical knowledge. It is a mystery beyond human contribution. We acknowledge this, but also recognise the call to work at growing in an ever-richer relationship with God, simply so that we can more effectively help those who are going through difficult, possibly overwhelming, circumstances. To this end we encourage trainees to gain every skill and bit of knowledge possible to optimise their counselling. There is no either/or here! The enterprise is very much a both/and process. Knowledge, skills, *and* incarnationality!

Appendix A

Here we offer a sample life-history questionnaire. It is very comprehensive. Feel free to adapt it to suit your own need.

Life-History Questionnaire

The following information will assist your therapist in facilitating your treatment program. Please answer the questions as fully as possible. Be assured this questionnaire will be treated in strict confidence as are all counselling sessions.

Date _____

Name _____ Date of birth _____

Address _____

_____ PC _____

Telephone _____ Mobile _____

Occupation _____

Marital Status _____ Partner's Name _____

If a parent, names and ages of your children:

Name _____ Age _____

Name _____ Age _____

Name _____ Age _____

Name _____ Age _____

Name _____ Age _____

List any prior counselling you have received

Year	Issues Addressed	Counsellor

State in your own words the nature and development of your main concerns

_____

_____

_____

_____

What feelings, thoughts, or behaviours do you want to change?

_____

_____

_____

_____

List your current medications and any observed results

Medication	Results/side effects

Please check any of the following that apply to you:

Headaches	Panic feelings	Cannot make decisions
Bowel/stomach disturbances	Rely on sedatives	High anxiety
Nightmares	Suicidal ideas	Lost appetite
Cannot make friends	Sexual problems	Insomnia
Memory problems	Dizziness	Fatigue

I often feel

Overwhelmed	Lonely	Shy	Stupid
Worthwhile	Evil	Competent	Ugly
Useless	Bored	Confident	Attractive
Unforgivable	Naive	Intelligent	Immoral
Unloved	Appreciated	Depressed	Inadequate

Medical History

Childhood Illnesses _____

Adolescent Illnesses _____

Surgical Operations and dates _____

_____

Current Medical Issues _____

_____

Menstrual History

Age of first period _____   How were you prepared? _____

Are you regular? _____   Duration? _____   Date of last period _____

What physical symptoms accompany your period? _____

_____

In what way do your periods affect your moods _____

_____

Sexual History

What was the parental attitude towards sex? _____

How were you educated about sex? _____

How adequate was your sex education? _____

How have you dealt with adverse feelings about your own sexual behaviours? _____

Do you recall any sexual abuse as a child or adult? Yes/No (please circle)

What sexual issues remain unresolved at this time? _____

_____

Marital History

Date of Marriage _____ How long have you known your partner

_____

List any previous marriages or permanent relationships and their duration

_____

Describe your partner

_____

_____

In what areas are there compatibility? _____

In what areas are there incompatibility? _____

Family History

Father: _____

Living: present age ____ occupation _____ Health Issues _____

Deceased: age at time of death _____ Cause of death _____

Your age at the time of his death _____

Describe his personality and attitude towards you (past and present)

_____

Complete the following:

My father was always _____

I wish my father had _____

Mother: _____

Living: present age ____ Occupation _____ Health Issues _____

Deceased: age at time of death _____ Cause of death _____

Your age at the time of his death _____

Describe her personality and attitude towards you (past and present)

_____

Complete the following:

My mother was always _____

I wish my mother had _____

SIBLINGS:

Number of sisters ____ Names and Ages _____

Number of brothers _____   Names and Ages _____

Describe your relationship with your siblings:

Past: _____

Present: _____

Home Life

Write your impressions of your home atmosphere:

_____

_____

What was the best memory you have of home life? _____

What was the most painful memory you had growing up? _____

PERSONAL IMPRESSIONS

I am a person who _____

_____

All my life I _____

_____

I feel very proud about _____

_____

I feel guilty about _____

_____

If I didn't worry about what others think I would _____

_____

Others can hurt me by _____

_____

When I was growing up I missed out on _____

_____

The worst thing about growing up is _____

_____

I am very angry about _____

_____

I could help myself a great deal more if I _____

_____

My goal for therapy is _____

To reach my goal I need to work on _____

Appendix B

Supervision Competency Checklist

In Incarnational Counselling emphasis is placed on the importance of ongoing supervision as non-negotiable for all beginning counsellors. Over the years the following competency-based checklist has been developed, to guide both those involved in the training of counsellors, and also supervisors of novitiate counsellors. Clearly, the competencies and indicators included here go beyond an initial counselling skills class. The checklist brings in competencies and performance indicators we include in our training, and expect to see in evidence in trainee counsellors by the end of the first two years of training.

1. Counselling Skills

(Demonstrates familiarity with, and the capacity to use, a broad range of basic counsellor responses, conducive to effective counselling.)

		Never Evident	Seldom Evident	Somewhat Evident	Often Evident	Always Evident
1.	Demonstrates the capacity to establish a therapeutic alliance (rapport) with the client.	1	2	3	4	5
2.	Demonstrates the capacity to attend to the client as he or she shares.	1	2	3	4	5

		Never Evident	Seldom Evident	Somewhat Evident	Often Evident	Always Evident
3.	Demonstrates the capacity to listen actively to the client's broad communication spectrum.	1	2	3	4	5
4.	Demonstrates the capacity to probe helpfully, encouraging further problem exploration by the client.	1	2	3	4	5
5.	Demonstrates the ability to respond empathically to client sharing.	1	2	3	4	5
6.	Demonstrates the capacity to, helpfully, share information, or correct misinformation, for the client.	1	2	3	4	5
7.	Demonstrates a thorough understanding of crisis counselling skills, and the capacity to use these as needed.	1	2	3	4	5
8.	Demonstrates the capacity to contract with the client.	1	2	3	4	5
9.	Demonstrates the capacity to share his or her own selective experience in ways that are helpful to the client.	1	2	3	4	5
10.	Demonstrates the capacity to focus, helpfully, on aspects of the therapeutic relationship that are affecting the counselling process.	1	2	3	4	5
11.	Demonstrates the capacity to track underlying themes in client sharing.	1	2	3	4	5
12.	Demonstrates the capacity to help the client stay focused in the counselling process.	1	2	3	4	5
13.	Demonstrates the capacity to identify issues below the client's level of conscious awareness.	1	2	3	4	5

	Never Evident	Seldom Evident	Somewhat Evident	Often Evident	Always Evident
14. Demonstrates the capacity to use Scaling constructively to aid assessment, encourage hope and develop action plans.	1	2	3	4	5
15. Demonstrates the capacity to discover, and help the client identify, strengths in his or her functioning.	1	2	3	4	5
16. Demonstrates the capacity to teach new skills, relevant to the therapeutic issues, to the client.	1	2	3	4	5
17. Demonstrates the capacity to "contain" the client's emotionality.	1	2	3	4	5
18. Demonstrates the capacity to promote hope for clients.	1	2	3	4	5

2. Theory-Based Practice

(Demonstrates a comprehensive knowledge of more than one traditional theory of counselling and works with clients from the bases of these.)

		Never Evident	Seldom Evident	Somewhat Evident	Often Evident	Always Evident
19.	Demonstrates an ability to conceptualise client issues from within traditional theories.	1	2	3	4	5
20.	Demonstrates an ability to plan appropriate interventions that derive from traditional theory.	1	2	3	4	5
21.	Actively seeks to increase knowledge of additional theories of counselling.	1	2	3	4	5
22.	Under supervision, works to extend range of appropriate interventions, building from new theoretical understandings.	1	2	3	4	5
23.	Demonstrates an understanding of at least one brief counselling theory.	1	2	3	4	5
24.	Demonstrates the capacity to conceptualise and work with clients from at least one brief counselling theory.	1	2	3	4	5

3. Diagnostic Skills

(Demonstrates the ability to recognise, or determine, the primary nature of a client's issues, in terms of some well-established and widely recognised nosology, such as DSM—IV.)

		Never Evident	Seldom Evident	Somewhat Evident	Often Evident	Always Evident
25.	Evidences the capacity to consult DSM—IV, or a similar diagnostic classification system, to clarify diagnoses.	1	2	3	4	5
26.	Evidences a clear understanding of the fundamental features of, and differences between, anxiety disorders, mood disorders and thought disorders.	1	2	3	4	5
27.	Is aware of diagnoses that require urgent referral, or consultation.	1	2	3	4	5
28.	Evidences a sound understanding of the symptoms of depression, including depression among children.	1	2	3	4	5
29.	Evidences a basic understanding of the broad features of a range of personality disorders.	1	2	3	4	5
30.	Demonstrates an awareness of the potential negatives associated with diagnostic labelling of clients.	1	2	3	4	5
31.	Evidences growing skills in differential diagnosis.	1	2	3	4	5

4. Assessment Skills

(Demonstrates the capacity to measure, in formal or informal ways, the functioning of clients, the severity of their symptoms and the extent of improvements they make.)

		Never Evident	Seldom Evident	Somewhat Evident	Often Evident	Always Evident
32.	Evidences awareness of the value of attempting to measure client functioning, symptom severity and client progress.	1	2	3	4	5
33.	Demonstrates knowledge of a range of useful assessment instruments, appropriate to their level of qualification.	1	2	3	4	5
34.	Shows evidence of understanding the limitations of the assessment instruments.	1	2	3	4	5
35.	Is able to use several assessment instruments helpfully.	1	2	3	4	5
36.	Demonstrates an ability to assess client issues using a developmental focus.	1	2	3	4	5
37.	Demonstrates an interest in extending their familiarity with a wider range of assessment instruments.	1	2	3	4	5

5. Ethical Awareness and Practice

(Is aware of the central principles of relevant Codes of Ethics, applicable to the professional association they belong to, and seeks to integrate these into their practice.)

		Never Evident	Seldom Evident	Somewhat Evident	Often Evident	Always Evident
38.	Demonstrates an appropriate awareness of their limits of competence, and seeks to consult, or refer clients where this is indicated.	1	2	3	4	5
39.	Demonstrates an awareness of the issue of confidentiality, and its limits, and observes this in practice.	1	2	3	4	5
40.	On occasions brings up ethical dilemmas, pertaining to a client, for discussion within supervision.	1	2	3	4	5
41.	Observes professional boundaries in relationships with clients.	1	2	3	4	5
42.	Is aware of the distinctive issues associated with working with suicidal clients and works responsibly with them.	1	2	3	4	5
43.	Is aware of the distinctive ethical issues associated with counselling minors and observes these, where relevant, in practice.	1	2	3	4	5
44.	Is sensitive to the impact of issues of gender, culture and power as they relate to the counselling process, and takes these into account in their practice.					

6. Professional Awareness and Practice

(Understands the legal requirements and propriety of professional functioning for counsellors/psychologists and demonstrates this in practice.)

		Never Evident	Seldom Evident	Somewhat Evident	Often Evident	Always Evident
45.	Is familiar with the legal requirements pertaining to counsellors/psychologists, including mandatory reporting requirements.	1	2	3	4	5
46.	Follows a program of supervision and ongoing professional development.	1	2	3	4	5
47.	Keeps case-notes and other records systematically and professionally.	1	2	3	4	5
48.	Evidences an awareness of the importance of referral to medical practitioners where the medication needs of a client require assessment.	1	2	3	4	5
49.	Demonstrates the capacity to liaise effectively with medical practitioners and other helping professionals in respect to clients.	1	2	3	4	5
50.	Demonstrates the ability to liaise ethically and helpfully with others (e.g. family members, teachers) where appropriate.	1	2	3	4	5
51.	Is sensitively aware of the controversy associated with Recovered Memories and does not "lead" clients or use disreputable techniques.	1	2	3	4	5

7. Self-Understanding

(Functions professionally out of an evident understanding of both professional strengths, and areas still needing further ongoing development.)

		Never Evident	Seldom Evident	Somewhat Evident	Often Evident	Always Evident
52.	Demonstrates a commitment to ongoing personal growth.	1	2	3	4	5
53.	Demonstrates the capacity to reflect critically on his or her counselling practice, and make changes as a result.	1	2	3	4	5
54.	Does not function defensively, but actively seeks feedback.	1	2	3	4	5
55.	Is able to accurately identify areas of relative strength in their counselling work.	1	2	3	4	5
56.	Is able to identify ongoing personal growth areas that pertain to improved professional functioning.	1	2	3	4	5
57.	Is familiar with the concepts of transference and counter-transference, and able to identify and label specific instances of these which affect personal and professional functioning.	1	2	3	4	5

Appendix C

Concluding Therapy—A Sample Counsellor Letter

The following letter, written near the conclusion of counselling, was directed to a client who had survived horrific abuse by her grandfather. She struggled with all the sequelae—intense anxiety, self-condemnation, suicidal thoughts and feelings, anorexic struggles, and so on. She was seen, on and off, over a period of eleven years, processing her experience. Progress fluctuated constantly, to the point where she was still quite suicidal just three months prior to the time of this letter. However, at this point, through God-ordained circumstances and because of an accident to her husband, she was forced to drive the family to their home from a country town four hours north. (She had a licence but, out of fear, had not driven for years.) Terrified, she nevertheless completed the journey and suddenly began to see herself differently. This letter clearly has a "narrative counselling flavour" and is directed at summarising the strengths demonstrated and the gains made. It was written shortly before the conclusion of counselling. Names have been changed.

* * * * * * * * *

Dear Lucy,

I've had it in mind to write to you since our last session, but it's taken a while to get around to it. Here are some of my reflections.

It was so encouraging to hear your report of what you have been experiencing. I truly believe a lot of the hard work by you and Ross, with God's help of course, are showing fruit.

Where should I start in detailing the "advances"? Driving more and more, including taking your daughter, Elise, to oboe lessons in peak hour on a busy city road, handling crises with Josie when she caught glandular fever, including taking her to the hospital (again during peak hour!), working in the garden, handling a three-day trip to Melbourne, and the list goes on!

The account of your driving Elise to the shopping centre on Saturday morning, and having a parking spot "provided" for you so that you could "test yourself" for half an hour on your own at the shops was a highlight. And no panic attack! I think that what excited me most was the realisation I had that in this new, re-authored story of who you are, there are not only these successes but also included is a new part of the story about a God who cares for his child. In the old story he was thought to be cold and uncaring, a punishing God. But in this new version, he even cares enough to provide an on-the-spot parking space so you can test yourself at the shops. I think that part of these changes is great too!

Of course, there'll still be lousy days. Be ready for them. Anxiety, fear, guilt, and self-blame don't pack up and leave without a lot of counterattack. But just survive those days, then get back on track, and keep counting your "successes." I want to hear about each one.

Lucy, you and Ross deserve to celebrate and savour each of these bits of progress. Talk about them, take delight in them, nurture them in your heart, thank God for them, and enjoy them. Celebrate them in every way you can. I truly believe you will never be the same.

Warm regards,

Appendix D

Psychopharmacology for Counsellors

Paul Meier, MD

Many clients experience such a severe time in their lives that they often need psychiatric medications so they can return to school or work or even a normal routine at home. These clients represent the 20 percent of the population who have genetic biochemical deficiencies that would benefit from proper, safe medications to correct the genetic imbalance. I have ADHD myself, for example, and get about twice as much accomplished on ADHD medication as I would without them. I feel God's pleasure at taking the medication I need to accomplish more good in the world. I have written more than ninety books, e-books, and tape series, and it is a gift I can accomplish easily on ADHD medication. But I am so distractible that I have trouble reading a book for very long without this medication.

If a person has a genetically low level of thyroid hormone, he or she takes thyroid medication or else suffers dry skin, hair loss, weight gain, constipation, sensitivity to cold, and depression—perhaps even a suicide that could have been completely prevented with proper diagnosis. People with pancreatic deficiencies take insulin to ward off diabetic disease processes, or else they would die. The brain is simply one more organ, having biochemical deficiencies in a minority of people. (Meier et al. 2006).

What Counsellors Should Know about Psychotropic Medications

Serotonin

Serotonin is needed for love, joy, peace, good sleep, and freedom from the obsessions, compulsions, and negative thinking that low levels cause. I remind my clients that they are not in charge of their lives if they have an untreated brain chemistry disorder. Their chemicals are influencing them. Serotonin medications bring happiness, peace, and good sleep, with less irritability. Low serotonin is like wearing glasses every day with cow manure smeared on them. Life looks worse than it already is, and you see yourself and others more negatively also.

We have more than a hundred billion brain cells, with tiny spaces (synapses) between them, where we have *reuptake sites* that absorb the old serotonin so it can be replaced with the new. Some people inherit serotonin reuptake sites that "work overtime"—causing depression, anxiety, and OCD. Most modern antidepressants are selective serotonin reuptake inhibitors (SSRIs). These antidepressants block some of these "drains," so to speak, so serotonin levels can rise back up to a normal level that allows the client to exhibit their true personality, not the irritable, sad, perfectionistic one caused by the deficiency.

Depending on the brand and dosage levels, SSRIs can take between five and ten weeks to bring serotonin to peak levels for a depressed client. If 20mg of a particular antidepressant alleviates the depression, it will usually take 30 or 40 mg of that same medication to eliminate the symptoms of OCD. If a client is bipolar (genetic regular mood swings), then the SSRI often will not work unless he or she takes a *mood stabiliser* with it (either a proper GABA medication or a proper *dopamine* medication). In fact, if a client has a first-degree relative (mom, dad, brother, sister, etc.) who has Bipolar Disorder, the antidepressant is likely not to work unless he also takes a low dose of a mood stabiliser. Even people with Schizoaffective Disorders will benefit from combinations of medications that include an antidepressant, a mood stabiliser, and an atypical antipsychotic to correct the dopamine component of the disorder. Often with this kind of combination people can regain their normal functioning as long as they continue to take their medication. If they quit the medications the entire disorder will generally show itself again within weeks accompanied by the original moods, and possibly delusions and/or hallucinations.

Norepinephrine

Norepinephrine, also known as noradrenalin, is like the fine-tuning system in your television set. A normal level gives us joy, like serotonin does, but norepinephrine is different in that it gives us more energy, focus, memory and motivation. Selective norepinephrine reuptake inhibitors (SNRIs) can often correct this imbalance within five to ten weeks.

Current SSRIs and SNRIs are effective about 75 percent of the time, so if one does not seem to work for a client, help him or her not be discouraged since eventually most people find a combination of medications that work for them.

Dopamine

Dopamine is a "pleasure" chemical that also is needed for sanity. It gives pleasure in life, improves sexual enjoyment, and helps one see things more realistically. If dopamine is out of balance in one way, it can cause Parkinsonism. If it is out of balance in other ways, it causes varying degrees of paranoia. People who are mildly to moderately paranoid become critical, controlling, self-righteous, condescending, and ascribe evil motives to others, mistrusting others too much rather than exhibiting a healthy scepticism. More severe paranoia leads to blunted affect (the person may have trouble laughing or even crying), marked ambivalence (inclined to be nice one minute and losing their temper rapidly the next), inability to have fun, blank staring, loose associations (e.g., losing their train of thought more than usual in the middle of sentences), and other symptoms. If more severe, the person can develop gross delusions that are grandiose, such as thinking they have special powers. They may also develop auditory hallucinations—thinking they hear audible voices saying negative things about them, and they can find themselves looking around the room to see who is speaking to them, only to find nobody else is there. The dopamine imbalance makes their own negative thoughts seem amplified into other voices. Some religious clients may start to believe that demons are talking to them, but since the voices go away 100 percent of the time on a proper dose of a dopamine medication (the atypical antipsychotics are the best), those "demons" are either allergic to dopamine medication or not demonic at all!

GABA

In scientific terms, GABA stands for gamma-amino butyric acid. It is the chemical in our brains that "puts the brakes on our worries." Proper levels bring peace and more stable moods, less irritability, and even less craving for alcohol, cannabis or other substances that bind to the GABA receptors. GABA medications that facilitate effective use of our natural GABA help prevent seizure disorders, stabilise our moods (some of them are superb for even severe bipolar disorders), take away anxiety, and often even decrease physical pain. Some, like topiramate (generic), can help also with weight loss. They are like "wonder drugs" in comparison to earlier drugs such as lithium.

In summary, psychopharmacology involves the use of medications (but also proper vitamins and amino acids) to correct imbalances in one or more of the brain amines. The imbalance may be a temporary one, not requiring ongoing medication, or it may be a genetic and permanent one, requiring lifelong medications.

As counsellors, encourage clients to see a psychiatrist to get their brains working the way they would have if they had not inherited or developed a chemical imbalance. Encourage them also to get a thorough physical exam, perhaps even laboratory studies from their family physician, since medical conditions such as hypothyroidism, hormone imbalances (like low testosterone), sleep apnoea, and others can make many people suicidally depressed or psychotic. A small percentage of psychiatric patients have a primary medical illness as the root cause, so this possibility should never be overlooked. These people are unlikely to respond to either counselling or psychiatric medications until they resolve the medical problem.

As time passes, psychiatric medications keep getting safer, quicker, and more effective than the year before. Most people don't need them. However, some clients do need them for a quicker and more complete recovery, possibly initially for six months or so. About twenty percent of the population would benefit from one or more lifelong psychiatric medications like an antidepressant, ADHD medication, or one of the other medications.

Further Reading

Meier, P., Clements, T., Bertrand, J, L., & Mandt, D. (2006). *Blue genes*. Carol Stream, IL: Tyndale House.

See also www.meierclinics.org.

References

Adams, J. E. (1970). *Competent to counsel.* Grand Rapids: Baker.

Anand, B. K., & Dua, S. (1956). Circulatory and respiratory changes induced by electrical stimulation of limbic system (visceral brain). *Journal of Neurophysiology.* 19: 393–400.

Antony, M.M., & Roemer, L. (2011). *Behaviour therapy.* Washington, DC: American Psychological Association.

APA, (1997). Guidelines for the provision of humanistic psychosocial services. *The Humanistic Psychologist,* 25(1).

Backus, W., & Chapian, M. (2000). *Telling yourself the truth.* Minneapolis, MN: Bethany.

Beck, A.T. (1963). Idiosyncratic content and cognitive distortions. *Arch Gen Psychiatry.* 9(4): 324–333.

Beck, J., & Beck, A. (2011). *Cognitive behaviour therapy: Basics and beyond.* 2nd Ed. New York: Guilford Press.

Bettenson, H. (1963). *Documents of the Christian church.* London: Oxford.

Bobgan, M. & D. (1979). *The psychological way/The spiritual way.* Grand Rapids: Bethany House.

Bowen, M. *Murray Bowen MD and the nine concepts in Family Systems Theory.* Retrieved from http://ideastoaction.wordpress.com/2007/10/11.

Brady, M. (2003). *The wisdom of listening.* Somerville, MA: Wisdom Publications.

Bufford, R. (1997). Consecrated counselling: Reflections on the distinctives of Christian counselling. *Journal of Psychology and Theology,* 25, 111–122.

Calvin J. (N.D). *Institutes of the Christian religion.* 2.2.15–16. Grand Rapids: Associated Publishers and Authors.

Carter, J., & Narramore. B. (1979). *The integration of psychology and theology.* Grand Rapids: Zondervan.

Collins G. (1977). *The rebuilding of psychology.* Wheaton, IL: Tyndale House.

Colman, A. M. (2009). *Oxford dictionary of psychology.* 3rd Ed. Oxford: Oxford University Press.

Conan Doyle, A. (1893/1993). Silver Blaze. In A. Conan Doyle *The bedside Conan Doyle,* London: Chancellor Press.

Cormier, S., Nurius, P. S., & Osborn, C. (2009). *Interviewing and change strategies for helpers.* Belmont, CA: Brooks Cole.

Cozolino, L. (2004). *The making of a therapist.* New York, NY: W. W. Norton and Co.

Crabb, L. (1975). *Principles of biblical counselling.* Grand Rapids, MI: Zondervan.

De Shazer, S. (1985). *Keys to solution in brief therapy.* New York, NY: Norton.

Dixon, T. (2003). *From passions to emotions: The creation of a secular psychological category.* Cambridge, UK: Cambridge University Press.

Dombeck, M., & Wells-Moran, J. Humanistic Theory. In *The psychological self-tools-online self-help book*. www.peakwellnesscenter.org. Accessed 22.01.2013

Ecker, B., & Hulley, L. (1996). *Depth-oriented brief therapy*. San Francisco, CA: Jossey-Bass.

Egan, G. (2010). *The skilled helper*. 9th ed. Belmont, CA: Brooks/Cole.

Egan, G. (2010). *Exercises in helping skills: A manual to accompany The Skilled Helper*. 9th ed. Belmont, CA: Brooks/Cole.

Ellis, A. (1977). *Handbook of rational-emotive therapy*. New York, NY: Springer.

Enright, R. D., & Fitzgibbons, R. P. (2000). *Helping clients forgive*. Washington, DC: American Psychological Association.

Fisher, P. C. (2006). The Link between Posttraumatic Growth and Forgiveness: An Intuitive Truth. In L. G. Calhoun & R. G. Tedeschi (Eds.), *Handbook of Posttraumatic Growth: Research and Practice*. Mahwah, NJ: Erlbaum.

Fortune, A. E., Pearlingi, B., & Rochelle, C. D. (1992). Reactions to termination of individual treatment. *Social Work*, 37, 171–8.

Fowler, J. W. (2004). Identity, intimacy, and 'hooking up.' *Ethics News and Views*, 13, (1), 2. Emory University: Centre for Ethics.

Fowler, J. W., Streib, H., & Keller, B. (2004). *Manual for faith development research*. 3rd ed. Bielefeld; Atlanta: Research Centre for Biographical Studies in Contemporary Religion, University of Bielefeld; Centre for Research in Faith and Moral Development, Emory University.

Gordon, T. (1970). P.E.T.: *Parent effectiveness training.* New York: Plume Books.

Gubi, P. M. (2008). *Prayer in counselling and psychotherapy.* Philadelphia, PA: Jessica Kingsley Publishers.

Harris, R., & Hayes, S. (2009). *ACT made simple.* Oakland, CA: New Harbinger.

Hart, A. (1991). *Issues in Christian counselling in congress proceedings.* Australian Congress on Christian Counselling. Melbourne: Elkanah.

Hayes, S., & Smith, S. (2005). *Get out of your mind and into your life: The new Acceptance and Commitment Therapy.* Oakland, CA: New Harbinger.

Henley, T. B., & Thorne B.M. (2005). The lost millennium: Psychology during the Middle Ages. *Psychological Record,* 55, 103–13

Holmes, A. F. (1977). *All truth is God's truth.* Grand Rapids: Eerdmans.

Horvath, A. O., & Luborsky. L. (1993). The role of the therapeutic alliance in psychotherapy. *Journal of Consulting and Clinical Psychology.* 61, (4), 561–73.

Hunsley, J., Aubry, T. D., Verstervelt, C. M., & Vito, D. (1999). Comparing therapist and client perspectives on reasons for psychotherapy termination. *Psychotherapy,* 36, 380–38.

Hurding, R. (1986). *Roots and shoots.* London: Hodder and Stoughton.

Inglis B. (1979). *Natural medicine.* Glasgow: William Collins and Sons.

James, W. (1890). *Principles of psychology.* New York: Holt.

James, W. (1982). *The varieties of religious experience.* New York: Penguin.

Johnstone, L., & Dallos, R. (Eds.). (2006). *Formulation in psychology and psychotherapy.* New York: Routledge.

Joyce, A. S., Piper, W. E., Ogrodniczuk, J. S., & Klein, R. H. (2007). *Termination in psychotherapy: A psychodynamic model of processes and outcomes.* Washington, DC: American Psychological Association

Kabat-Zinn, J. (2012). *Mindfulness for beginners.* Boulder, CO: Sounds True Inc.

Kennedy-Moore, E., & Watson, J.C. (1999). *Expressing emotion: myths, realities, and therapeutic strategies.* New York: The Guilford Press.

Kirwan, W. (1984). *Biblical concepts for Christian counselling.* Grand Rapids: Baker

Kottler, J. (2010). *On being a therapist.* 4th ed. San Francisco: John Wiley and Sons.

Lake, F. (1966). *Clinical theology: A theological and psychiatric basis to clinical pastoral care.* London: Darton, Longman and Todd.

Levy, D., & Kilpatrick, J. (2011). *Gray matter: A neurosurgeon discovers the power of prayer.* Carol Stream, IL: Tyndale.

Linehan, M. (1993). *Cognitive behavioural treatment of borderline personality disorder.* New York: The Guilford Press.

Linehan, M. (1993). *Skills training manual for cognitive behavioural treatment of borderline personality disorder.* New York: The Guilford Press.

Lord, P. (2011). *Hearing God: An easy-to-follow, step-by-step guide to two-way communication with God.* Bloomington, MN: Chosen Books.

Lovallo, W. R. (2005). *Stress and health.* London: Sage.

Martin, D. G. (2011). *Counselling and therapy skills.* Long Grove, IL: Waveland Press.

Maslow, A. H. (1943). A theory of human motivation. *Psychological Review,* 50(4), 370–396.

McCullough, M. E., Pargament, K. I., & Thoreson, C. (Eds.). (2000). *Forgiveness: Theory, research, and practice.* New York: Guilford Press.

McKenzie, G. J. (1940). *Psychology, psychotherapy, and evangelicalism.* London: Allen and Unwin.

McMinn, M. (1996). *Psychology, theology, and spirituality in Christian counselling.* Carol Stream, IL: Tyndale.

Mehrabian, A. (1971). *Silent messages: Implicit communication of emotion and attitudes.* Belmont, CA: Wadsworth.

Meier, P. D. (1977). *Christian parenting and child care.* Grand Rapids: Baker.

Miller, G. (1997). *Becoming miracle workers: Language and meaning in brief therapy.* New York: Aldine de Gruyter.

Miller, W. R., & Rollnick, S. (2002). *Motivational interviewing.* New York: Guilford Press.

Minirth, F. B. (1990). *Christian psychiatry.* Grand Rapids: Fleming Revell.

Monk, G., Winslade, J., Crocket, K., & Epston, D. (1997). *Narrative therapy in practice.* San Francisco: Jossey-Bass.

Muran, J.C. & Barber, J.P. (2010). *The therapeutic alliance: An evidence based guide to practice.* New York: Guilford Press.

Neibhur, H, R. (1951). *Christ and culture.* New York: Harper and Row.

Nelson-Jones, R. (2011). *Basic counselling skills: A helper's manual.* London: Sage.

O'Connell, W., and Palmer, S. (2003). *Handbook of solution-focused therapy.* London: Sage.

Pacheco, A., Palha M., & Estevez, M. (1991). The origin of dementia praecox. *Schizophrenia Research,* 28, (2), 99–103.

Pekarik, G. (1980). *Psychotherapy abbreviation.* London: Haworth Press.

Powell, C. J., & Barker, G. A. (1998). *Unloading the overload: Stress management for Christians.* Sydney: Strand.

Rogers, C. (1961). *On becoming a person.* New York: Houghton and Mifflin.

Seligman, L. (2004). *Diagnosis and treatment planning in counselling.* 3rd Ed. New York, NY: Springer.

Shirer, P. C. (2011). *Discerning the voice of God.* Chicago: Moody Publications.

Siegel, R. (2011). *The mindfulness solution.* New York: Guilford Press.

Skinner, B. F. (1938). *The behaviour of organisms: An experimental analysis.* New York: Appleton-Century.

Skovholt, T. M. (2012). *Becoming a therapist: On the path to mastery.* Hoboken, N.J: John Wiley and Sons.

Sommers-Flanagan, J., & Sommers-Flanagan, R. (2012). *Counselling and psychotherapy theories in context and practice.* New Jersey: John Wiley and Sons.

Stafford, T. (1993). How Christian psychology is changing the church. *Christianity Today,* 17 May, 1993.

Stevenson, D. H. (2007). *Introduction in psychology, Christianity, and integration.* Batavia IL: CAPS.

Tan, S. Y. (2011). *Counselling and psychotherapy.* Grand Rapids: Baker Academic.

Thurman, C. (1999). *The lies we believe.* New York: Nelson

Tournier P, (1957). *The healing of persons.* New York: Harper and Row.

VanZant, J. C. (2010). *Prayer in counselling: The practitioner's handbook.* Bloomington, IN: WestBow Press.

Virkler, M., & Virkler, P. (2005). *How to hear God's voice.* Shippensburg, PA: Destiny Image.

Westbrook, D., Kennerley, H., & Kirk, J. (2007). *An introduction to cognitive behaviour therapy: Skills and applications.* London: Sage.

Willard, D. (2012). *Hearing God.* Downer's Grove, IL: Intervarsity Press.

Williams, M.,& Penman, D. (2011). *Mindfulness: An eight-week plan for finding peace in a frantic world.* New York: Rodale Inc.

Wimberly, E. P. (1994). *Using scripture in pastoral counselling.* Nashville, TN: Abingdon Press.

Windy Dryden, W. (2008). *The therapeutic alliance as an integrating framework*. Thousand Oaks, CA: Sage.

Wolters, C., (Ed.). (1978). *The cloud of unknowing and other works*. Harmondsworth, UK: Penguin.

Woodward, B. (2012). *Understanding psychotherapy for adults*. Rochester, NY: Mayo Foundation for Medical Education and Research.

Zuckerman, A., & Mitchell, C. L. (2004). Psychology interns' perspectives on the forced termination of psychotherapy. *The Clinical Supervisor, 23*, 55–70.

CPSIA information can be obtained at www.ICGtesting.com
Printed in the USA
LVOW06s1448191115

463342LV00003B/473/P